The Visible and the Revealed

John D. Caputo, *series editor*

PERSPECTIVES IN
CONTINENTAL
PHILOSOPHY

JEAN-LUC MARION

The Visible and the Revealed

TRANSLATED BY CHRISTINA M. GSCHWANDTNER
AND OTHERS

FORDHAM UNIVERSITY PRESS
New York ▪ 2008

With the exception of Chapters 5 and 8, this book was published in French as Jean-Luc Marion, *Le visible et le révélé* © *Les Éditions du Cerf,* 2005. The author has graciously allowed us to add these two essays for the English translation.

Library of Congress Cataloging-in-Publication Data is available from the publisher.

Marion, Jean-Luc, 1946–
   [Visible et le révélé. English]
   The visible and the revealed / Jean-Luc Marion ; translated by Christina M. Gschwandtner and others.
      p.   cm.
   Includes bibliographical references (p.   ).
   ISBN-13: 978-0-8232-2883-6 (cloth : alk. paper)
   ISBN-13: 978-0-8232-2884-3 (pbk. : alk. paper)
   1. Christianity—Philosophy.   2. Philosophy and religion.   3. Phenomenology.
   I. Title.
   B2430.M283V5713   2008
   210—dc22

                                                                        20080-19667

Printed in the United States of America
10 09 08   5 4 3 2 1
First edition

Contents

Preface

In order to know if he is a God, I ask only one thing of you: that is to open your eyes.

—**Voltaire,** *Histoire de Jenni ou l'athée et le sage*

The publication of a new book is not always justifiable. In fact, it rarely is. Often the trees it consumes would have given far more—and far purer—air to breathe. Such an ethical and ecological concern serves as even stronger discouragement for any untimely reprinting of essays that have already appeared. Often they merit neither cluttering the bookstores a second time nor inflicting new boredom on the (rather rare) readers. In light of these formidable arguments, maybe I should have stuck with my first impulse, namely, to do nothing. Morality would thus have conspired with sloth to achieve a delightful and unassailable position. Since, despite all that, I imprudently follow the other path, with the hope that its greater difficulty grants it at least some virtue, I must give reasons for such a questionable effort. And I do have several good reasons to defend this choice.

The first derives from the patient yet insistent friendship of Philippe Capelle, dean of the faculty of philosophy at the Institut catholique. For several years now, he has not only maintained the honor of Christian thought, continually threatened (most immediately by Christianity itself), but above all he has not ceased to gather together in many academic events all those (whether Christian or not) who take seriously the really central and decisive question of the relationship between the Revelation

of Christ and philosophy in all its states. Like many others, I have bene-
fited from his sympathic and critical attention. In it I have many times
found the courage to persevere in an increasingly difficult work, in increasingly dangerous but—in my eyes at least—also fascinating areas.
Consequently, the promise that I had made of entrusting a book to the
series he edits at the Éditions du Cerf had to be kept. That promise has
been fulfilled today.

The second reason derives from the both opposing and approving interest that readers (to my surprise, rather less rare than I had foreseen) have
brought not only to my fully constructed books but also to articles that I
had considered mere outlines or rough drafts, forgotten as soon as published (as intellectual hygiene recommends, anyway). This has been particularly so during recent discussions, conferences, or studies devoted to the
topics of givenness,[1] the gift, and the saturated phenomenon, where have
resurfaced works that are much earlier, at times very old and often lost in
marginal publications. Certainly for the foreign reader or one removed
from the dense French microcosm, ignorance of the original context and
the questions that first gave rise to these texts can cause them to be read
badly or even to be misunderstood entirely. It is claimed, for example, that
I have simply assumed the concepts of "first philosophy," "metaphysics,"
"negative theology," or "Christian philosophy," whereas I precisely take
the opportunity of orders given by others to try to get rid of them. Given
that people in fact persist in taking into account what happens in the background of the atelier and in the innermost recesses of the laboratory, it
seems to me that it would be better for me to bring these materials back to
light by presenting them as they are, in chronological order and in context
(therefore the "Note on the Origin of the Texts" below). If one is to have
a discussion, at least it should be conducted on a clear basis. I have therefore not made any alterations to the following texts, even when they seem
insufficient to me or even bluntly erroneous. I have merely harmonized
some of the references in the notes, or even suggested some cross-refer-
ences from one article to another, but without additions or updates.[2] Unless noted otherwise, any translations are my own.

Yet a third reason remains. This is the real reason and less anecdotal. To
the extent that, being a historian of philosophy, I take an interest in the
constitution of metaphysics, I have better understood why and how its
"end" and its "destruction" belong as intimately to metaphysics as its
birth, indeed do so in virtue of this birth itself. As I repeated the stages of
this doubled twilight, I noticed that the history of philosophy was not sufficient to describe it (although this discipline itself found its possibility and

its unique place in this twilight), but that in order to describe it as a philosopher, I must risk stepping onto nonmetaphysical ground or (for want of such a transgression) at least one that would be metaphysically neutral, in this case, phenomenology. As I entered phenomenology, I was persuaded that this thought could become what it is not yet fully, namely, precisely nonmetaphysical, only by being radically reformulated as a phenomenology of givenness, broadened to include all that is given, considered as such and without a priori conditions. Yet (as somewhat forewarned by Christian theology) right from the first step on this journey I faced a final difficulty: Christ's Revelation is given as an event that *appears* within history and in the present; it appears rightfully and even as a phenomenon par excellence. Not only is "God [himself] revealed" (Romans 1:19) in the light of this visibility, but anything else also becomes fully visible, as it never would otherwise. Revelation reveals any phenomenon to itself, according to the oft-repeated principle that "nothing is hidden that will not be disclosed" (Luke 8:17; see 12:2 and Mark 4:22). This statement of Revelation resonates as if it suggested a phenomenology of the revealed. The difference between the two spellings (upper-case and lower-case) marks the difficulty exactly here: if "the light appears in the darkness" (John 1:5), then what light is at stake? That of a revealing phenomenology or a completely different one, that of Revelation revealing itself? Or maybe one must admit only one, which makes all things visible as different as they might appear? This question can be formulated with two opposing meanings.

Theologically: the event of Revelation implies the transition of what does not show itself to that which makes itself visible. Yet this metamorphosis is deployed on the stage of *this* world. It presents not only God, "whom no one has ever seen" (John 1:18), but also the things of the world, which up to this point all believe they have always seen. Henceforth we discover them in a completely new light (by the light of charity and its judgment). Must one not admit that a radically new and infinitely powerful phenomenality is in play here? What is its nature? Can theology avoid thinking the phenomenality that it cannot refuse to implement? Is it sufficiently concerned even to confront that task?

In turn, in order to become what it claims to be, phenomenology must enlarge the production of everything that can appear in the world as far as possible, hence especially what at first glance and most often *does not yet appear there*. But, taking the easiest and quickest path, it always falls back on what appears to it most easily and most rapidly—*objects*, which one can constitute, and, in the best case, *beings*, which are. Yet phenomena that are neither objects nor beings are not lacking, and they do not cease to vindicate their manifestation and (without authorization from philosophy) succeed in accomplishing it. Among these phenomena, which I call saturated phenomena, must one not also include the phenomena of revelation, which alone correspond formally to what Revelation claims to accomplish?

Notwithstanding various subjective and arbitrary prejudices, one must ask of phenomenology: To what kinds of phenomena can it grant access? Which others does it refuse to admit, and according to what criteria? I certainly do not rule out that one might have the right or even the duty to limit the field of phenomenality and to relinquish accepting in it everything that claims to appear—for example, to push the radiance of the Resurrection or the evidence of theophanies into the shadows. But one must take the time and the trouble to justify this exclusion and to wonder about possible types of phenomena and degrees of phenomenality. One would certainly have to wonder whether this repression does not do more wrong to phenomenology itself (which would thus contradict its principal intention) than to the phenomena that it censures and that, despite this rejection, do not cease to manifest themselves. At the very least, one would have to redo, in phenomenological terms, what Spinoza and Hume, Kant and Fichte have attempted to do, namely, to criticize the possibility of any revelation in general by risking an even more radical defeat regarding this prohibition than did the Enlightenment philosophers.

By contrast, broadening phenomenality to include phenomena of revelation, by granting the *possibility* of phenomenalizing Revelation (according to its own modalities) might fulfill phenomenology as essentially as it would liberate the rights of theology. Finally, it might be possible that the refusal to want to see or even to be able to see does not disqualify what one denies, but rather the one who denies it. Blindness does not call light into question. And voluntary blindness even less so.

Responding to questions such as these poses immense difficulties. Simply causing them to be heard and acknowledged gives rise to questions just as great or even greater. It is therefore a pleasant duty for me to thank the steadfast interlocutors of the essays collected here. My gratitude is directed to those whom I will never convince as much as to those who at times have agreed with me: Jocelyn Benoist, Serge-Thomas Bonino, John D. Caputo, Vincent Carraud, Jean-François Courtine, Emmanuel Falque, Giovanni Ferretti, Didier Franck, Emmanuel Gabellieri, Jean Greisch, Kevin Hart, Vincent Holzer, Ralf Kühn, Jean-Yves Lacoste, Claude Romano, Barbara Stiegler, Katheryn Tanner, David Tracy, Stijn van den Bossche, Ruud Welten, and Marlène Zarader, without forgetting Dominique Janicaud, who has helped so much.

September 2004

Note on the Origin of the Texts

1. "The Possible and Revelation" originally appeared in French in P. J. M. van Tongeren et al., eds., *Eros and Eris: Contributions to a Hermeneutical Phenomenology*, Liber amicorum for Adriaan Peperzak, *Phaenomenologica*, no. 127 (Dordrecht: Kluwer Academic Publishers, 1992), 217–32. It was initially published in German translation by Rudolf Funk, "Aspekte der Religionsphänomenologie: Grund, Horizont und Offenbarung," in *Religionsphilosophie heute*, ed. Alois Halder, Klaus Kienzler, and Joseph Möller (Düsseldorf: Patmos, 1988), 84–103, and has recently been reprinted in *Von der Ursprünglichkeit der Gabe: Jean-Luc Marions Phänomenologie in der Diskussion*, ed. M. Gabel and H. Joas (Freiburg: Karl Alber, 2007). Since then, its theses have been taken up in a more direct manner in "À Dieu, rien d'impossible" (For God nothing is impossible), *Communio: Revue catholique internationale* 14.5 (Paris: September 1989). [The essay appears here in English for the first time.] The concept of the "saturating/saturated phenomenon" is announced in this essay for the first time.

2. "The Saturated Phenomenon" appeared in *Phenomenology and the "Theological Turn": The French Debate*, ed. Dominique Janicaud, Jean-François Courtine, et al. (New York: Fordham University Press, 2000), 176–216. An earlier translation appeared in *Philosophy Today* 40.1–4 (1996): 103–24; the original French version appeared in *Phénoménologie et théologie*, ed. Jean-François Courtine (Paris: Critérion, 1992), 79–128.

Although I now consider it out of date, I reproduce here this early stage in my understanding of the saturated phenomenon and its schema, to ensure that it is *not* confused with the later version established in *Étant donné: Essai d'une phénoménologie de la donation* (Paris: Presses Universitaires de France, 1997); *Being Given: Toward a Phenomenology of Givenness*, trans. Jeffrey L. Kosky (Stanford: Stanford University Press, 2002). In effect, as I pointed out in *De surcroît: Études sur les phénomènes saturés* (Paris: Presses Universitaires de France, 2001); *In Excess: Studies of Saturated Phenomena*, trans. Robyn Horner and Vincent Berraud (New York: Fordham University Press, 2002), this first study included Revelation directly among the saturated phenomena by numbering it in fourth position, whereas the later study takes the precaution of distinguishing the four types of saturated phenomena (event, idol, flesh, and *icon*, thus established in their specificity) from "the phenomenon of revelation," which "concentrates the four types of saturated phenomena" in a "fifth type" (327/235). This distance between the saturated phenomenon in its quadruple banality, on the one hand, and the phenomenon of revelation (hence the possibility of Revelation), on the other, makes it possible to maintain a neat distinction between phenomenology (even of givenness) and theology (even of Revelation).

3. "Metaphysics and Phenomenology: A Relief for Theology" was first published in French in the *Bulletin de littérature ecclésiastique* 94.3 (Toulouse: July 1993), 189–206; English translation by Thomas A. Carlson in *Critical Inquiry* 20.4 (1994): 572–91. Originally it was the text for a presentation delivered at the conference The Future of Metaphysics, organized by the Institut catholique de Toulouse (January 29–31, 1993). It would be proper to place it in a larger context, consisting first of "Phenomenology of Givenness and First Philosophy," published in French successively in the review *Philosophie* 49 (1996), in *Le statut contemporain de la philosophie première*, ed. P. Capelle, (October 9, 1995), 29–50, and then finally as the first chapter in *De surcroît* (*In Excess*). It was first translated by Thomas A. Carlson under the title "The Other First Philosophy and the Question of Givenness," *Critical Inquiry* 25.4 (1999): 784–800. These two essays share the search for a new philosophical paradigm for theology. In both cases, this question was posed to me in terms that are not really mine: neither that of "metaphysics" (in 1993), nor that of "first philosophy" (in 1995). I therefore each time attempted to take up and then leave behind these two instances, with the goal of moving on to the paradigm of phenomenology in general (in 1993) or the phenomenology of givenness in particular (in 1995). In this I follow the progression of the elaboration underway in *Being Given*. This sequence does not mask the

insufficiency of the present text, which is clearly due to the fact that the concept of phenomenology is still very vague. Phenomenology is not a univocal term, such that it could remain (at least partially) metaphysical, in particular when it is supposed to be transcendental. (See my preface to G. Planty-Bonjour and Jean-Luc Marion, eds., *Phénoménologie et métaphysique* [Paris: Presses Universitaires de France, 1984].) Phenomenology must first become radically phenomenological to be able really to offer "relief" to metaphysics, a possibility that has not yet been actualized. It must first be rethought as a phenomenology of givenness. This was barely outlined in 1993.

The other point of reference for this essay can be found in "Saint Thomas d'Aquin et l'onto-théo-logie," a presentation given at a conference of the same title, organized on June 3, 1994, by the Institut catholique de Toulouse. It was published first in the *Revue thomiste* 95.1 (1995), then in 2002 in the 3rd edition (the 2nd in "Quadrige") of *Dieu sans l'être: Horstexte* (Paris: Arthème Fayard, 1982); "Saint Thomas Aquinas and Onto-theo-logy," trans. B. Gendreau, R. Rethy, and M. Sweeney, in *Mystic: Presence and Aporia*, ed. M. Kessler and C. Sheppard (Chicago: University of Chicago Press, 2003), 38–74. As the preface added to this new edition specifies, "my own position has changed since 1982, and even today I defend the apparent paradox that Thomas Aquinas did not identify the question of God or of the divine names with Being, at least the kind of Being understood by metaphysics" (*Dieu sans l'être*, 7). That was already the position taken in the prefaces to the Italian translation by A. Dell'Asta, *Dio senza l'essere* (Milan, 1987), 9–11, and to the English translation by Thomas A. Carlson, *God Without Being* (Chicago: University of Chicago Press, 1991), xxii and following. Here it is a matter of distinguishing between St. Thomas Aquinas's thought and "metaphysics" understood in the strict sense of the onto-theo-logical constitution of metaphysics.

This debate obviously implies a decidedly historical definition (if not a concept) of metaphysics. This I outlined in a presentation to the Twenty-seventh Congress of ASPLF [L'Association des Sociétés de Philosophie de Langue Française], organized by the University of Laval, Quebec, on August 18, 1998, which was published under the title "La science toujours recherchée et toujours manquante," in *La métaphyique: son histoire, sa critique, ses enjeux*, ed. J.-M. Narbonne and L. Langlois (Paris-Quebec: J.Vrin-Presses Universitaires de Laval, 1999). Furthermore, this debate demands a determination, itself *historical*, of the equivocal uses of theology: I suggested this in "Théo-logique," in *Encyclopédie philosophique universelle*, ed. A. Jacob, vol. 1, *L'Univers philosophique* (Paris: Presses Universitaires de France, 1989), 17–25.

The concept of the "being-given" was first articulated in this context.

4. "'Christian Philosophy': Hermeneutic or Heuristic?" originally appeared in English; it has not previously been published in French. This presentation was initially delivered under the title "Christian Philosophy: Hermeneutic or Heuristic?" at the conference The Question of Christian Philosophy Today, organized at Georgetown University, Washington, D.C., on November 25, 1993. It was published in *The Question of Christian Philosophy Today*, ed. Francis J. Ambrosio (New York: Fordham University Press, 1999), 247–64. A shortened and adapted version of this argument has been published under the title "Philosophie chrétienne et herméneutique de la charité" (Christian philosophy and hermeneutic of charity), in *Communio: Revue catholique internationale* 18.2 (Paris, March 1993), 89–96.

Being the response to a set question, this essay is merely an attempt to restore a "Christian philosophy." On the one hand, this appears to me today in some sense useless and illegitimate. On the other hand, though, it could become an attempt to rediscover the original *theological* concept of *philosophia christiana* by pursuing the path of giving phenomenological evidence for what Pascal understood (without making it manifest) by the "third order" of charity. In this context, one should compare this text with two other sketches: "De la 'mort de Dieu' aux noms divins," *Laval théologique et philosophique* 41.1 (1985): 25–42 and "La fin de la fin de la métaphysique," *Laval théologique et philosophique* 42.1 (1986): 23–33.

5. ["Sketch of a Phenomenological Concept of Gift" first appeared as "Esquisse d'un concept phénoménologique du don," *Archivo di Filosofia* 62.1–3 (1994): 75–94. An earlier English translation appeared in *Postmodern Philosophy and Christian Thought*, ed. Merold Westphal (Bloomington: Indiana University Press, 1999), 122–43; it appears here by permission of the publisher. The essay has been added for the English edition and is not included in the French version of this book. As the title indicates, the text outlines a first attempt at sketching a phenomenological concept of the gift and considering its import for phenomenology and theology. It was reworked much more thoroughly in the second part of *Being Given*, which concentrates on the phenomenological concept of the gift. It is included here not only because it fits well with the other essays of the volume but because of its frequent mention in the English secondary literature on Marion's work.—Trans.]

6. "What Cannot Be Said: Apophasis and the Discourse of Love" appeared in *Proceedings of the American Catholic Philosophical Association* 76 (2002): 39–56. The French text, "Ce qui ne se dit pas—l'apophase du discours amoureux," first appeared in *Biblioteca dell'archivio di filosofia* 29,

ed. Marco M. Olivetti (Rome, 2002), 43–69. This presentation was first delivered at a conference organized by E. Castelli, La théologie negative, on January 4–7, 2002, then at the conference entitled Philosophy at the Boundary of Reason of the American Catholic Philosophical Association, in Cincinnati, Ohio, on November 1–3, 2002, under the title "What Cannot Be Said: Love as Apophasis."

It anticipates *Le phénomène érotique* §28, "Des mots pour ne rien dire" (Paris: Grasset, 2003); "Words for Saying Nothing," *The Erotic Phenomenon*, trans. Stephen E. Lewis (Chicago: University of Chicago Press, 2007), 143–50, which articulates and develops these arguments in a much more explicit context. It constitutes an example of a saturated phenomenon that is accessible to anyone and indisputable, yet for certain people much more privileged because it is not directly theological. But it may *possibly* end up in a theological paradigm.

7. "The Banality of Saturation" was originally in English; it is previously unpublished in French. A first version was presented under the title "Saturation and Counter-Experience" at the conference In Excess: Jean-Luc Marion and the Horizon of Modern Theology, organized by Kevin Hart at the University of Notre Dame, on May 9–11, 2004. It is published in *Counter-Experiences: Reading Jean-Luc Marion*, ed. Kevin Hart (Notre Dame, Ind.: Notre Dame University Press, 2007), 383–418, and appears here by permission of the publisher. At stake here is a final attempt—without grand illusions—to respond to several objections to the attempt to introduce the concept of the saturated phenomenon into phenomenology by underlining its status in phenomenality in general: not as an exception but as a paradigm. This takes up the position already sustained in *Being Given* §22 and §23 and even in Chapter 2 ("The Saturated Phenomenon") of the present work.

8. ["Faith and Reason," not previously published in English, was first delivered on February 13, 2005, the first Sunday of Great Lent, in the context of a series of Lenten lectures at the cathedral of Notre Dame de Paris, organized by Jean-Marie Cardinal Lustiger. The title of the series was Dialogue between Faith and Contemporary Thought, and Marion gave the first lecture, outlining how a "Christian philosopher" might approach this question of dialogue between faith and reason. It is not included in the French version of this book.—Trans.]

The Visible and the Revealed

The Possible and Revelation

1

Can phenomenology contribute in a privileged way to the development of a "philosophy of religion"? In other words, can "philosophy of religion" become a "phenomenology of religion"? The context in which the present contribution first appeared presupposed this without a doubt.[1] One might also attempt to establish it by looking at the many works devoted to religion that (methodologically or thematically) claim to go back to or call upon the spirit of phenomenology. Yet these arguments do not suffice. First, facts (even when there are many) do not justify applying phenomenology to religion, as if by right, or recognizing phenomenological method as in any way particularly suitable for religion. Furthermore, there is only one legitimation for phenomenology, namely, return to the things themselves. To confirm that religion could offer a possible field for phenomenology, one would have to show that it uses the phenomenological method to make manifest phenomena that without it would have remained masked or simply missing in the religious domain. Phenomenology could then be applied both to religion and to potential phenomena. This double requirement—justifying religion to phenomenology as a possible phenomenon, justifying phenomenology to religion as a suitable method—imposes a single instruction: the use of a possible phenomenology of religion cannot be surreptitiously presupposed but must be deduced, in the sense in which Kant defines deduction: "the explanation of the manner in which concepts can thus relate a priori to objects."[2] How, then, can phenomenological concepts be related to objects of religion a priori? How must one proceed phenomenologically in order to return to "the things themselves" of religion?

These two questions doubtless share a special difficulty: the possibility of acknowledging a concept of revelation. I presuppose two points here. (a) Religion attains its highest figure only when it becomes established by and as a revelation, where an authority that is transcendent to experience nevertheless manifests itself experientially. Such an experience, effectively beyond (or outside of) the conditions of possibility of experience, is affirmed not only by its affidavit from privileged or designated individuals, but by words or expositions rightly accessible to everyone (e.g., the Scriptures). Revelation takes its strength of provocation from what it speaks universally, yet without this word being able to ground itself in reason within the limits of the world. As long as this paradox is not admitted, or at least thought honestly, the phenomenon of religion remains misunderstood. (b) Understood as metaphysics, philosophy is accomplished by continually (from Descartes to Hegel) radicalizing the implications of the principle of sufficient reason: all that is (being, *étant*) exists to the extent to which a *causa* (actuality) *sive ratio* (concept) gives an explanation either for its existence, for its nonexistence, or for its exemption from any cause. The emergence of the principle of reason forces metaphysics to assign each being its concept and its cause, to the point of dismissing any beings irreducible to a conceptualizable cause as illegitimate and hence impossible. It is therefore no fortuitous coincidence that the thinkers of the *causa sive ratio* (Spinoza, Malebranche, Leibniz, etc.) also disqualified the possibility of miracles and revelation in general. In this context, religion remains admissible only by renouncing revelation in the full sense. Consequently, it remains thinkable for metaphysics only by deserting its ultimate accomplishment. On the one hand, religion may be understood to remain metaphysically legitimate. In that case, it must submit to the requirements of the principle of reason, in short, be content with the limits of simple reason, and thus finally repudiate revelation inasmuch as the latter by definition eludes the grasp of the concept, of cause, and of reason. Or, on the other hand, religion may be understood to remain faithful to revelation, which excludes it from the world. But then it must first renounce concept, cause, and all reason, to the point where it comes to be expelled from metaphysical rationality under the nickname of *Schwärmerei* [religious enthusiasm, or fanaticism].

This is not an artificial dilemma. In fact, it indicates the two principal positions that metaphysicians who do not simply cede to irreligion sustain in face of the hypothesis of a revealed religion. The second part of the dilemma is illustrated by Kant's thematic in *Religion Within the Limits of Reason Alone* (1793) and Fichte's in *Attempt at a Critique of All Revelation* (1792). For them, only the universal has the value of a priori truth in the practical domain. Yet this universal is implemented by the categorical imperative and the moral law. Any revelation's claim to decree moral duty must hence be measured by the norm of the universal moral law. Unless it renounces leaning on revelation altogether, religion will only call upon revelation by submitting it to a moral hermeneutic exercised by the categorical imperative. Any other hypothesis would betray fanaticism.

> For the theoretical part of ecclesiastical faith cannot interest us morally if it is not conducive to the performance of all human duties as divine commands (what constitutes the essence of all religion). Frequently, this interpretation may in the light of the text (of the revelation), appear forced—it may often really be forced; and yet if the text can possibly support it, it must be preferred to a literal interpretation which either contains nothing at all [helpful] to morality or actually works counter to moral incentives.[3]

Revelation will be reduced to an imperative, hence to the moral law, or it will founder outside of all reason, hence outside of all possibility. In either case it disappears as such.

The first moment of the dilemma is exemplified in a theme in Hegel (if not the early Schelling): here revelation is no longer opposed to reason, but by contrast it essentially contributes to reason. In God's incarnation, revelation actually reveals that the absolute dwells among humans, hence that spirit is reconciled to its proper negativity. Revelation reveals that spirit manifests itself absolutely. "Consequently, in this religion the divine Being is *revealed* [*geoffenbart*]. Its being-revealed [*Offenbarsein*] obviously consists in this, that what it is, is known. But it is known precisely in its being known as Spirit, as a Being that is essentially a *self-conscious Being*."[4] The fact of revealing or even of being revealed goes back to manifesting or to being manifest. Revealed (*geoffenbarte*) religion exhausts itself in the end in the manifest (*offenbare*) evidence of the spirit to itself. Revelation finally has no other content than the manifestation and the consciousness of the concept. It is hence only justified by being abolished in manifestation in general. Revelation escapes being disqualified by metaphysics when it limits itself strictly to what admits of reason (Kant) or identifies itself simply with the work of the concept (Hegel). In both cases, it must renounce its specificity: announcing an event, explicating a word that surpasses the conditions of the possibility of experience and submitting to the requirements of the principle of reason.

Without a doubt, numerous classical aporias in the philosophy of religion result from its presupposition and (what shows up here again) from its method, namely, knowing that it is not possible to test the possibility of an impossibility. For the possible possibility of impossibility would imply that possibility cannot be limited to what sufficient reason ensures, hence possibility cannot be restricted to the actuality that produces the cause. Not to limit possibility in the sense in which, since Aristotle, "it is obvious that actuality precedes potentiality [φανερον οτι προτερον ενεργεια δυναμεωζ εστιν]"[5] would, by contrast, force us to understand how "*possibility* stands higher than actuality [*höher als die Wirklichkeit steht* die Möglichkeit]"; or, following Heidegger, "understanding phenomenology consists in nothing other than seizing it as possibility."[6] If by recognizing phenomena without the preliminary condition of a *causa sive ratio*, but in the way as and insofar as they are given, phenomenology is able to return to the things themselves, then does it not become the highest priority to free the thought of revelation in general? Phenomenology would hence be the only appropriate philosophy, not only for religion in its essence but also for knowledge as revelation.

2

Phenomenology goes back to the things themselves. This watchword would remain a slogan even if detailed procedures did not make it explicit. From the *Logical Investigations* onward, Husserl clears a decisive path toward the things themselves. Despite Kantian prohibitions, he recognizes the given as such by the simple fact that it is given. Essences are given invariable and in themselves, for example, although they are so only through a vision of essence and not by a sensible intuition. Without a doubt Husserl maintains the Kantian equivalence between givenness and intuition, but he doubles its scope. (a) What is intuited is at the same time given: thus signification is verified if sensible intuition fills the directed intention. (b) But inversely (against Kant), what is given testifies also, in the same measure, to what is intuited, even if no sensible intuition notices it: the founding acts that permit us to apply the categories imply a (categorial) intuition, since they are effectively given to consciousness. "In general, whether a givenness [*Gegebenheit*] manifests what is merely represented or what truly exists, what is real or what is idea, what is possible or what is impossible, it is a given in the cognitive phenomenon, in the phenomenon of a thought in the widest sense of the term."[7] In other words, givenness precedes intuition and abolishes its Kantian limits, because the fact of being given to consciousness (in whatever manner) testifies to the right of phenomena to be received as such, that is to say, as they give themselves. To return to the things themselves amounts to recognizing phenomena as themselves, without submitting them to the (sufficient) condition of an anterior authority (such as thing in itself, cause, principle, etc.). In short, it means liberating them from any prerequisite other than their simple givenness, to which consciousness bears witness before any constitution. Since it makes possible the return to the things themselves, the principle of all principles should perhaps be understood as a suspension of the principle of sufficient reason insofar as the phenomenon is not indebted to any reason, because its givenness itself justifies it: "The *principle of all principles, that every originarily giving intuition* [Anschauung] *is a source of right* [Rechtsquelle] *for cognition*, that everything that offers itself to us originarily in 'intuition' [*"Intuition"*] is to be taken quite simply as it gives itself out to be, but also only within the limits in which it is given there."[8] Intuition counts here as a source not only de facto but also de jure (*Rechtsquelle*). Why this change? Intuition is exercised as a *de* jure source [*source* de *droit*] because the source *of* right [*source du droit*], namely, givenness itself, is exercised in it more originally. What gives itself (inevitably by intuition of whatever type), in the measure and the limits within which it gives itself (inevitably to consciousness), must be accepted simply and purely (*einfach*) for what it is. The question *cur existat?* should not be answered with another *ratio* or another *causa* but only with: *es gibt das, was sich gibt*; "there is [lit. it gives] what gives itself"; hence, this gives what this gives. Not only the rose, but any phenomenon is without *why*, since any phenomenon is as it gives itself.

Such a breakthrough opens the imperial road of access to the things themselves inasmuch as phenomenology attains the received phenomenon as it gives itself without prerequisites. Yet it would not make sense to assume that a phenomenon could happen without cause or reason, since at the very least it would be given to consciousness, and inasmuch as given, it would exist. By thus lifting the prohibition of sufficient reason, phenomenology liberates possibility and hence opens the field possibly even to phenomena marked by impossibility. Among other possibilities, religious phenomena would reappear again in philosophy, as *facts* justified de jure since given *in fact*: the lived states of consciousness and the intentionalities of praise, of demand, of veneration, of repentance, of reconciliation, of confidence, etc., beliefs (from theological faith to various "holding as true"), the volitions of charity, of fraternity, of peace, of sacrifice, etc., not scientific but experiential types of knowledge (vision, "presences," internal dialogues, words said in the heart, etc.)—all these lived experiences of consciousness would hence appear as phenomena by full right, at least to the extent to which they are given to consciousness. When an allegedly adequate explanation is missing for them, that is to say, in fact their cause or sufficient reason, their legitimacy as phenomena is not thereby put into question, but only their objectivity beyond the limits of immanence. Givenness remaining immanent does not prohibit a phenomenon's actually being given: first because phenomenality cannot be reduced to objectivity; then because an intentionality can aim at an object correctly without intuition fulfilling intention adequately (that is even the most frequent case) or without intention being defined exactly by a formalized signification (as is the case in natural language). Without a doubt, a similar broadening of phenomenality does not fail to raise particular difficulties in the case of lived experiences and specifically religious intentions. Are these lived experiences really intentional (that is to say, are they really focused on an object), and, reciprocally, can these intentional aims of objects lay claims to merely partial intuitive fulfillment? Nevertheless, these questions can legitimately be examined in a phenomenological framework that respects their possibility.

What appears is as and according to how it gives itself. In other words: "As much appearance, so much being (whether it is recovered or falsified by its fact)." This equivalence as it is formulated by Husserl, although it contradicts classical metaphysics in a revolutionary way, will be taken up again literally by Heidegger: "As much appearing, so much being."[9] He will take it up in order to radicalize it, since it is now a matter of widening the concept of the phenomenon beyond the limits Husserl fixed for it. In order really to open access to a "phenomenon of Being,"[10] or, in other words, in order to include Being [*l'être*] inasmuch as different from being [*l'étant*] in phenomenality, one must admit that the absence of being gives itself.[11] From the ontic point of view, Being as such strictly amounts to nothing. Hence it gives itself inasmuch as it gives nothing, indeed gives the nothing. This paradox of a givenness without given is repeated for visibility: if it is a matter of making manifest, Being can manifestly not manifest itself visibly; just as easily, Heidegger will later speak of a "phenomenology of the unapparent."[12] Being can therefore only reach phenomenality if phenomenology also concerns what, at first glance, precisely does not manifest itself. In the case of the nonphenomenon of Being, phenomenology hence will attempt to include even what does *not* give itself phenomenally: "And it is precisely because phenomena are proximally or for the most part *not* given, that there is need for phenomenology."[13]

With this intention Heidegger will restore "indication" among the other meanings of the phenomenon (*Schein, Phänomene, Erscheinung*): for the indication announces (*anmelden*) a term that can make itself known while remaining invisible—in this way Being will announce itself in *Dasein* as a privileged being. By understanding the phenomenon as the *Sich-an-ihm-selbst-zeigende*, the phenomenological concept of the phenomenon also includes within it referral by indication, in such a way that, despite the unapparent nothingness of Being, it "means, as that which shows itself, the Being of being, its sense, its modifications and derivatives."[14] Husserl therefore had restored any intuited given inasmuch as intuited to the phenomenon and hence had legitimated the validity of religious lived experience inasmuch as it is given intuitively. In the same way, Heidegger integrates into phenomenality all that shows itself (*sich zeigt*) only by indication (*Anzeige*), inasmuch as the "showing itself" is still accomplished "from itself"—and hence he legitimates the possibility of a phenomenology of the unapparent in general. Certainly, the analytic of *Dasein* already discovers several unapparent phenomena (Being-for-death opened by anxiety, the *Nichts* by the *Gewissen*, possibility by being-in-the-world, etc.). Yet by beginning with the same *Dasein* or with another determination of privileged being, other analyses could make visible other unapparent phenomena. More precisely, one of the objections most often posed by metaphysics to the possibility of revelation and, in general, of religious phenomena is raised here: that through its lived experiences consciousness aims intentionally at an invisible object of the sort that could never be given directly. Nevertheless, this objection fails, because, on the one hand, even the most subjective or the most abstract intuition suffices to establish an actual givenness (Husserl) and, on the other hand, because even the invisible can be considered to be an authentic phenomenon, provided that it show itself beginning from itself, even if indirectly (Heidegger). The two constitutive terms of any phenomenon (lived experience, signification) are broadened in such a way that they allow revelation to enter into phenomenality. If one maintains the provisional definition of revelation introduced above—to know an instance transcendent to experience that nevertheless is manifested experientially—then one must admit that it is inscribed among phenomena, hence in experience (Husserl) of an intentional object that would be invisible and indirect, hence transcendent to experience (Heidegger). And transcendence must be understood here both in the sense of Kant and that of Husserl. The so-called religious lived experiences of consciousness give intuitively, but by indication, intentional objects that are directly invisible: religion becomes manifest and revelation phenomenal. What philosophy of religion tends to close, phenomenology of religion could open. Phenomenology offers a method not only to ontology (Heidegger), but to any region of phenomena not directly visible and hence immediately invisible—hence exceedingly to religion inasmuch as it concerns revelation. In short, phenomenology would be the method par excellence for the manifestation of the invisible through the phenomena that indicate it—hence also the method for theology.

3

One question nevertheless remains: If, when it recognizes religion as legitimate phenomenon, phenomenology gets beyond the limits of metaphysics' "Platonism" by radically broadening the conditions of givenness in presence, it thereby merely broadens what is given in presence.[15] Does such a broadening of manifestation really amount to a liberation of revelation? Furthermore, can (at least Husserlian) phenomenology not always pursue the enterprise of metaphysics with other means, namely, by leading every given back to givenness *in presence*? In this case, would not the conditions of possibility for presence always determine in advance the very givenness of phenomena? Would not such presuppositions merely reverse the metaphysical prohibitions regarding revelation, in such a way that, despite or because of its broadening of givenness, phenomenology would equally forbid the possibility of revelation by assigning to it a determined possibility? If that were so, it would be necessary to show that certain presuppositions of phenomenology restrict revelation. To achieve this, I will examine three of them, in order to clear three potential obstacles to the possibility of revelation.

By definition, phenomenology carries out a reduction—or rather, multiple reductions. For Husserl, it is a matter of reducing [*réduire*], or of leading back [*reconduire*], the world to the things themselves, that is to say, to what the *I* effectively experiences as given in the flesh: any possible phenomenon must be led back to one or several lived experiences of consciousness, hence to the *I* as intersection of these lived experiences (at least). No phenomenon can escape this automatic requirement: all that is, is experienced as *Erlebnis*, and what is not experienced in this way (even in the smallest manner) absolutely does not reach phenomenality at all. For Heidegger, reduction can become operative as soon as one transposes the *I* into *Dasein* and recognizes an analogy to lived experiences in the *Stimmungen* [moods or attunement], which give rise to *Dasein* as the fact of being-in-the-world. Following the opening of *In-der-Welt-sein*, nothing is constituted as a phenomenon that does not allow itself to be led back to *Dasein*, affected by diverse *Stimmungen* from the beings of its world. In short, the givenness of phenomena presupposes the point of reference that accommodates their givenness. As broadened as this givenness may appear, it nevertheless only allows things to appear to an *I*. It matters little that the *I* has different statuses (immanent, transcendent, constituting, constituted-constituting, *Dasein*, etc.), since it always precedes the phenomena as their condition of possibility regarding lived experiences.

What is the import of this for revelation? A question can at least be outlined here: Does whoever receives a revelation constitute it as one would constitute any other phenomenon? Obviously, one must doubt this: revelation really only merits its name if it surprises any anticipation of perception and surpasses any analogy to perception. The *I* has not the slightest idea, notion, or expectation regarding who or what is revealed. Furthermore, not only does what revelation reveals without a doubt shy away from being constituted by any sort of *I*, but occasionally it is possible that no lived experiences of the *I* correspond to it. What is experienced in revelation can be summed up as the powerlessness to experience whatever it might be that one experiences. The recipient of revelation does not retain common measure with what revelation communicates; otherwise, revelation would not have been necessary. In this way, whether due to excess or due to deficiency, the *I* in its finitude cannot register all that happens to it as a lived experience of consciousness. What is revealed is not necessarily experienced, because it transgresses the dimensions of *Erlebnis*. What one so improperly calls an exstasis in fact goes back to the "night of the senses," where the revealed imposes itself precisely because it cannot be experienced.

The dysfunction of *Erlebnis* in revelation is also confirmed *a contrario*, since revelation is annulled when *Erlebnis* persists in exhausting it. Thus Rudolf Bultmann, at the time of his greatest familiarity with Heidegger, attempted to define revelation by beginning with the *I* and its lived experiences, and by underlining that, if *fides ex auditu*, the event of Jesus comes to me by the word that "it announces" to me today: "Preaching itself is Revelation." Hence preaching, as actually experienced, counts as a lived experience. Yet what intentional object is the aim of this lived experience of the revealed? Or rather, what does the revealed lived experience reveal? No other revelation than the *fact* of Jesus: "Jesus is sent as the one who reveals [*als Offenbarer*]; and what does he reveal? That [*daß*] he is sent as the one who reveals." The revealed lived experience reveals the empty fact of revelation, which then, far from opening onto absolute possibility, sends lived experience back to itself: "Outside faith, Revelation is not visible; nothing is revealed in (regard to) what one believes."[16] The lived experience of faith remains because the *I* that experiences it first believes; but it cannot reach Jesus historically as its intentional object because the received lived experience (preaching), as a screen, returns the spirit of the *I* to itself in a repeated lived experience (faith). The phenomenological method here is applied to theology only by reducing the revealed to the lived experience of the revealed, hence obscuring the revealed revealing itself. The phenomenological reduction provokes demythologization, and *sola fides* reduces revelatory transcendence to real immanence in consciousness. Although it believes, consciousness does not reach any transcendent (thus revealed) object but is nourished by the immanent lived experience of its solitary faith. In 1929, Bultmann merely draws the consequences of the phenomenological definition of theology given by Heidegger in 1927. As Christian religion remains regional by relation to the analytic of *Dasein*, faith must be understood as a tonality of *Dasein*: "Faith is a mode of existence of human *Dasein*." Revelation hence cannot be understood as the communication of information to *Dasein* (thus of other intentional objects) but only as a participation in an event, that of faith itself. Revelation is confused with "the existence that Revelation has encountered."[17] This entails two possible consequences. On the one hand, if the thought of revelation is subjected to the phenomenological requirement of being reduced to the immanence of lived experience (or to modes of existence), hence to the *I* (or to *Dasein*), then the revealed is confined to revealed lived experience (faith, etc.), without any possibility of receiving the revealed revealing itself. Or, on the other hand, if thought claims to remain open to Revelation as such, it must be liberated from its immanence in the *I* (or in *Dasein*). Because it institutes the *I* (or *Dasein*) as the originary instance of phenomenality, the very concept of reduction damages the possibility of revelation as such.

Phenomenology presupposes a horizon for presenting the phenomena it reduces and constructs. Among other possible forms, this horizon assumes that of Being (Heidegger). In this exemplary case our guiding question could again be tested: Does phenomenology tolerate the general possibility of revelation? By establishing the unconditioned priority of ontological difference over any other question, Heidegger always includes God within it: as one among beings, even if the highest, God is given ontic appearance by the opening arranged by Being itself, the truth of Being precedes the light of the being-God: "Only from the truth of Being can the essence of the holy [*Heiligen*] be thought. Only from the essence of the holy is the essence of divinity to be thought. Only in the light of the essence of divinity can it be thought or said what the word 'God' is to signify."[18] The condition for thinking and saying the word "God" does not belong only to God, but depends finally on Being alone through the intermediaries of the divine, of the holy, and of the "whole" (*Heile*). Therefore, since thinking and saying the word "God" does not depend first and solely on God, one must conclude that God cannot be said or thought directly from himself, in short, that he cannot reveal himself. Without a doubt the being-God is seen as always granting the right to manifestation, but to a manifestation determined a priori according to the dimensions of a horizon, the horizon of Being: "But the holy [*das Heilige*], which alone is the essential sphere of divinity, which in turn alone affords a dimension for the gods and for God, [the sacred] comes to radiate only when being itself beforehand and after extensive preparation has been cleared and is experienced in its truth."[19] In other words, God (placed among the rank of the gods!) cannot appear (*ins Scheinen kommen*), that is to say "become phenomenon," except by entering into a *Wesensraum*, a "space of manifestation," which is measured by the dimensions of Being and not those of God. Hence here (*zuvor*) as in the previous text (*erst*), Being precedes God, for whom it limits manifestation in advance as his horizon. The *Wesensraum*, the *Dimension*, even the *Aufenthalt*,[20] define the parameters of the necessarily finite horizon of any manifestation of God. God can no longer reveal himself freely, but must manifest himself according to the conditions superimposed by the whole, the sacred, and the divine, thus finally by Being. Container [*Écrin*] of any being, Being plays, in the case of God, the function of a screen [*écran*]. It precedes the very initiative of revealing, it fixes the frame of revelation, and it imposes the conditions of reception on the revealed gift.

Even Christian theology can be tempted to reduce the Revelation of God by God to the measure of the ontological horizon of manifestation. Thus Karl Rahner radicalizes what may have been one of Heidegger's profoundest intuitions by constructing an "ontological Christology" (*ontologische Christologie*), not a "squared circle" but a transcendental demarcation of the dimensions of Christology according to the a priori of Being. Any revelation legitimizes itself by beginning from a *Vorbegriff auf das Sein*, because love and knowledge of God have as their condition an *ontological* mediation operated by Christ: "Self-mediation according to Being must be comprehended in advance as the condition of possibility for the immediate personal knowledge of God and for love of him."[21] The possibility of loving God admits a condition of possibility: ontological self-mediation (identified with Christ). Furthermore, this self-mediation must legitimate itself and, in turn, be legitimated according to a being: "An intimate understanding and an ontological legitimacy of such a concept of self-mediation is to find in the transcendental experience of the return of each finite being an absolute Being and the secret of God." Mediation in the person of Christ is hence inscribed into the horizon of Being according to the transcendental dimension of being. This dimension manifests him in his truth, according to the "ontological essence of this self-mediation,"[22] but does not reveal itself in its proper infinite. Put differently: Does Christology reveal God's free charity or does it manifest the transcendental (a priori, ontological) conditions of finite being? The ambiguity results from assuming that a phenomenological horizon is necessary for revelation. Without a doubt, this ambiguity would be confirmed by other instances of phenomenological horizons. By imposing an a priori dimension or abode and therefore a limit for revelation, the concept of the horizon itself disqualifies the possibility of revelation, while at the same time making any manifestation possible.

The obstacles to revelation thus coincide with the conditions of manifestation. One of Husserl's doctrines confirms explicitly that the reduction (to the *I* or to *Dasein*) and the presupposition of a horizon (of Being, etc.) lead to closing phenomenology to the proper conditions of possibility. An absolutely given truth (in conformity with the "principle of principles") imposes itself on any consciousness whatsoever without any restriction: "What is true is absolutely, intrinsically true: truth is one and the same [*identisch Eine*], whether humans or non-humans, angels or gods apprehend and judge it." The conditions of evidence impose the evidence of their condition on any mind whatsoever, even on God: "Thus we see that not only for us human beings *but also for God* . . . whatever has the character of a spatial thing, is intuitable only through appearances, wherein it is given, and indeed must be given, as changing 'perspectively' in varied yet determined ways, and thereby presented in changing orientations."[23] Givenness to presence—the principle of all the principles—is absolutely essential: if God knows, he must see according to given appearances. It follows that he would not be able to give himself to see except according to the requirements of this same principle. Revelation will either be impossible or it will come down to a common law phenomenal manifestation. A second aporia confirms this first one, namely, the Husserlian impossibility of justifying knowledge of the other as such phenomenologically (at least in the *Cartesian Meditations*). The other cannot appear as other because the phenomenological conditions of appearance (reduction to the *I*, horizon, and constitution) allow only the appearance of an object or the assumption of an *alter ego*. The other either amounts to another object still constituted by an *I* or will be reached only indirectly (*appresentation*), as invisible observer of the same object as *I* am. The horizon of objectivity and the reduction to an *I* confine givenness in the manifestation of objectivity to the point of excluding revelation of an Other [*Autre*] who is authentically such.

Givenness in presence, by which phenomenology surpasses metaphysics and the principle of reason, nevertheless does not permit it to attain the givenness of revelation. The principle of principles presupposes the primacy of the *I* or of *Dasein*. Phenomenology does not liberate the possibility of a theology. "My immediate aim concerns not theology but phenomenology, however important the bearing of the latter on the former may indirectly be"[24] (Husserl). "There is no such thing as a neo-Kantian, or axiological, or phenomenological theology, just as there is no phenomenological mathematics"[25] (Heidegger).

4

Phenomenology cannot give its status to theology, because the conditions of manifestation contradict or at least are different from the free possibility of revelation. Yet the result is not necessarily a divorce, since a final hypothesis remains conceivable: could theology not suggest to phenomenology certain modifications of method and processes in virtue of its own requirements and only for formulating them? In other words, could one not inquire into the (unconditional) conditions to which the phenomenological method would have to subscribe in order to attain a thought of revelation? Inversely, could not the requirements of theology permit phenomenology to transgress its proper limits, in order finally to attain the free possibility at which it has pretended to aim since its origin?

Phenomenology refuses to admit the full possibility of revelation, because it imposes two limits on possibility in general: the *I* and the horizon. Hence even the question of a phenomenology of religion, like that of a phenomenology of revelation, suggests calling into question the axiomatic character of these two presuppositions. In at least one way, the Husserlian *I* persists in Heideggerian *Dasein* despite all their polemics: With *Being-in-the-world* intentionality does not disappear but is radicalized, since in both cases only the originally possibilizing opening of the *I* (or of *Dasein*) can take aim at, reach, or experience either an object or, more generally, an intra-mundane being. Intentionality opens a world; *being-in-the world* "worlds": whether as objectivity or as world, such opening is decided in a center that always reverts back to the *I*. This presupposition raises two difficulties within phenomenology itself.

(a) The *I* constitutes objects according to its axis of intentionality. Yet supposing that the constitution of the world is accomplished without remainder (hence that a revelation could be demarcated a priori), one would still have to ask whether the *I* is constituted by itself, to what extent and by what authority. Husserl himself constantly confronted this multiform difficulty although he never resolved it. Merleau-Ponty and Sartre attempted to split the *I* in two, one aspect constituted (transcendence of the ego), one aspect not constituted (prereflexive). Although Heidegger shifted the emphasis from the question of constitution to that of *Entschlossenheit*, he possibly did not, for all that, surpass it. But if the inherent locus of constitution according to the intentional axis remains itself undetermined, does not the very ground of reduction begin to shift?

(b) It does so because a different property of the *I* turns out to be problematic in a parallel fashion: Does the *I* define itself essentially as the origin of intentionality? Even *Dasein* keeps the privilege of opening (on) beings from itself. This polarization of the *I* according to the intentional axis can nevertheless be contested phenomenologically: either by challenging absolutely the intentional ecstasy (subject-object split) from the self-affectivity of the *me*, an original and self-immanent passivity;[26] or by deforming the constituted and the constituting *I* all the way to the givenness in person (*Selbstgegebenheit*) of the original flesh (*Leib*), in such a way that it would precede the gap between immanence and transcendence, constituting and constituted, and hence all intentionality;[27] or, finally, by invalidating the intentional axis through the ethical injunction, which the I no longer exercises but which it receives and suffers from the face of the other—without representation, passively, forever the other obliges the *I* to relinquish any *Jemeinigkeit*, any intentional source, any constitution, in order to become an *I* in the accusative (*me*, not *ego*) convoked, summoned, affected by the other.[28] A single paradox is outlined in these three attempts: one of the instances that restrict phenomenology's acceptance of the full possibility of revelation, namely, to know the *I* (and its equivalents), does not offer any certain phenomenological guarantee. What phenomenology opposes to revelation—the *I* as origin—is perhaps not phenomenologically legitimate: Who is the *I*? Is the *I* original or derived? If it is derived, from where, from what—from whom? Consequently, would it not be suitable to reverse the relation and the dependence? Far from the *I* restricting the possibility of a revelation phenomenologically, would one not have to venture that maybe the *I* can only attain its proper phenomenological possibility from a givenness that cannot be constituted, cannot be objectified and is prior to it—maybe even from a revelation?

Phenomenology returns to the things inasmuch as it makes them visible or phenomenal. It presents the things themselves. This presentation is deployed within a horizon. The horizon can vary: objectivity (Husserl), Being (Heidegger), ethics (Levinas), the body of the flesh (Merleau-Ponty), etc. The principle of horizon always remains. This requirement raises a double question. (a) What sort of horizon could allow for a revelation? While the horizon of objectivity quickly and generally has been recognized as inadequate and theology consequently is acknowledged as a nonobjectifying knowledge, must one therefore uphold the horizon of Being as the indisputable frame for any possible revelation? Fundamental ontology's neutrality—and especially its "appearance of an individualistic and radical atheism to the extreme"[29]—closes down the possibility of revelation, first by leading revelation back precisely to the manifestation of a being, but especially by prejudging that revelation already concerns a being. Of course, one can object: Can revelation retain any meaning without the horizon of Being? Certainly, since the substitution of ethics for Being as horizon already opens phenomenology; no longer is it closed to the invisible phenomenon of the face of the other. The injunction inverts intentionality, and concrete morality appears. But for all that, it is not certain that by passing from Being to ethics (or to the body's flesh) phenomenology has made sufficient progress in the direction of the possibility of revelation, of possibility as revelation. In any case, possibility actually submits straightaway to the restriction of a horizon. Any horizon that determines the scene of incoming phenomena in a priori fashion delimits the possible, hence limits (or forbids) revelation.

(b) Thus the second question: Does revelation admit of a horizon (still to be identified), or does it exclude being presented by any horizon whatsoever in principle? The difficulty of the dilemma increases as soon as one notes that neither of these hypotheses is acceptable. If revelation admits of a horizon, it acknowledges the horizon a priori and therefore renounces possibility. It really then renounces itself and regresses to the rank of a simple constituted manifestation. If revelation excludes any horizon on principle, it can no longer present itself anywhere, to no gaze nor as any phenomenon: thus it would lose any relation with phenomenology and its presentation, certainly with phenomenality as such (*schlechthin*). How should one therefore think the relation of revelation to the horizon (thus to phenomenology), if the two extremes cannot be admitted? Revelation entails a presentation. Hence it condescends to assume a horizon, but it nevertheless challenges any a priori condition imposed on its possibility.

Even so these paradoxical requirements indicate the correct response: revelation presents itself in a horizon only by *saturating* it. Without a doubt, a horizon remains acquired and all visibility takes place within the measure of its scope—revelation can allow itself to be refracted on the horizon of Being, of the other, of the body's flesh, etc. Yet what is thus revealed fulfills at this point the dimensions and the possibilities that this frame imparts to it, so that the resulting phenomenon damages itself. The strength and the scope of what allows itself to be presented can enter the limits of the phenomenological horizon only by disrupting it: each line of the phenomenon interferes with all the others, as if they crossed or reflected each other or interacted within their respective frames.[30] This confusion does not indicate any disarray internal to revelation, but only the incommensurability of any revelation with any phenomenological horizon whatsoever. The confusion of the horizon by revelation marks, as saturation, the *correct*, that is to say, the paradoxical relation of one to the other: revelation does not enter phenomenality except under the figure of a paradox—as saturated phenomena that saturate the entire horizon of phenomenality. "Saturated phenomenon" means: instead of common phenomenality striving to make intuition adequate to intention, and usually having to admit the failure in givenness of an incompletely intuited though fully intended object, revelation gives objects where intuition surpasses the intentional aim. Under the regime of revelation, intuition offers neither as much nor less than but *infinitely more* than intention, hence than the significations elaborated by the *I*. Similar intuitions (still) without intention, without signification, even without expressible objectivity thus play freely (*imaginatio vaga*), interfere with each other, escape constitution, saturate the horizon. Thus revelation forces phenomenology to question that truth could be boiled down to the lived experiences of truth—to know that "evidence would be the 'lived experience' of truth"[31] (and this lived experience would refer unreservedly to *Dasein*'s opening). "Being true, as much as being revelatory, is a mode of the being of *Dasein*."[32] Truth, at least the truth given without restraint by revelation, does not discover (itself) so much as it recovers from intuition all intentions, inundates significations with (albeit extravagant) objectivities, and saturates the horizon with its givenness without measure. In this situation, truth no longer comes from δοξα, (true or false) appearance, but from παραδοξον, an appearance that contradicts opinion or appearance, and above all saturates the horizon.

The conditions under which phenomenology would be able to do justice to the possibility of revelation (to possibility as revelation) can hence, at least summarily, be expressed in this way: (a) that the *I* admit its nonoriginal character and think it all the way to an inherent givenness; (b) that the horizon allow itself to be saturated by givenness instead of insisting on determining it a priori, and that truth accordingly change from the evidence of δοξα to the παραδοξον of the revealed. A definitive response to these two conditions could only be possible after long and difficult investigations, which are to a great extent still to come. If phenomenology would at least begin to approach and to confront them candidly, it might accomplish what previous philosophy of religion has never more than outlined: freeing the possibility of revelation, hence possibility as revelation, from the grip of the principle of sufficient reason, under-stood as the a priori condition of possibility (hence of impossibility) for any event to come. Certainly, freeing the possibility of revelation doubt-lessly would force phenomenology to liberate itself from its pretensions to self-constitution (*I*, the horizon), but this requirement is so radical that it merely confirms how radical the liberation in question will have to be.

—Translated by Christina M. Gschwandtner

The Saturated Phenomenon

What comes into the world without troubling merits neither consideration nor patience.

—**René Char**

1

The field of religion could be defined simply as whatever philosophy excludes or at best subjugates. Such constant antagonism cannot be reduced to any given ideological opposition or anecdotal prejudice. In fact, it rests upon perfectly reasonable grounds: any possible "philosophy of religion" would have to describe, produce, and constitute phenomena. It would then find itself confronted with a disastrous alternative: it would be a question either of addressing phenomena that are objectively definable but lose their religious specificity or of addressing phenomena that are specifically religious but cannot be described objectively. A phenomenon that is religious in the strict sense—that is, belongs to the domain of a "philosophy of religion" distinct from the sociology, history, and psychology of religion—would have to render visible what nevertheless could not be objectivized. The religious phenomenon thus amounts to an impossible phenomenon, or at least it marks the limit from which the phenomenon in general is no longer possible. Thus, beyond the question of the possibility of religion, the religious phenomenon poses the question of the general possibility of the phenomenon.

Once this boundary is acknowledged, several ways of understanding it remain. Religion could not strike with impossibility the possibility of the phenomenon in general if the very possibility of the phenomenon were not defined: When does it become impossible to speak of a phenomenon, and according to what criteria of phenomenality? Yet the possibility of the phenomenon (and therefore the possibility of declaring a phenomenon impossible, that is, invisible) in turn could not be determined without also establishing the terms of possibility taken by itself. By subjecting the phenomenon to the jurisdiction of possibility, philosophy in fact brings its own definition of naked possibility fully to light. The question concerning the possibility of the phenomenon implies the question of the phenomenon of possibility. Or better, the rational scope of a philosophy that is measured by the extent of what it renders possible is also assessed by the range of what it renders visible, thus, according to the possibility of phenomenality within it. Depending, hence, on whether it is accepted or rejected, the religious phenomenon becomes a privileged index of the possibility of phenomenality.

I will begin by relying on Kant. In Kant the metaphysical definition of possibility is stated as follows: "What agrees with the formal conditions of experience, that is, with the conditions of intuition and of concepts, is possible [*mit den formalen Bedingungen der Erfahrung . . . überein-kommt*]."[1] Surprising here is the intimate tie that Kant establishes between possibility and phenomenality: possibility results explicitly from the conditions of experience. Among these conditions is intuition, which indicates that experience takes the form of a phenomenality, that experience has a form ("formal conditions") precisely because it experiences sensible forms of appearance. Hence here possibility depends on phenomenality. Should we conclude from this that the phenomenon imposes its possibility, instead of being subject to the conditions of possibility? Not at all, because the possible does not agree with the object of experience but with its "formal conditions": possibility does not follow from the phenomenon, but from the *conditions* set for any phenomenon. Thus a formal requirement is imposed on possibility, just as Kant indicates a little later: "The postulate of the possibility of things requires [*fordert*] that the concept of things should agree with the formal conditions of experience in general."[2] The access of the phenomenon to its own manifestation must submit to the requirement of possibility; but possibility itself depends upon the "formal conditions of experience." How, then, on final appeal, are established these "formal conditions" that determine phenomenality and possibility together? Kant indicates an indirect but unambiguous answer by underlining that "the categories of modality . . . express only the relation of the concept to the power of knowing."[3] The formal conditions of knowledge are here joined directly to the power of knowing. This means that intuition and the concept determine in advance the possibility for any phenomenon to appear. The possibility—and therefore also and especially the impossibility—of a phenomenon is ordered by the measure of the "power of knowing," that is, concretely, the measure of the play of intuition and of the concept within a finite mind. Any phenomenon is possible that matches the finitude of the power of knowing and its requirements.

In this way, Kant merely confirms a decision already made by Leibniz. To be sure, the one thinks phenomenal possibility starting from a finite mind, while the other thinks it starting from an infinite (or indefinite) mind, but both lead to the same conditional possibility of the phenomenon. Indeed, metaphysics obeys the "Great Principle . . . which holds that nothing is done without sufficient reason, that is, that nothing happens without it being possible for the one who sufficiently knows things to give a Reason that suffices to determine why it is so and not otherwise."[4] Thus, nothing "is done," nothing "happens," in short, nothing appears without the attestation that it is "possible"; this possibility, in turn, is equivalent to the possibility of knowing the sufficient reason for such an appearance. As for Kant, for Leibniz the right to appear, the possibility of the phenomenon, depends on the power of knowing that implements the sufficiency of reason, which (whatever it might be) precedes what it renders possible. As the "power of knowing" will establish the conditions of possibility, sufficient reason already suffices to render possible what would have remained impossible without it. This dependence is indicated with particular clarity in the case of the sensible. To be sure, "sensible things" appear and deserve the name of "phenomena," but they owe that name to another "reason," a reason that is different from their appearance and that alone suffices to qualify that appearance as a phenomenon: "The truth of sensible things consisted only in this relation of the phenomena, which had to have its reason."[5] When, among the beings that he recognizes as permanent (*Creatura permanens absoluta*), Leibniz opposes full being (*Unum per se, Ens plenum. / substantia / Modificatio*) to the diminished being that he likens to the phenomenon (*Unum per aggregationem. Semiens, phaenomenon*),[6] one should not commit the error of imagining that the phenomenon would be ranked as half a being or a half-being only because it would suffer from an insufficiency of reason. On the contrary, it is precisely because it enjoys a perfectly sufficient reason that the phenomenon regresses to the rank of half a being; it is precisely as "well-grounded phenomena [*phaenomena bene fundata*]"[7] that phenomena admit their being grounded and therefore conditioned by a reason that alone is sufficient and that they themselves do not suffice to ensure. If reason can ground phenomena, this is so because it must save them. Yet reason would not have to save them if one did not first admit that, left to themselves, these phenomena would be lost. It is not sufficient to justify the possibility of appearance for it to appear in fact. Appearance must still resort to reason. Although itself refraining from appearing, reason alone makes possible the brute actuality of appearance, because it renders this possibility real. The phenomenon attests to its lack of reason when and because it receives that reason, for it appears only under condition, as a conditional phenomenon—under the condition of what does not appear. In a metaphysical system, the possibility of appearing never belongs to what appears, nor phenomenality to the phenomenon.

2

It is this aporia that phenomenology escapes by opposing the "principle of all principles" to the principle of sufficient reason and thus surpassing conditional phenomenality through a phenomenality without condition. The "principle of all principles" posits that "*every originarily giving intuition* [Anschauung] *is a source of right* [Rechtsquelle] *for cognition*, that everything that offers itself to us originarily in 'intuition' ["*Intuition*"] is to be taken quite simply as it gives itself out to be, but also only within the limits in which it is given there."[8] There can be no question concerning the decisive importance of this principle, nor of its function within the group of other principles of phenomenology.[9] It will suffice to underscore some of its essential traits.

According to the first essential trait, intuition no longer intervenes simply as a de facto source of the phenomenon, a source that ensures its brute actuality without grounding it in reason, but as a source of right justifying itself. Intuition is itself attested through itself, without the background of a reason that is yet to be given. In this way, the phenomenon according to Husserl foreshadows Heidegger's definition of the phenomenon as that which shows itself on the basis of itself—to put it plainly: from itself as pure and perfect appearance of itself and not on the basis of something other than itself, another that would not appear (a reason). Intuition is sufficient for the phenomenon to justify its right to appear without any other reason: far from having to give a sufficient reason, it is enough for the phenomenon to give itself through intuition according to a principle of sufficient intuition. But intuition becomes sufficient only inasmuch as it operates without any background, originarily, as Husserl says. Now, it operates originarily, without any presupposition, only inasmuch as it furnishes the originary data, inasmuch, therefore, as it gives itself originarily. Intuition is de jure justified from itself only by making a claim to be the unconditioned origin. It cannot justify this claim without miming the sufficient reason to be rendered (*reddendae rationis*), that is, by rendering itself, by giving itself directly. Indeed, *givenness* alone indicates that the phenomenon ensures in a single gesture both its visibility and the full right of that visibility, both its appearance and the reason for that appearance. Nevertheless, it still remains to be verified whether the "principle of all principles" in point of fact ensures a right to appear for all phenomena, whether it really opens for them an absolutely unconditioned possibility, or whether it still renders them possible only under some condition. Now, it happens that the principle of the giving intuition does not authorize the absolutely unconditioned appearance, and thus the freedom of the phenomenon that gives itself on the basis of itself. To be sure, this is not because intuition as such limits phenomenality, but because as intuition it remains framed by two conditions of possibility, conditions that themselves are not intuitive but that are nevertheless assigned to every phenomenon. The second and third traits of the "principle of all principles" contradict the first, as conditions and limits—a condition and a limit—contradict the claim to absolute possibility opened by the giving intuition.

Let me first consider a second trait of the "principle": it justifies every phenomenon, "but also only [*aber auch nur*] within the limits in which" that phenomenon is given. This restriction attests to a twofold finitude of the giving instance of intuition. First, there is a factual restriction: intuition admits "bounds [*Schranken*]": these bounds, in whatever way one understands them (since Husserl hardly makes them clear), indicate that not everything is capable of being given perfectly. Right away, intuition is characterized by scarcity, obeys a logic of shortage, and is stigmatized by an indelible insufficiency. One will have to ponder the motivation, the status, and the presuppositions of this factual shortcoming. Yet, second, this restriction can already be authorized by a de jure limitation: any intuition, in order to give within certain factual "bounds," must first be inscribed by right within the limit (*Grenze*) of a horizon. Likewise, no intentional aim of an object, signification, or essence can operate outside of a horizon. Husserl indicates this point in an argument that is strengthened by its paradox: considering what he nevertheless names "the limitlessness [*Grenzenlosigkeit*] that is presented by the immanent intuitions when going from an already-fixed lived experience to new lived experiences that form its horizon, from the fixing of these lived experiences to the fixing of their horizon; and so on," he admits that any lived experience is continually referred to new, as yet unknown lived experiences and therefore to a horizon of novelties that are irreducible because continually renewed. Yet this irrepressible novelty of the flux of consciousness remains by right always comprehended within a horizon, even if these new lived experiences are not yet given: "a lived experience that has become an object of an ego's gaze and that therefore has the mode of something observed, has its horizon of non-observed lived-experiences [*Danach hat ein Erlebnis, das zum Objekt eines Ich-Blickes geworden ist, also den Modus des Erblickten hat, seinen Horizont nichterblickter Erlebnisse*]."[10] The horizon, or, according to its etymology, the delimitation, is exerted over experience even where there are only lived experiences that are not looked at, that is, where experience has not taken place. The outside of experience is not equivalent to the experience of the outside, because the horizon in advance seizes the outside, the nonexperienced, the nonobserved. One cannot escape the feeling of a fundamental ambiguity here. With this horizon, is it a question of what is not looked at as not looked at, a question of the simple recognition that all lived experience is grasped in the flux of consciousness, and therefore oriented in advance toward other lived experiences that are yet to arise? Or is it not rather a question of the treatment in advance of non–lived experiences that are not looked at as the subjects of a horizon, and therefore a question of inclusion within a limit—albeit that of the flux of consciousness—of anything that is not seen, a question of the a priori inscription of the possible within a horizon? Thus one must ask whether the "principle of all principles" does not presuppose at least one condition for givenness: the very horizon of any givenness. Does not the second trait of the "principle of all principles," that of some horizon or other, contradict the absoluteness of intuitive givenness?

The third trait of the "principle of all principles" has to do with the fact that intuition gives what appears only by giving it "to us." There is nothing trivial or redundant about this expression; it betrays a classic ambiguity of the *Ideas*: The givenness of the phenomenon on the basis of itself to an *I* at every instant can veer toward a constitution of the phenomenon through and on the basis of the *I*. Even if one does not overestimate this constant threat, one must at least admit that givenness can give and justify nothing except before the tribunal of the *I*, precisely because the *I* keeps its originary and justifying function. Transcendental or not, the phenomenological *I* remains the beneficiary, and therefore the witness and even the judge, of the given appearance. It falls to the *I* to measure what does and does not give itself intuitively, within what limits, according to what horizon, following what intention, essence, and signification.

Even if it shows itself on the basis of itself, the phenomenon can do so only by allowing itself to be led back, and therefore reduced, to the *I*. Moreover, the originary primacy of the *I* maintains an essential relation with the placement of any phenomenon within the limits of a horizon. Indeed, "every *now* of a lived-experience has a horizon of lived-experiences—which also have precisely the originary form of the 'now,' and which as such produce *an originary horizon* [Originaritätshorizont] *of the pure I*, its total originary *now* of consciousness."[11] In this way the "principle of all principles" still presupposes that all givenness must accept the *I* as its "now." The requirement of a horizon is one with that of the reduction: it is always a matter of leading phenomenological givenness back to the *I*. But that being so, if every phenomenon is defined by its reducibility to the *I*, must one not exclude straightaway the general possibility of an absolute and autonomous, in short, irreducible phenomenon? By the same token, is not all irreducible possibility decidedly jeopardized?

By originarily giving intuition, "the principle of all principles" undoubtedly frees phenomena from the duty of rendering a sufficient reason for their appearance. But it thinks that givenness only on the basis of determinations that threaten its originary character: the horizon and the reduction. Phenomenology would thus almost immediately condemn itself to missing what the giving intuition indicates to it as its goal: to free the possibility of appearing as such. One should stress that it is obviously not a question here of envisaging a phenomenology without any *I* or horizon, for clearly phenomenology itself would then become impossible. On the contrary, it is a question of taking seriously the claim that since the formulation of the "principle of all principles" "*possibility* stands higher than actuality"[12] and of envisaging this possibility radically. Let me define it provisionally: As regards phenomenality, what would happen if an intuitive givenness were accomplished that was absolutely unconditioned (without the limits of a horizon) and absolutely irreducible (to a constituting *I*)? Could one not envision a type of phenomenon that would reverse the condition of a horizon (by surpassing it, instead of being inscribed within it) and that would reverse the reduction (by leading the *I* back to itself, instead of being reduced to the *I*)? To declare this hypothesis impossible, without first resorting to intuition, would betray a phenomenological contradiction. Consequently, I will here assume the hypothesis of such a phenomenon, at least as an imaginary variation, permitting us to test the limits of all phenomenality and again to experience what possibility means—or better, what it might give. Some limits remain irrefutable and undoubtedly indispensable in principle. Yet this does not mean that what contradicts them cannot for all that, paradoxically, be constituted as a phenomenon. Quite the contrary, by playing on the limits of phenomenality, certain phenomena not only can appear at those limits, but appear even better there. On this hypothesis, the question of a phenomenology of religion might arise in new terms, as much for religion as for phenomenology.

3

Evoking the possibility of an unconditioned and irreducible phenomenon, that is, of a phenomenon par excellence, would be justified only inasmuch as such a possibility is truly opened. It would therefore have to be established that this possibility cannot be reduced to an illusion of possibility by moving to the limit in a way that would exceed nothing other than the conditions of possibility of phenomenality in general. In short, I will have to establish that an unconditioned and irreducible phenomenon, with neither delimiting horizon nor constituting *I*, presents a true possibility and does not amount to "telling tales." To support this claim, I will first proceed indirectly by examining the common definition of the phenomenon, since such a definition exists as much in Kant's metaphysics as in Husserl's phenomenology. Then I will attempt to specify whether that definition, which subjects every phenomenon to a horizon of appearance and a constituting *I*, is justified by an opening of phenomenality or whether it does not, rather, confirm phenomenology's essential closure. In other words, at stake will be specifying the ground of the limitation imposed upon the phenomenon by its common definition, in order to indicate, by contrast, exactly what possibility would remain open to an unconditional and irreducible sense of phenomenality.

All along the path of his thinking, Husserl maintains a definition of the phenomenon that is determined by its fundamental duality: "The word 'phenomenon' is ambiguous [*doppelsinnig*] in virtue of the essential correlation between appearance and that which appears [*Erscheinen und Erscheinendem*]."[13] This correlation is organized according to several different but connected pairs—intention/intuition, signification/fulfillment, noesis/noema, and the like—and thus only establishes the phenomenon more firmly as what appears as a correlate of appearance. This is indeed why the highest manifestation of any phenomenon, that is to say, its highest possible phenomenality, is achieved with perfect adequation between these two terms: the subjective appearing is equivalent to what appears objectively. "And so also, *eo ipso*, the idea of every fulfillment, and therefore of a *significative* fulfillment, is sketched for us; the *intellectus* is in this case the thought-intention, the intention of meaning. And the *adequatio* is realized when the objectness meant is given in intuition in the strict sense, and given precisely as it is thought and named. No thought-intention could fail to find its fulfillment, and certainly its final fulfillment, insofar as the fulfilling medium of intuition has itself lost all implication of unsatisfied intention."[14] It is certainly important to stress the persistence here, in a nevertheless phenomenological territory, of the most metaphysical definition of truth as *adequatio rei et intellectus*. But it is even more important to stress the fact that adequation defines not only truth but above all "the idea of ultimate fulfillment."[15] This limit case of perception is equivalent to what Husserl, in a Cartesian fashion, names "evidence." More precisely, objective truth is achieved subjectively through evidence, considered as the experience of adequation made by consciousness. Now this ideal of evidence, which is supposed to designate the maximum and the extreme of any ambition to truth, nevertheless with a very strange modesty claims only an "adequation," a simple equality. The paradigm of ideal equality weighs so heavily that Husserl does not hesitate to repeat it in no fewer than four figures: (a) "the full agreement between the meant and the given as such [*die Übereinstimmung zwischen Gemeintem und Gegebenem*]"; (b) "the idea of the absolute adequation [*Adäquation*]" between ideal essence and the empirically contingent act of evidence; (c) the "ideal fulfillment for an intention"; (d) and, finally, "truth as rightness [*Rechtigkeit*] of our intention."[16] What is surprising, however, resides not so much in this insistent repetition as in the fact that the adequation it seeks so explicitly remains, nonetheless, a pure and simple ideal: "The ideal of an ultimate fulfillment," "that is ideally fulfilled perception," and "idea of absolute adequation as such."[17] Now, how can one fail to understand these two terms in a Kantian manner, where the ideal is the object of the idea? Consequently, since the idea remains a concept of reason such that its object can never be given through the senses, the ideal as such (as object of the idea) will never be given.[18] Thus, if adequation, which produces evidence subjectively, still constitutes an "ideal" for Husserl, one must conclude that it is realized never or at least only rarely. And truth itself is rarefied or made inaccessible together with evidence. Why, then, does adequate evidence most often remain a limit case or even an excluded case? Why does the equality between *noesis* and *noema*, essence and fulfillment, intention and intuition, seem inaccessible (or almost so) at the very moment when it is invested with the dignity of truth? Why does Husserl compromise the return to the things themselves by investing evidence and truth with ideality?

Answer: because the equality that Husserl maintains de jure between intuition and intention remains intolerable for him. Intention (almost) always (partially) lacks intuition, just as signification almost always lacks fulfillment. In other words, intention and signification surpass intuition and fulfillment. "A surplus in signification [*ein Überschuss in der Bedeutung*] remains, a form that finds nothing in the phenomenon itself to confirm it," because in principle "the realm of signification is much wider than that of intuition."[19] Intuition remains essentially lacking, poor, needy, indigent. The adequation between intention and intuition thus becomes a simple limit case, an ideal that is usually evoked by default. One could not argue against this by putting forward the fact that evidence is regularly achieved in mathematics and formal logic; for this fact, far from denying the failure of evidence, confirms it. Indeed, the ideal of adequation is realized only in those domains where the intention of signification requires merely a pure or formal intuition (e.g., space in mathematics), or even no intuition at all (e.g., empty tautology in logic) in order to be fulfilled in a phenomenon. Mathematics and formal logic offer, precisely, only an ideal object—that is, strictly speaking, an object that does not have to give itself in order to appear, in short, a minute or zero degree of phenomenality. Evidence is adequately achieved because it requires only a poor or empty intuition. Adequation is realized so easily here only because it is a matter of phenomena without any (or with weak) intuitive requirements.[20] There would be good reason, moreover, to wonder about the privilege that is so often granted to logical and mathematical phenomena by theories of knowledge (from Plato to Descartes, from Kant to Husserl). They are erected as models for all other phenomena, while they are distinguished from them by their shortage of intuition, by the poverty of their givenness, or even by the unreality of their objects. It is not self-evident that this marginal poverty could serve as a paradigm for phenomenality as a whole, nor that the certitude it ensures would be worth the phenomenological price one pays for it. Whatever the case may be, adequation becomes an ideal in the strict sense if the ideal of evidence is realized only for intuitively poor phenomena, when, on the contrary, it is a matter of plenary phenomena (that is, of the appearance of the "things themselves" to be given intuitively). Adequation then becomes an event not (entirely) given, due to a (at least partial) failure of intuition. This equality required de jure between intuition and intention is lacking—for lack of intuition. The senses deceive, not at all through a provisional or an accidental deception, but through an inescapable weakness: even an indefinite sum of intuited outlines will never fill intention with the least real object. When it is a question of a thing, the intentional object always exceeds its intuitive givenness. Its presence remains to be completed by appresentation.[21] What keeps phenomenology from allowing phenomena to appear without reserve is therefore first the fundamental deficit of intuition with which it endows them, without appeal or recourse. But the phenomenological "breakthrough" postulates this shortage of intuition only as a result of metaphysical decisions—in short, Husserl here suffers the consequences of decisions made by Kant.

It was Kant who, always defining truth by *adaequatio*,[22] first inferred this parallel between intuition and the concept, both of which are supposed to play a tangentially equal role in the production of objectivity. "Without sensibility no object would be given to us, without understanding no object would be thought. Thoughts without content are empty, intuitions without concepts are blind. It is, therefore, just as necessary to make our concepts sensible (that is, to add the object to them in intuition), as to make our intuitions intelligible (that is, to bring them under concepts). These two powers or capacities cannot exchange their functions. The understanding can intuit nothing, the senses can think nothing."[23] In principle, the phenomenon, and therefore the real object, appears to the strict measure that the intuition and the concept are not only synthesized but balanced in that synthesis. *Adaequatio*, and therefore truth, would thus rest on the equality of the concept with intuition. However, Kant himself does not hesitate to disqualify this parallelism. For if the concept corresponds to intuition, it nevertheless radically depends on it. Indeed, to the extent that the concept thinks, it is limited to rendering intelligible (after the fact and by derivation) what intuition alone can give, principally and originarily: "Our knowledge springs from two fundamental sources of the mind. . . . Through the first [receptivity] an object is given [*gegeben*] to us, through the second the object is thought." "There are two conditions under which alone the knowledge of an object is possible, first, intuition, through which it is given, though only as phenomenon [*nur als Erscheinung gegeben wird*]; second, the concept, through which an object is thought corresponding to this intuition."[24] To be sure, intuition remains empty, but blindness is here worth more than vacuity: for even blinded intuition remains giving, whereas the concept, even if it alone can make visible what is first given to it, remains as such perfectly empty, and therefore incapable of seeing anything at all. Intuition without concept, although still blind, nevertheless already gives matter to an object, whereas the concept without intuition, although not blind, nevertheless no longer sees anything, since nothing has yet been given to it to be seen. In the realm of the phenomenon, not the concept but intuition is king: before an object is and in order for it to be seen, its appearance must be given. Even if it does not see what it gives, intuition alone enjoys the privilege of giving: "the object cannot be given to a concept otherwise than in intuition [*kann nicht anders gegeben werden, als in der Anschauung*]"; for "the category is a simple function of thought, through which no object is given to me, and by which alone what can be given in intuition is thought [*nur was in der Anschauung gegeben werden mag*]." Or again, "intuitions in general, through which objects can be given to us [*uns Gegenstände gegeben werden können*], constitute the field, the whole object, of possible experience." Thus, intuition does not offer a simple parallel or complement to the concept but ensures the concept's very condition of possibility: "intuitions in general, through which objects can be given to us [*gegeben werden können*], constitute the field or whole object of possible experience [*möglicher Erfahrung*]."[25] The phenomenon is thought through the concept; but in order to be thought it must first be given; and it is given only through intuition. The intuitive presentation [*mise en scène*] conditions conceptual objectivation. Inasmuch as it gives alone and earlier, intuition breaks its parallelism with the concept. Henceforth, the scope of intuition establishes that of phenomenal givenness. Phenomenality is indexed according to intuition.

Now, in a stunning tactical reversal, Kant stresses this privilege of intuition only in order better to stigmatize its weakness. Although intuition alone gives objects, it only reverts to human finitude as a similarly finite and in this case sensible intuition. Consequently, all possible objects that would necessitate an intellectual intuition are excluded from the possibility of appearing. Phenomenality remains limited by the defect of what renders it partially possible: intuition. What gives (intuition inasmuch as sensible) is of a piece with what is lacking (intuition inasmuch as intellectual). Intuition determines phenomenality as much by what it refuses as by what it gives. "Thought is the act which relates given intuition [*gegebene Anschauung*] to an object. If the mode of this intuition is not in any way given [*auf keinerlei Weise gegeben*], then the object is merely transcendental and the concept of understanding has only transcendental employment."[26] To think is more than to know the objects given by (sensible) intuition; it is to think all those objects that no (intellectual) intuition will ever give, to measure the immense cenotaph of phenomena that have never appeared and never will appear—in short, to presume intuition's absence from possible phenomena. For intuition, which alone gives, is essentially lacking. What gives the gift is lacking [*ce qui fait don fait défaut*]. A paradox follows: henceforth, the more phenomena give themselves in sensibility, the more the silent number increases of all the phenomena that cannot and need not claim to give themselves in sensibility. The more intuition gives according to the sensible, the more evident becomes its failure to let what is possibly phenomenal appear—a phenomenality that is henceforth held to be impossible. As much as the directly given phenomena, the limitation of intuition to the sensible indirectly shows the shadow of all those that it cannot let appear. The (in Kant's view "necessary") permanence of the idea attests to the finitude of intuition. The idea, although, or rather because, it is a "rational concept to which no corresponding object can be given in the senses [*in den Sinnen*]," remains nevertheless *visable*,[27] if not visible in all the sensible appearances from which it is excluded. "Absent from every bouquet," the flower of thought, according to the "glory of long desire,"[28] calls for sensible flowers and survives them. Likewise the idea, in letting itself be aimed at *outside* of the conditions established for phenomenality, marks its limits that much more. In the quasi-phantomlike mode of a nonobject, the idea attests to the limits of an intuition that was not able to give the idea. It is therefore by not being sensible that the idea proves the failure of sensible intuition—in it and in general.

The phenomenon is characterized by its lack of intuition, which gives it only by limiting it. Kant confirms that intuition is operative only under the rule of limitation, of lack and of necessity, in short, of nothingness [*néant*], by undertaking to define reciprocally the four senses of nothingness, starting from intuition. It is as if nothingness could be defined in all its dimensions only when one begins with intuition, and with intuition considered as essentially lacking, failing, and limited. The list of the four senses of nothingness actually amounts to a review of four modes of intuition's failure. (a) Nothingness can be taken as *ens rationis*. This is defined as "the object of a concept to which there corresponds no intuition that might be given [*keine anzugebende Anschauung*]." Intuition first produces nothingness in being unable to give any intuition corresponding to a rational being. Its limitation to the sensible finally leads to a first nothingness. (b) Nothingness can be taken as *nihil privativum*. This is defined as "the concept of the lack of an object," that is, as a double lack of intuition: first as a concept, and therefore as what by definition lacks intuition; then as the concept representing the lack of intuition, which alone gives an object. This double lack of intuition produces a second nothingness. (c) Nothingness can be taken as *nihil imaginativum*. This acceptation is paradoxically significant: in principle, imagined nothingness would have to be disconnected from nothingness, since here a minimum of intuition (precisely, the imagined) must give a minimum of being. But Kant does not grant even this positivity to intuition, admitting only a "simple form of intuition" and reducing it to an "empty intuition." It should be noted that "empty" elsewhere returns to the concept, and that intuition here does not even have any further right to its "blind" solitude—since it is true that here the form of intuition is reduced to a third nothingness. (d) Finally, nothingness can be taken as *nihil negativum*. As an "empty object without concept," it would seem to be defined by the failure within it of the concept and not of intuition; likewise, as "the object of a concept that contradicts itself," it would seem to admit of a purely logical explanation, and not an intuitive one. Strangely, such is not the case, since Kant puts forward as example a two-sided rectilinear figure that can be conceived only in space, and therefore in intuition. Moreover, as he specifies earlier, "there is no contradiction in the concept of a figure that is enclosed between two straight lines, since the concepts of two figures and of their meeting contain no negation of a figure; the impossibility does not arise from the concept in itself, but in connection with its construction in space."[29] The concept lacks because the object contradicts itself. Yet this contradiction is not logical; it results from the contradiction of the conditions of experience—here from the requirements of construction in space; it is therefore a matter of a contradiction according to intuition, and thus according to the finitude of that intuition. Nothingness is expressed in many ways, as is Being elsewhere, but that polysemy is organized entirely on the basis of different absences of finite and sensible intuition. Intuition's failure characterizes it fairly essentially, so that nothingness might itself be inflected in its voids.

I was asking: How is the phenomenon defined when phenomenology and metaphysics delimit it within a horizon and according to an *I*? Its definition as conditioned and reducible is accomplished through a de-*finition*: phenomena are given through an intuition, but that intuition remains finite, either as sensible (Kant), or as most often lacking or ideal (Husserl). Phenomena suffer from a deficit of intuition, and thus from a shortage of givenness. This radical lack has nothing accidental about it but results from a phenomenological necessity. In order that any phenomenon might be inscribed within a horizon (and there find its condition of possibility), it is necessary that that horizon be delimited (it is its definition) and therefore that the phenomenon remain finite. In order for a phenomenon to be reduced to an obviously finite *I* who constitutes it, the phenomenon must be reduced to the status of finite objectivity. In both cases, the finitude of the horizon and of the *I* is indicated by the finitude of the intuition itself. Phenomena are characterized by the finitude of givenness in them, so as to be able to enter into a constituting horizon and be led back to an *I*. But, conversely, one could also conclude from this equivalence of the determinations that unconditioned and irreducible phenomena would become possible only if a nonfinite intuition ensured their givenness. But can a nonfinite intuition ever be envisioned?

4

The impossibility of an unconditioned and irreducible phenomenon thus results directly from the determination of the phenomenon in general by the (at least potential) failure of intuition in it. Every phenomenon would appear as lacking intuition and as marked by this lack to the point of having to rely on the condition of a horizon and on the reduction toward an *I*. There would be no phenomenon except that which is essentially poor in intuition, a phenomenon with a reduced givenness.

Having arrived at this point, one can pose the question of a strictly inverse hypothesis: In certain cases still to be defined, must one not oppose to the restricted possibility of phenomenality a phenomenality that is in the end absolutely possible? To the phenomenon that is supposed to be poor in intuition, can one not oppose a phenomenon that is saturated with intuition? To the phenomenon that is most often characterized by a defect of intuition and therefore by a disappointment of the intentional aim and, in particular instances, by the equality between intuition and intention, why would there not correspond the possibility of a phenomenon in which intuition would give *more, indeed immeasurably more*, than intention ever would have intended or foreseen?

This is not a matter of a gratuitous or arbitrary hypothesis. That is so, first, because in a certain way it falls to Kant, although he is the thinker of the intuitive shortage of the common phenomenon, to have envisioned and defined what I am calling a "saturated phenomenon." There is nothing surprising in that. Indeed, if the "rational idea can never become a cognition because it contains a concept (of the supersensible) for which no adequate intuition can ever be given," namely, a phenomenon that is not only poor in but deprived of intuition, it nevertheless offers only one of the two faces of the idea. This idea is defined in general as the representation of an object according to a principle such that it nonetheless can never become the knowledge of this principle. Thus, to the rational idea (a representation according to the understanding) corresponds the "aesthetic idea" (a representation according to intuition), which itself can never become a cognition, but for an opposite reason: "because it is an intuition (of the imagination) for which no adequate [*adäquat*] concept can ever be found."[30] Inadequation always threatens phenomenality (or, better, suspends it). Yet it is no longer a matter of the nonadequation of the (lacking) intuition that leaves a (given) concept empty; at stake rather, is a failure of the (lacking) concept that leaves the (overabundantly given) intuition blind. Henceforth, it is no longer intuition but the concept that is lacking. Kant stresses this unambiguously: in the case of the aesthetic idea, the "representation of the imagination furnishes much to think [*viel zu denken veranlasst*], but no determinate thought, or concept, can be adequate to it [*adäquat sein kann*]." The excess of intuition over any concept also prohibits "that any language ever reach it completely and render it intelligible,"[31] in short, allow an object to be seen in it. It is important to insist on this in particular: this failure to produce the object does not result from a shortage of givenness (as with the ideas of reason) but from an excess of intuition and thus from an excess of givenness—which "gives much to think." It is an excess of givenness and not simply of intuition, since according to Kant (and, for the main part, Husserl) it is intuition that gives. Kant formulates this excess in a rare term: the aesthetic idea remains an "inexposable [*inexponible*] representation of the imagination." One can understand this in the following way: because it gives "much," the aesthetic idea gives more than any concept can expose; to "expose" here amounts to arranging (ordering) the intuitive given according to rules. The impossibility of this conceptual arrangement issues from the fact that the intuitive overabundance is no longer exposed within rules, whatever they may be, but overwhelms them. Intuition is no longer exposed within the concept, but saturates it and renders it overexposed— invisible not by lack but by excess of light. The fact that this very excess should prohibit the aesthetic idea from organizing its intuition within the limits of a concept, and therefore from giving a defined object to be seen, nevertheless does not disqualify what it is, this "inexposable representation" operates according to its "free play."[32] The difficulty consists simply in attempting to comprehend (and not only to repeat) what phenomenological possibility is put into operation when the excess of giving intuition thus begins to play freely.

Now the path one must follow opens more clearly. One must develop as far as possible the uncommon phenomenological possibility glimpsed by Kant. In other words, contrary to most phenomena, which are poor in intuition and defined by the ideal adequation of intuition to intention, one must attempt to describe the traits of a phenomenon that would be characterized by an excess of intuition, and thus of givenness, over the intention, the concept, and the aim. Such a phenomenon will doubtless no longer allow the constitution of an object, at least in the Kantian sense. But it is not self-evident that objectivity should have all the authority in fixing phenomenology's norm. The hypothesis of a phenomenon saturated with intuition can certainly be warranted by its outline in Kant, but above all it must command our attention because it designates a possibility of the phenomenon in general. And in phenomenology, the least possibility is binding.

5

In sketching a description of the saturated phenomenon, I will take as a guiding thread the categories of the understanding established by Kant. But in order to do justice to the excess of intuition over the concept, I will use them in a negative mode. The saturated phenomenon exceeds the categories and the principles of understanding—it will therefore be invisable[33] according to quantity, unbearable according to quality, absolute according to relation, and incapable of being looked at [irregardable] according to modality.

First, the saturated phenomenon cannot be aimed at. This impossibility stems from its essentially unforeseeable character. To be sure, its giving intuition ensures it a quantity, but such that it cannot be foreseen. This determination is better clarified by inverting the function of the axioms of intuition. According to Kant, quantity (the magnitudes of extension) is declined through a composition of the whole on the basis of its parts. This "successive synthesis" allows one to compose the representation of the whole according to the representation of the sum of the parts. Indeed, the magnitude of a *quantum* has the property of implying nothing more than the summation of the *quanta* that make it up through addition. From this homogeneity follows another property: a quantified phenomenon is "foreseen in advance [*schon . . . angeschaut*] as an aggregate [a sum of parts given in advance; *vorher gegebener*]."[34] Such a phenomenon is literally foreseen on the basis of the infinite number of its parts and of the magnitude of each one among them.

Now, these are precisely the properties that become impossible when a saturated phenomenon is at stake. Indeed, since the intuition that gives it is not limited, its excess can be neither divided nor put together again by virtue of a homogeneous magnitude and finite parts. It could not be measured on the basis of its parts, since the saturating intuition surpasses the sum of these parts by continually adding to them. Such a phenomenon, which is always exceeded by the intuition that saturates it, would instead have to be called incommensurable, not measurable (immense), disproportionate. Furthermore, this excessiveness does not always or initially operate through the enormity of an unlimited quantity. It is marked more often by the impossibility of applying a successive synthesis to it, a synthesis allowing one to foresee an aggregate on the basis of the sum of its parts. Since the saturated phenomenon exceeds any summation of its parts—which, moreover, often cannot be counted—one must forsake successive synthesis in favor of what I will call an instantaneous synthesis. Its representation precedes and goes beyond that of possible components, rather than resulting from them according to foresight.

Amazement constitutes a privileged example of this. According to Descartes, this passion strikes us even before we know the thing, or rather, precisely because we know it only partially: "One can perceive of the object only the first side that has presented itself, and consequently one cannot acquire a more particular knowledge of it."[35] The "object" delivers to us only a single "side" (one could also say *Abschattung*) and immediately imposes itself on us, with such force that we are overwhelmed by what shows itself, possibly to the point of fascination. And yet the "successive synthesis" was suspended as early as its first term. This is because another synthesis has been achieved, a synthesis that is instantaneous and irreducible to the sum of possible parts. Any phenomenon that produces amazement imposes itself upon the gaze in the very measure (or, more precisely, in the very lack of measure) that it does not result from any foreseeable summation of partial quantities. Indeed, it amazes because it arises without any common measure with the phenomena that precede it, without announcing it or explaining it—for, according to Spinoza, it "has no connection with the others [*nullam cum reliquis habet connexionem*]."[36] Thus, for at least two phenomenological reasons, the saturated phenomenon could not be foreseen on the basis of the parts that would compose it through summation. First, because intuition, which continually saturates the phenomenon, prohibits distinguishing and summing up a finite number of finite parts, thus annulling any possibility of foreseeing the phenomenon. Next, because the saturated phenomenon most often imposes itself thanks to amazement, where it is precisely the nonenumeration and the nonsummation of the parts, and thus unforseeability, that accomplish all intuitive givenness.

Second, the saturated phenomenon cannot be borne. According to Kant, quality (intensive magnitude) allows intuition to give a degree of reality to the object by limiting it, possibly as far as negation: every phenomenon will have to admit a degree of intuition, and that is what perception can anticipate. The foresight at work in extensive magnitude is found again in intensive magnitude. Nevertheless, an essential difference separates them: foresight no longer operates in a successive synthesis of the homogeneous, but in a perception of the heterogeneous—each degree is marked by a break with what precedes, and therefore by an absolutely singular novelty. Since he privileges the case of the poor phenomenon, Kant analyzes this heterogeneity only on the basis of the simplest cases: the first degrees starting from zero, imperceptible perceptions, and so on. But in the case of a saturated phenomenon, intuition gives reality without any limitation (or, to be sure, negation). It reaches an intensive magnitude without (common) measure, such that, starting from a certain degree, the intensity of the real intuition exceeds all the anticipations of perception. In the face of that excess, perception not only can no longer anticipate what it is going to receive from intuition, but above all it can no longer bear the degree of intuition, for intuition, which is supposed to be "blind" in the realm of poor phenomena, proves instead to be blinding in a truly radical phenomenology. The intensive magnitude of the intuition that gives the saturated phenomenon is unbearable for the gaze, just as this gaze could not foresee that intuition's extensive magnitude.

Bedazzlement characterizes what the gaze cannot bear. Not bearing does not amount to not seeing, for one must first perceive, if not see, in order to experience this incapacity to bear. It is, rather, a question of something visible that our gaze cannot bear. This visible something is experienced as unbearable to the gaze because it weighs too much; the glory of the visible weighs and weighs too much. What weighs here is neither unhappiness, nor pain, nor lack, but indeed glory, joy, excess: "O / Triumph! / What Glory! What human heart would be strong enough to bear / That?"[37] Intuition gives too intensely for the gaze truly to be able to see what it already can no longer receive, or even confront. Indeed, this blinding concerns the intensity of the intuition and it alone, as is indicated by cases of blinding in the face of spectacles where the intuition remains quantitatively ordinary, even weak, but of an intensity that is out of the ordinary: Oedipus blinds himself for having seen his transgression, and therefore a quasi-moral intensity of intuition; and he whom no one can see without dying blinds first by his holiness, even if his coming is announced by a simple breath of wind. Because the saturated phenomenon, due to the excess of intuition in it, cannot be borne by any gaze that would measure up to it ("objectively"), it is perceived ("subjectively") by the gaze only in the negative mode of an impossible perception, the mode of bedazzlement. Plato describes this perfectly in connection with the prisoner in the cave: "let one untie him and force him suddenly to turn around [ανιστασθαι] . . . and to lift his gaze toward the light [προς το φως αναβλεπειν], he would suffer in doing all that, and, because of the bedazzlements, he would not have the strength to see face on [δια τας μαρμαρυγας αδυνατοι καθοραν] that of which previously he saw the shadows." It is indeed a question of "suffering" in seeing the full light, and of fleeing it by turning away toward "the things that one can look at [α δυναται καθοραν]." What keeps one from seeing are precisely "eyes filled with splendor."[38] Moreover, this bedazzlement is just as valid for intelligible intuition as it is for sensible intuition: first, because the myth of the cave, in the final analysis, concerns the epistemological obstacles to intelligibility, of which the sensible setting explicitly offers a figure; then, because the idea of the Good also and especially offers itself as "difficult to see [μογις ορασθαι]," certainly not by defect, since it presents "the most visible of beings," but by excess—because "the soul is incapable of seeing anything . . . saturated by an extremely brilliant bedazzlement [υπο λαμπροτερου μαρμαρυης εμπεπλησται]."[39] What in all these cases prohibits one from seeing is the sensible or intelligible light's excess of intensity.

Bedazzlement thus becomes a characteristic of an intuitive intensity that goes beyond what a gaze can sustain and what can be universalized to any form of intuition. This is not a question of some exceptional case, which one could mention merely as a matter of interest along with the poor phenomena, thought to be more frequent and thus more or less normative. On the contrary, it is a question of an essential determination of the phenomenon, which is rendered almost unavoidable for two reasons. (a) Although it is in other respects original and true, the Kantian description of intensive magnitudes nevertheless maintains a resounding silence concerning the most characteristic notion of intensive magnitude: the maximum. Even if it can undoubtedly not be defined objectively, there is always a subjective maximum, the threshold of tolerance. Bedazzlement begins when perception passes beyond its subjective maximum. The description of intensive magnitudes would necessarily first have to take into consideration their highest degrees, and therefore the subjective maximum (or maximums) that bedazzlement signals. (b) Like unforeseeability, bedazzlement designates a type of intuitive givenness that is not only less rare than it would seem to a hasty examination but above all decisive for a real recognition of finitude. Finitude is experienced (and proved) [s'éprouve (et se prouve)] less in the shortage of the given before our gaze than in that this gaze sometimes no longer measures the amplitude of givenness. Or rather, measuring itself against that givenness, the gaze experiences it, sometimes in the suffering of an essential passivity, as having no measure with itself. Finitude is experienced as much through excess as through lack—indeed, more through excess than through lack.

6

Neither visable according to quantity, nor bearable according to quality, a saturated phenomenon would be absolute according to relation, as well: that is, it would shy away from any analogy to experience. Kant defines the principle of such analogies as follows: "Experience is possible only through the representation of a necessary connection of perceptions." Now, simple apprehension by empirical intuition cannot ensure this necessary connection. On the contrary, the connection will have to produce itself at once through concepts and in time: "Since time cannot itself be perceived, the determination of the existence of objects in time can be made only through their connection in time in general, and therefore only through concepts that connect them in general."[40] This connection links via three operations: inherence of accident in substance, causality between cause and effect, and community between several substances. But Kant establishes them only by bringing three presuppositions into play. The possibility of questioning them will again define the saturated phenomenon.

First presupposition: in all cases, a phenomenon can manifest itself only by respecting the unity of experience, that is, by taking place in the tightest possible network of ties of inherence, causality, and community. These assign to the phenomenon, in a hollow, so to speak, a site and a function. This is a matter of strict obligation: "This entire manifold must be unified [*vereinigt werden soll*]." "An analogy of experience is, therefore, only a rule according to which the unity of experience must arise from perceptions [*entspringen soll*]."[41] For Kant, a phenomenon appears, therefore, only in a site that is predefined by a system of coordinates, a system that is itself governed by the principle of the unity of experience. Now it is here that another question creeps in: Must every phenomenon without exception respect the unity of experience? Can one legitimately rule out the possibility that a phenomenon might impose itself on perception without, for all that, being able to assign to it either a substance in which to dwell as an accident, or a cause from which it results as an effect, or even less an interactive *commercium* in which to be relativized? Further, it is not self-evident that the phenomena that really arise—as opposed to the phenomena that are poor in intuition, or even deprived entirely of intuition—can right from the first and most often be perceived according to such analogies of perception. Quite the contrary, it could be that they occur without, at least at first, being inscribed in the relational network that ensures experience its unity, and that they matter precisely because one could not assign them any substratum, any cause, or any communion.

To be sure, after a bit of analysis most can be led back to the analogies of perception, at least approximately. But those that do not lend themselves to this leading-back (and they are not all that rare) henceforth assume the character and the dignity of an event: an event or a phenomenon that is neither foreseeable (on the basis of the past), nor exhaustively comprehensible (on the basis of the present), nor reproducible (on the basis of the future); in short, absolute, unique, occurring. One could also say a "pure event." I am here taking that which has the character of event [*l'événementiel*] in its individual as much as in its collective dimension. Henceforth, the analogies of experience could concern only a fringe of phenomenality, the phenomenality typical of the objects constituted by the sciences, exhaustively knowable and reproducible, while other layers would be excepted—historical phenomena first among them.

The second presupposition concerns the elaboration of the procedure that allows one to ensure the necessity (at once temporal and conceptual) and thus the unity of experience. Kant presupposes that this unity must always be achieved by recourse to an analogy. For "all the empirical determinations of time must [*müssen*] stand under the rules of the general determination of time, and the analogies of experience . . . must [*müssen*] be rules of this kind."[42] In short, it is up to the analogies of experience and to them alone actually to exercise the regulation of experience by necessity, and thus to ensure its unity. Now, at the precise moment of defining these analogies, Kant himself recognizes the fragility of their phenomenological power: indeed, in mathematics, analogy remains quantitative, such that it gives itself the fourth term through calculation and constructs it truly. In this way the equality of these two relations of magnitude is "always constitutive" of the object and actually maintains it in a unified experience. But, Kant specifies, "in philosophy, on the contrary, analogy is not the equality of two *quantitative* relations but of two *qualitative* relations; and from three given members we can obtain a priori knowledge only of the relation to a fourth, not of the fourth member itself. . . . An analogy of experience therefore will be a rule according to which the unity of experience . . . must arise from [*entspringen soll*] perceptions, and it will be valid as the principle of objects (phenomena) in a manner that is not *constitutive* but only *regulative*."[43] To put it plainly, when it is a question of what we have called poor phenomena (here, mathematical ones), intuition (here, the pure intuition of space) is not such that it could saturate the phenomenon and contradict it in the unity and the preestablished necessity of experience. In this case, the analogy remains quantitative and constitutive. In short, there is analogy of experience provided that the phenomenon remains poor. Yet as soon as the simple movement to physics (not even to speak of a saturated phenomenon) occurs, analogy can no longer regulate anything except qualitatively: if *A* is the cause of effect *B*, then *D* will be in the position (quality) of effect with respect to *C*, without it being possible to identify what *D* is or will be, and without it being possible to construct it (by lack of pure intuition) or to constitute it. Within the analytic of principles Kant's predicament culminates in the strange employment of principles whose use remains purely "regulative," which can be understood in only one sense: the analogies of experience do not really constitute their objects, but instead express subjective needs of the understanding. Let's suppose, for the moment, that the analogies of perception, thus reduced to a simple regulative usage, must treat a saturated phenomenon: the latter already exceeds the categories of quantity (unforeseeable) and quality (unbearable); it gives itself already as a pure event. Henceforth, how could an analogy (especially one that is simply regulative) assign to the phenomenon (especially one that is necessarily and a priori) a point whose coordinates would be established by the relations of inherence, causality, and community? This phenomenon would escape all relations because it would not maintain any common measure with these terms. It would be freed from them, as from any a priori determination of experience that could possibly claim to impose itself on the phenomenon. In this sense, I will speak of an "absolute phenomenon": one untied from any analogy with any object of experience whatsoever.

This being the case, the third Kantian presupposition becomes questionable. The unity of experience is developed on the basis of time, since it is a matter of "the synthetic unity of all phenomena according to their relation in time."[44] Thus, Kant posits, and is the first no doubt to do so, not only time as the ultimate horizon of phenomena, but above all that no appearance can dawn without a horizon that receives it and that it rejects at the same time. This signifies that before any phenomenal breakthrough toward visibility, the horizon waited in advance. And it means that, by appearing, every phenomenon is in fact limited to actualizing a portion of the horizon, which otherwise remains transparent. A current question concerns the identity of the horizon (time, Being, the Good, and so on). This should not, however, mask another question that is simpler, albeit rougher: Could certain phenomena exceed every horizon? I should specify that this is not a matter of dispensing with a horizon in general—which would undoubtedly prohibit all manifestation—but of freeing oneself from the delimiting anteriority proper to every horizon, an anteriority that will always enter into conflict with a phenomenon's claim to absoluteness. Let me assume a saturated phenomenon that has just gained its absolute character by freeing itself from the analogies with experience. What horizon can it recognize? On the one hand, the excess of intuition saturates this phenomenon so as to make it exceed the frame of ordinary experience. On the other hand, a horizon, by its very definition, defines and is defined; through its movement to the limit, the saturated phenomenon can manage to saturate its horizon. There is nothing strange about this hypothesis—even in strict philosophy: with Spinoza, for example, the unique substance, by absorbing all the determinations and all the individuals corresponding to it, manages to overwhelm the horizon of Cartesian metaphysics with its infinitely saturated presence (*infinitis attributis infinitis modis*) by leaving no more free space for the finite (absolute and universal necessity) in this horizon.

Such saturation of a horizon by a single saturated phenomenon presents a danger that cannot be underestimated, since it is born from the absolutely real, in no way illusory, experience of totality, with neither door nor window, with neither other [*autre*] nor Other [*autrui*]. But, strangely, this danger results less from the saturated phenomenon itself than from its misapprehension. Indeed, when it arises, it is most often treated as if it were only a common-law phenomenon or a poor phenomenon and as if a single horizon could not also saturate it. In fact, the saturated phenomenon maintains its absoluteness and dissolves its danger at the same time, when one recognizes it without confusing it with other phenomena and therefore when one allows it to operate on several horizons at once. Since there are spaces with $n + 1$ dimensions (whose properties saturate the imagination), there are phenomena with $n + 1$ horizons. One of the best examples of such an arrangement is furnished by the doctrine of transcendentals: the irreducible plurality of being (*ens*), the true (*verum*), the good (*bonum*), and the beautiful (*pulchrum*) allows one to decline the saturated phenomenon from the first principle in perfectly autonomous registers, where it gives itself to be seen, each time, only according to one perspective, which is total as well as partial; their convertibility indicates that the saturation persists, but that it is distributed within several concurrent horizons. Or rather, the saturation increases because each perspective, already saturated in itself, is blurred a second time by the interferences of other saturated perspectives in it.[45] The plurality of horizons therefore allows as much that one might respect the absoluteness of the saturated phenomenon (which no horizon could delimit or precede), as that one might render it tolerable through a multiplication of the dimensions of its reception.

Nevertheless, there remains one last thinkable, although extreme, relation between saturated phenomenon and horizon: that no horizon or any combination of horizons tolerates the absoluteness of the phenomenon precisely because it gives itself as absolute, that is, as free from any analogy with common-law phenomena and from any predetermination by a network of relations, with neither precedent nor antecedent within the already seen (the foreseen): in short, a phenomenon saturated to the point where the world could not accept it. Having come among its own, they did not recognize it; having come into phenomenality, the absolutely saturated phenomenon could find no room there for its display. But this opening denial, and thus this disfiguration, still remains a manifestation. Thus, in giving itself absolutely, the saturated phenomenon also gives itself as absolute: free from any analogy with the experience that has already been seen, objectivized, and comprehended. It frees itself from such analogy because it depends on no horizon. On the contrary, the saturated phenomenon either simply saturates the horizon, or it multiplies the horizon in order to saturate it that much more, or it exceeds the horizon and finds itself cast out from it. But this very disfiguration remains a manifestation. In any case, it does not depend on that condition of possibility par excellence—a horizon, of whatever kind. I will therefore call this phenomenon unconditioned.

7

Neither *visable* according to quantity, nor bearable according to quality, nor absolute according to relation, that is, unconditioned by horizon, the saturated phenomenon finally gives itself as incapable of being looked at according to modality. The categories of modality are distinguished from all the others, Kant insists, in that they determine neither objects themselves, nor their mutual relations, but simply "their relation to thought in general," in that they "express only the relation to the power of knowing," "nothing other than the action of the power of knowing."[46] In fact, between the objects of experience and the power of knowing, it is not only a question of "a simple relation," but of the fact that they "agree."[47] This agreement determines the possibility for phenomena to be (and therefore also their actuality and necessity) in the measure of their suitability to the *I* for and through whom the experience takes place. "The postulate of the possibility of things requires [*fordert*] therefore that their concept agree [*zusammenstimme*] with the formal conditions of an experience in general."[48] The phenomenon is possible in the strict measure that it agrees with the formal conditions of experience, thus with the power of knowing that fixes its attention on them, and therefore finally with the transcendental *I* itself. The possibility of the phenomenon depends on its reduction to the *I*.

This being the case, one can envisage a reversal of Kant's pronouncement and ask: What would occur phenomenologically if a phenomenon did not "agree" with or "correspond" to the *I*'s power of knowing? The Kantian answer leaves hardly any doubt: this phenomenon quite simply would not appear; or better, there would not be any phenomenon at all, but an objectless perceptive aberration. If this answer remains meaningful for a poor or common-law phenomenon, does it still hold for a saturated phenomenon? In fact, the situation in this case becomes very different. In the face of saturation, the *I* most certainly experiences the disagreement between the at least potential phenomenon and the subjective conditions of its experience; consequently, the *I* cannot constitute an object in them. But this failure to objectivize in no way implies that absolutely nothing appears: intuitive saturation, precisely inasmuch as it is invisible, intolerable, and absolute (unconditioned), imposes itself in the capacity of a phenomenon that is exceptional by excess, not by defect. The saturated phenomenon refuses to let itself be looked at as an object, precisely because it appears with a multiple and indescribable excess that suspends any effort at constitution. To define the saturated phenomenon as a non-objective or, more exactly, nonobjectivizable phenomenon in no way indicates a refuge in the irrational or the arbitrary. This definition refers to one of its distinctive properties: although exemplarily visible, it nevertheless cannot be looked at. I here take "to look at"—*regarder*—literally: *regarder* exactly reproduces *in-tueri* and must therefore be understood on the basis of *tueri, garder* [to protect or guard]—but in the sense of "to keep an eye on," "to keep half an eye on," "to have (to keep) in sight." *Regarder* therefore implies being able to keep the visible that is seen under the control of the one who is seeing and who is, consequently, a seer [*voyeur*]. And it is certainly not by chance that Descartes entrusts the *intuitus* with maintaining in evidence what the ego reduces to the status of *objectum*. To define the saturated phenomenon as incapable of being looked at [*irregardable*] amounts to envisioning the possibility of a phenomenon imposing itself with such an excess of intuition that it could neither be reduced to the conditions of experience, and thus to the *I* who sets them, nor thereby forego appearing.

Under what figure, then, would it appear? It appears in spite of and in disagreement with the conditions of possibility for experience, namely, by imposing an impossible experience (if not already an experience of the impossible). Of the saturated phenomenon only a counter-experience would be possible. Confronted with the saturated phenomenon, the *I* cannot not see it, but neither can it look at it [*le regarder*] as its object. It has the eye to see it, but not to look after it [*pour le garder*]. What, then, does this eye without gaze [*cet œil sans regard*] actually see? It sees the overabundance of intuitive givenness, not as such but as it is blurred by the overly short lens, the overly restricted aperture, the overly narrow frame that receives it—or rather, that no longer welcomes it. The eye apperceives not so much the appearance of the saturated phenomenon as the blur, the fog, and the overexposure that this phenomenon imposes on its normal conditions of experience. The eye sees not so much another spectacle as its own naked impotence to constitute anything at all. It sees nothing distinctly, but clearly experiences its impotence before the excessiveness of the visible, and thus above all experiences a perturbation of the visible, the noise of a poorly received message, damage to finitude. Through sight it receives a pure givenness, precisely because it no longer discerns any objectivizable given therein. Let me call this phenomenological extreme a paradox. The paradox not only suspends the phenomenon's relation of subjection to the *I*, it actually inverts that relation. Far from being able to constitute this phenomenon, the *I* experiences itself as constituted by it. It is constituted and no longer constituting because it no longer has at its disposal any dominant point of view over the intuition that overwhelms it. In space, the saturated phenomenon engulfs it with its intuitive flood; in time, it precedes it through an interpellation that is always already there. The *I* loses its anteriority and finds itself, so to speak, deprived of the duties of constitution, and is thus itself constituted: it becomes a *me* rather than an *I*. It is clear that on the basis of the saturated phenomenon one meets here with what I have thematized elsewhere under the name of the subject at its last appeal: the *interloqué*.[49] When the *I* finds itself, from the constituting *I* that it remained in the face of common-law phenomena, constituted by a saturated phenomenon, it can identify itself as such only by admitting the precedence of such a phenomenon over itself. This reversal leaves it interlocuted [*interloqué*], essentially surprised by the more original event that detaches it from itself.

Thus, the phenomenon is no longer reduced to the *I* that would look at it. Incapable of being looked at, it proves irreducible. There is no drift or turn here, not even a "theological" one, but, on the contrary, an accounting for the fact that in certain cases of givenness the excess of intuition could no longer satisfy the conditions of ordinary experience and that the pure event that occurs cannot be constituted as an object and leaves the durable trace of its opening only in the *I/me* that finds itself, almost in spite of itself, constituted by what it receives. The constituting subject is succeeded by the constituted witness. As a constituted witness, the subject remains the worker of truth, but is no longer its producer.

8

In order to introduce the concept of the saturated phenomenon in phenomenology, I have just described it as *invisable* (unforeseeable) according to quantity, *unbearable* according to quality, but also *unconditioned* (absolved from any horizon) according to relation, and *irreducible* to the *I* (incapable of being looked at) according to modality. These four characteristics imply the term-for-term reversal of all the rubrics under which Kant classifies the principles and thus the phenomena that these determine. However, in relation to Husserl, these new characteristics are organized in a more complex way; the first two, the invisable and the unbearable, offer no de jure difficulty for the "principle of all principles," for what intuition gives can quantitatively and qualitatively exceed the scope of the gaze. It is sufficient that intuition actually give it. The case is not the same for the last two characteristics: the "principle of all principles" presupposes the horizon and the constituting *I* as two unquestioned presuppositions of anything that would be constituted in general as a phenomenon. Yet the saturated phenomenon, inasmuch as it is unconditioned by a horizon and irreducible to an *I*, lays claim to a possibility that is freed from these two conditions. It therefore contradicts and exceeds the "principle of all principles." Husserl, who surpassed the Kantian metaphysics of the phenomenon, must himself be surpassed in order to reach the possibility of the saturated phenomenon. Even and especially with the "principle of all principles," Husserl maintains a twofold reserve toward possibility. Yet that reserve of Husserl *toward* possibility can prove to be a reserve of phenomenology itself—which still maintains a reserve *of* possibility, in order itself to be surpassed toward a possibility without reserve. Because it gives itself without condition or restraint, the saturated phenomenon offers the paradigm of the phenomenon without reserve. Thus, following the guiding thread of the saturated phenomenon, phenomenology finds its ultimate possibility: not only the possibility that surpasses actuality, but the possibility that surpasses the very conditions of possibility, the possibility of unconditioned possibility—in other words, the possibility of the impossible, the saturated phenomenon.

The saturated phenomenon must not be understood as a limit case, an exceptional, vaguely irrational, in short, a "mystical" case of phenomenality. On the contrary, it indicates the coherent and conceptual fulfillment of the most operative definition of the phenomenon: it alone truly appears as itself, of itself, and starting from itself,[50] since it alone appears without the limits of a horizon and without reduction to an *I*. I will therefore call this appearance that is purely of itself and starting from itself, this phenomenon that does not subject its possibility to any preliminary determination, a "revelation." And I insist that here it is purely and simply a matter of the phenomenon taken in its fullest meaning.

Moreover, the history of philosophy has a long-standing knowledge of such saturated phenomena. One could go so far as to maintain that none of the most important metaphysicians has avoided the description of one or more saturated phenomena, even at the price of a head-on contradiction of its own presuppositions. Among many fairly obvious examples, let me simply call to mind Descartes and Kant. (a) Descartes, who everywhere else reduces the phenomenon to the idea and the idea to the object, nevertheless thinks the idea of infinity as a saturated phenomenon. According to quantity, the idea of infinity is not obtained by summation or successive synthesis, but *tota simul*. Thus, the gaze (*intueri*) becomes the surprise of admiration (*admirari*).[51] According to quality, it admits no finite degree, but a *maximum*: "the most clear and distinct [*maxime clara et distincta*]," "the most true [*maxime vera*]."[52] According to relation, it maintains no analogy with any idea at all: "nothing univocal [*nihil univoce*]." Indeed, it exceeds every horizon, since it remains incomprehensible, capable only of being "touched by thought [*attingam quomodolibet cogitatione*]."[53] According to modality, far from letting itself be led back to a constituting *I*, it comprehends the *I* without letting itself be comprehended by it: "not to take hold of it as much as surrendering to it [*non tam capere quam a ipsa capi*],"[54] such that perhaps even the *ego* could also be interpreted at times as one who is called [*un interloqué*]. Moreover, might it not be sufficient to translate "idea of infinity" word for word by "saturated phenomenon" to establish my conclusion?

(b) Kant furnishes an example of the saturated phenomenon that is all the more significant insofar as it does not concern rational theology, as does that of Descartes: in fact, it is a question of the sublime. I relied above on the "aesthetic idea" to challenge the principle of the shortage of intuition and to introduce the possibility of a saturation. In fact, already the doctrine of the sublime may be said to deal with a saturated phenomenon. Indeed, according to quantity, the sublime has neither form nor order, since it is great "beyond all comparison," absolutely and not comparatively (*absolut, schlechthin, bloss*).[55] According to quality, it contradicts taste as a "negative pleasure," and it provokes a "feeling of inadequacy," a feeling of "monstrosity."[56] According to relation, it very clearly escapes any analogy and any horizon since it literally represents "unlimitedness [*Unbegrenztheit*]."[57] According to modality, finally, far from agreeing with our power of knowing, "it can appear [*erscheinen mag*] in its form to contradict the purpose [*zweckwidrig*] of our faculty of judgment." The relation of our faculty of judgment to the phenomenon is therefore reversed, to the point that it is the phenomenon that hereafter "gazes at" the *I* in "respect."[58] The Kantian example of the sublime would thus permit widening the field of application for the concept of the saturated phenomenon.

Let me recapitulate. Phenomena can be classified, according to their increasing intuitive content, in three fundamental domains. (a) Phenomena that are deprived of intuition or that are poor in intuition: for example, formal languages (endowed with categorial intuition by Husserl) or mathematical idealities (whose pure intuition is established by Kant). (b) Common-law phenomena, whose signification (aimed at by intention) can ideally receive an adequate intuitive fulfillment but that, right at the start and most of the time, do not reach such fulfillment. In these first two domains, the constitution of objects is rendered possible precisely because the shortage of intuition authorizes comprehension, foresight, and reproduction. (c) There remain, finally, saturated phenomena, which the excess of intuition shields from objective constitution. For convenience, one can distinguish two types. (i) First, pure historical events: by definition nonrepeatable, most often they occur without having been foreseen. Since through an excess of intuitive given they escape objectivation, their intelligibility excludes comprehension and demands that one turn to hermeneutics.[59] Intuitive saturation surpasses a single horizon and imposes multiple hermeneutics within several horizons. Finally, the pure historical event not only occurs to its witness (the nonconstituting *I*) without the latter comprehending it, but itself, in turn, comprehends the *I* (the constituted *I*): the *I* is comprehended on the basis of the event that occurs to it in the very measure that the *I* itself does not comprehend the event. Pure events offer a type of saturated phenomenon that is historical, and thus communal and in principle communicable. (ii) Such is not always the case for the second type: the phenomena of revelation. Let me repeat that by "revelation" I here intend a strictly phenomenological concept: an appearance that is purely of itself and starting from itself, that does not subject its possibility to any preliminary determination. Such revealed phenomena occur principally in three domains: first, the painting as a spectacle that, due to excess of intuition, cannot be constituted but still can be looked at (the idol); next, a particular face that I love, which has become invisible not only because it dazzles me, but above all because in it I want to look and can look only at its invisible gaze weighing on mine (the icon); finally, the theophany, where the excess of intuition leads to the paradox that an invisible gaze visibly envisages me and loves me. And it is here that the question of the possibility of a phenomenology of religion would be posed in terms that are simple if not new (for it is only a matter of pushing the phenomenological intention to its end). In any case, recognizing saturated phenomena comes down to thinking seriously "that which none greater can be conceived [*aliquid quo majus cogitari nequit*]"—which means thinking it as a final possibility of phenomenology.[60]

—Translated by Thomas A. Carlson

Metaphysics and Phenomenology

A Relief for Theology

> My immediate intention is not theology but phenomenology, although one may well say much for the other.
>
> **—Husserl, *Ideas* I, §51**

1

The question of God certainly does not begin with metaphysics. But it seems—or at least it managed to appear—that, since metaphysics was coming to an end, being completed, and disappearing, the question of God was also coming to a close. Throughout the past century, everything happened as if the question of God would have to make common cause, whether positively or negatively, with the destiny of metaphysics. Everything also happened as if, in order to keep the question of God open so as to permit a "rational worship" of him (Rom. 12:1), it was absolutely necessary to stick to the strictly metaphysical meaning of all philosophy.

But could one not, and thus should one not, also pose an entirely different and opposing preliminary question? Is philosophy really equivalent to metaphysics? In order to remain rational, must the question concerning God necessarily and exclusively take the paths that lead to the "God of the philosophers and the scholars" just because those paths issue necessarily from the decision of metaphysics?[1] On the one hand, this reversal of the question might surprise and even disturb, or, on the other hand, it might appear to dodge the radicality of the past century's philosophical situation. Nevertheless, it seems to me inevitable, since only such a reversal still truly leaves open the possibility of taking into proper account at least three questions. I will evoke them here without claiming to answer them explicitly. (1) At least as regards its historical destiny, did metaphysics not reach its end positively with Hegel and negatively with Nietzsche? (2) Was philosophy not devoted throughout an entire century to overcoming that end by assuming nonmetaphysical forms, of which the most powerful (I am not saying the only) remains phenomenology? (3) Does Christian speculative theology, understood in its exemplary figures (and here I am obviously thinking first of Saint Thomas Aquinas), belong to metaphysics in the strict sense, or has it responded to the peculiar conceptual demands of the revelation that prompted it?

In succession, then, I will examine the metaphysical figure of philosophy and the thought of God that it actualizes, then the phenomenological figure of philosophy and the possibility it keeps in store for God.

2

The mere evocation of the concept of an "end of metaphysics" gives rise to controversy. That controversy could undoubtedly be avoided if care were taken to agree first on a precise and verifiable concept of "metaphysics" itself. This is even truer insofar as that concept can be defined historically in an almost univocal manner. In fact, it appears relatively late, but with a clear definition. One of the first to accept it (which does not imply that he made it his own, since he hardly uses it except in commentary on Aristotle and elsewhere with caution), Aquinas establishes its theoretical field precisely: "*Metaphysics* simultaneously determines [how things stand] concerning being in general and concerning the first being, which is separated from matter [Metaphysica *simul determinat de ente in communi et de ente primo, quod est a materia separatum*]."[2] Despite some decisive modifications concerning, among other things, the meaning of being in general as an objective concept of being, this dual definition was sanctioned by Francisco Suarez as early as the opening of his *Disputatione Metaphysicae*, a work that itself definitely imposes the concept and the word *metaphysics* on modern philosophy: "This science abstracts from sensible and from material things . . ., and it contemplates, on the one hand, the things that are divine and separated from matter and, on the other hand, the common reason of being, which [both] can exist without matter [*Abstrahit enim haec scientia a sensibilibus, seu materialibus rebus . . ., et res divinas et materia separatas, et communes rationes entis, quae absque materia existere possunt, contemplatur*]."[3] This duality of one and the same science that treats simultaneously beings par excellence and being in general will lead, with the "scholastic metaphysics" (*Schulmetaphysik*) of the seventeenth and eighteenth centuries, to the canonical schema of "metaphysics" as divided into "general metaphysics," or *metaphysica generalis (sive ontologia)*, and "special metaphysics," or *metaphysica specialis (theologia rationalis, psychologia rationalis, cosmologia rationalis).*[4] Kant's critique stands entirely within this arrangement, since, as is often forgotten, the threefold refutation of special metaphysics in the "Transcendental Dialectic" of the *Critique of Pure Reason* rests on the rejection of the "proud name of . . . ontology" in the "Analytic of Principles."[5] Thus, by a simple survey of a history of concepts, *metaphysics* is defined as follows: the system of philosophy from Suarez to Kant as a single science bearing at one and the same time on the universal common being and on being (or beings) par excellence. This textual fact seems hard to contest.

But the fact remains to be interpreted. The historically narrow sense of *metaphysics* follows from its strict definition, but can this notion be confirmed conceptually? Can one read in it anything more than a mere scholastic or even pedagogical nomenclature that is without any authentically speculative scope and that, in any case, would be incapable of bringing us to the heart of the question of metaphysics? This suspicion would be a serious threat if we did not have at our disposal a conceptual elaboration of this common notion of "metaphysics"—namely, the elaboration furnished by Heidegger in the section of *Identity and Difference* entitled "The Onto-theological Constitution of Metaphysics." I will focus here on only one thesis from that decisive text. Indeed, the principal difficulty of metaphysical science stems from the problematic character of its unity. How can one and the same (*una et eadem*) science treat at the same time (*simul*) common being (and therefore no being in particular) and the being par excellence (and therefore a supremely particular being)? To be sure, in both cases it is a question of an abstraction, but taken in two opposite senses: in one case, an abstraction in regard to all real being and thus an abstraction only of reason; in the other case, an abstraction with a view to being that is all the more concrete insofar as no materiality affects it, and thus a real abstraction. Now Heidegger goes beyond this superficial but traditional opposition by proposing to read the relation between the two functions of the same "metaphysics" as the relation of two intersecting and reciprocal foundations:

Being [*das Sein*] shows itself in the unconcealing overcoming as that which allows whatever arrives to lie before us, as the grounding [*Gründen*] in the manifold ways in which beings are brought about before us. Beings [*das Seiende*] as such, [namely, as] the arrival that keeps itself concealed in unconcealedness, is the grounded [*Gegründete*], which, as grounded and thus effected [*Erwirktes*], grounds in its way, namely, effects, and therefore causes [*gründet, nämlich wirkt, d.h. verursacht*]. The conciliation of the grounding and the grounded [*von Gründendem und Gegründetem*] as such does not hold them one outside of the other, but one for the other.[6]

The inner unity of "metaphysics," which allows it not to fall apart into two unconnected sciences, stems from the fact that, between the science of being in general and the science of the being par excellence, the single institution of the ground is at work, in modes that are intrinsically conciliated. Common Being grounds beings, even beings par excellence; in return, the being par excellence, in the mode of causality, grounds common Being: "Being grounds being, and being, as what is most of all, causes Being [*gründet Sein das Seiende, begründet das Seiende als das Seiendste das Sein*]."[7] In and beyond the scholastic notion of metaphysics, the onto-theo-logical constitution thus brings out the ultimate concept of "metaphysics" by recognizing its unity in the intersecting conciliation of the ground (by beings as such) with the ground in the mode of causality (by the supreme being). I suggest that we have no other rigorous determination of "metaphysics" at our disposal, that is, no other determination that is historically confirmed and conceptually operative. Because the determination remains precise, it renders thinkable both the possibility and the impossibility of "metaphysics." And for this reason, too, the determination maybe renders intelligible the relief that goes beyond metaphysics and takes it up again in a higher figure.

3

The definition that renders "metaphysics" intelligible also makes possible the thought that it might become impossible. The demarcation of the possible necessarily implies both these postulations, with equal right. In my view, the reciprocal foundation of onto-theo-logy offers the most powerful working hypothesis for the historian of philosophy. It also allows us to understand how it was possible to speak of an "end of metaphysics." Nietzsche's critique of philosophy as a Platonism to be inverted and subverted is in fact perfectly in line with the Heideggerian hypothesis, for that critique amounts above all to a critique of the concept of being in general, reduced to the undistinguished level of one of the "'highest concepts,' which means the most general, the emptiest concepts, the last smoke of evaporating reality."[8] Nietzsche here contests the legitimacy of a general abstraction from matter and from the sensible, and thus the traditional condition of possibility for a science of being in general (*metaphysica generalis*). Reciprocally, Nietzsche denies that any being par excellence might exercise the function of foundation over common being from some invisible netherworld (his problematic of "vengeance" is added to this). No concept of *causa sui* is admissible, whether as logical principle, as universal cause, or as "moral God." Why would beings as such, that is, as sensible, necessitate that another being overdetermine them as their ground? Why would what *is* have to be given a further ground, instead of answering for itself by itself alone? The original function of the science of the being par excellence (*metaphysica specialis*) is thus called into question. This double disqualification is finally unified in the single identification between becoming (common being, *metaphysica generalis*) and Being (the being par excellence, *metaphysica specialis*): "To impose the seal of Being on becoming . . .—the height of speculation!"[9] Nothing can become ground since nothing calls for or necessitates a ground. Metaphysics no longer has grounds for being, nor Being a metaphysical ground [*La métaphysique n'a plus lieu d'être, ni l'être de lieu métaphysique*]. Nietzsche therefore confirms negatively the Heideggerian definition of *metaphysics* as an onto-theo-logical system of reciprocal foundation between the being par excellence and common being.

What must be concluded from this? First, something obvious: the definition of *metaphysics* that is historically and conceptually the most pertinent also allows one to challenge it. The thought of the ground, precisely because it can account for beings as a whole, can also be denied as ground. If the ground imposes itself metaphysically through its universal capacity to respond to the question "Why a being rather than nothing?" it exposes itself to the nihilistic refutation that asks "Why a reason rather than nothing?" The ground ensures the legitimacy of metaphysics but not of itself. Now, the self-evidence of the question "Why?" can (and undoubtedly must) always become blurred when faced with the violence of the question that asks "Why ask 'why'?" And if metaphysics is indeed defined as thought about a universal ground, it will founder when the self-evidence of the obligation to found being is called into question. This limitation of "metaphysics" is even stronger, first, insofar as it results directly from its definition, which is maintained but turned back against itself, and, second, insofar as a mere suspicion ("why ask 'why'?") and not even a demonstration is enough for metaphysics to be invalidated in point of fact. The "end of metaphysics" is thus in no way an optional opinion; it is a fact of reason. Whether one accepts it or not, it inevitably holds sway over us as an event that has arisen. The very fact that one can deny it and that, in order to do this, one must argue against it and therefore acknowledge it, confirms it sufficiently.[10] It is a question of a fact, and of a fact that is in some way neutral, admitting and affecting all theoretical options equally. Moreover, to refuse the fact of the "end of metaphysics" seems even less defensible insofar as it is a matter of a transitive concept. Its transitivity is formulated as follows: just as the onto-theo-logical definition of *metaphysics* directly implies at least the possibility of the "end of metaphysics," so the "end of metaphysics" directly implies the possibility of the "end of the end of metaphysics."[11] There is no paradox in this: as soon as "metaphysics" admits of a concept that is precise, historically verifiable, and theoretically operative, it follows that this concept can undergo a critique proportionate to its limits, but, thanks to those very limits, it can also offer the possible horizon of its overcoming. In contrast, so long as a concept of metaphysics is lacking, the question concerning the philosophy to come, and thus present philosophy, also remains closed, even beyond its crisis. The "end [*Ende*]," Heidegger suggested, remains fundamentally a "place [*Ort*]." If the concept of "metaphysics" fixes its limits and thus sets its end, that end remains fertile, with a purpose for philosophy still intact. The transitivity of "metaphysics" leads not only to its "end" but also to its own overcoming—more than a metaphysics at its limit, a meta-metaphysics.

At present the "end of metaphysics" affects most visibly at one privileged point, the being par excellence. Indeed, if the figure of the ground no longer allows us to legitimate the concept of "metaphysics" in general, it follows that the assimilation of God to the function of ultimate ground in particular becomes (or can become) illegitimate. This identification runs through the entire course of philosophy and its metaphysical figure. It always interprets this ground on the basis of effectivity or actuality: "active being by essence," according to Aristotle; "no pure act without any potentiality [*purus actus non habens aliquid de potentialitate*]" for Aquinas; "self-caused cause [*causa sui*]" following Descartes; "sufficient Reason for the universe," with Leibniz.[12] By "God," metaphysics therefore means the being par excellence that operates as and through efficiency such that it can ensure a ground for every common being through the *metaphysica specialis*. The "end of metaphysics" provokes the "death" of *this* "God." Yet one must measure its true scope against the aggressive or resigned platitudes that seize upon this theoretical event. At issue is not denying any greatness to this determination of the divine by the efficiency of the ground, nor is it a matter of underestimating its theoretical fecundity. It is simply a matter of honestly posing this question: Does the effectivity of the ground really allow us to think the way in which God is God, even in philosophy? Even for the "God of the philosophers and the scholars," do *causa sui*, "sufficient Reason," *purus actus*, or *energeia* offer a sufficiently divine name to make God appear? At the very least, it is impossible today not to admit at least the possibility of such a suspicion. Now, this simple possibility suffices for recognizing the "death of God" in the "end of metaphysics," for it should not be possible for the divinity of God to be lacking. If it *is* lacking, if only imperceptibly, then God is already no longer at issue—but rather "God," who is stigmatized as an idol by these quotation marks.

4

If the "death of God" in philosophy belongs essentially to the "end of metaphysics" and if the latter follows essentially from the concept of "metaphysics," then the overcoming of onto-theo-logy becomes the condition for surpassing the naming of "God" in philosophy as efficient ground.

The question of whether philosophy itself can escape its metaphysical figure and thus its metaphysical destiny remains open. To be sure, Heidegger postulated a strict equivalence between "metaphysics" and "philosophy," to the advantage of "thought." But besides the fact that in certain decisive periods even after 1927 he himself claimed that "thought" would have to be introduced into "metaphysics," *Being and Time*, his first step back out of "metaphysics," remains strictly philosophical. How can that be so? By presupposing phenomenology as the method for ontology (understood in a sense radically renewed by ontological difference). In this way, he was content with simply repeating Husserl's gesture, who posited the equivalence between phenomenology and phenomenological philosophy in the *Ideas* of 1913. Despite the hesitations of the two greatest phenomenologists, one should therefore not speak of an ambiguous or undecided relation between phenomenology and metaphysics. One can simply grant that the radical innovation that phenomenology accomplishes in (and for) philosophy has perhaps not yet been measured fully in its most decisive meaning. It must therefore be sketched out, if only in broad strokes.

Phenomenology begins with a tautological principle, the "principle of nonpresupposition," which is formulated as early as 1900 in the opening of the second volume of the *Logical Investigations*: "strict exclusion of all statements not permitting of a comprehensive phenomenological realization."[13] The tautology is real but nevertheless meaningful. There is phenomenology when and only when a statement gives a phenomenon to be seen; what does not appear in one fashion or another does not enter into consideration. To understand is ultimately to see. To speak is to speak in order to render visible, thus to speak in order to see. Otherwise, to speak means nothing. But how are we to see? How does the statement make itself seen, taking on the status of a phenomenon? Husserl will respond more explicitly to this second question in the opening of the *Ideas* of 1913, where he posits the "principle of principles," which states "*that every originarily giving intuition is a source of right for cognition*, that everything that offers itself [*sich darbietet*] to us in originary 'intuition' (so to speak, in its fleshly actuality) must be received exactly as it gives itself out to be [*als was es sich (da) gibt*]."[14] To be realized as a phenomenon means to be given in an actuality without reserve, a "fleshly [*leibhaft*] actuality." For a statement to appear phenomenally amounts to its assuming flesh; the phenomenon shows the flesh of the discourse. How does a statement obtain this phenomenal flesh? Through intuition (*Anschaung* or *Intuition*, equally). One intuition of whatever kind is sufficient for the phenomenon, the flesh of the discourse, to occur. Indeed, intuition operates an absolutely indisputable hold and an ultimate cognition, since only another intuition can contradict a first intuition, so that in the final instance an intuition always remains. Intuition accomplishes the most fleshly acts of cognition. The flesh of the discourse appears to the flesh of the mind— the phenomenon to intuition. Phenomenology calls this encounter a givenness [*donation*]: intuition gives the phenomenon, the phenomenon gives itself through intuition. To be sure, this givenness can always be examined, can always be authenticated or not, can always admit limits—but it can never be questioned or denied, except by the authority of another intuitive givenness. The universal validity of the "principle of principles" confirms this.

One could not meditate too much on the scope of this principle, although it is often underestimated. (1) Setting intuition to work as the ultimate instance of givenness, the "principle of principles" gives rise to the extension of intuition beyond the Kantian prohibition. The intuition of essences and categorical intuition are added to sensible intuition. (2) Since intuition gives in the flesh, the Kantian caesura between the (solely sensible) phenomenon and the thing-in-itself must disappear. This is accomplished through intentionality. (3) Since intuition alone gives, the *I* (even the transcendental and constituting *I*) must remain held *by* and hence *in* an intuition. The "originary impression" temporally precedes consciousness precisely insofar as the latter remains pure. It imposes a facticity on consciousness that is not at all derivative, but originary. (4) As determinative as they may be (and none of the later phenomenologists called them into question), these doctrinal decisions must not divert our attention from their source. The "principle of principles" posits that in the beginning[15] (of philosophy and, first, of experience), there is only intuition. Yet insofar as it gives every phenomenon and initiates phenomenality in general, intuition is at work prior to any a priori as an originary a posteriori. An essential paradox emerges: the sole legitimate a priori in phenomenology becomes the a posteriori itself. The formula "principle of all principles" must not lead us astray. The principle here is that there is no principle at all, at least if by principle we mean what precedes, "that starting from which."[16] Or, in other words, what takes the place of a principle—namely, intuition as givenness—always precedes the consciousness of it, which we receive as if after the fact. The reduplication of "principle" in the "principle of principles" therefore must not be understood as the statement of another principle (after those of identity or of sufficient reason) that would be more essentially a priori than the preceding ones. Instead one must think of it in the manner of a superlative, as the (non)principle that surpasses all the previous principles insofar as it states that in the beginning there is no (transcendental) a priori principle but indeed an intuitive a posteriori: givenness precedes everything and always. Hence phenomenology goes unambiguously beyond metaphysics in the strict sense that it gets rid of any a priori principle in order to admit givenness, which is originary precisely insofar as it is a posteriori for the one who receives it. Phenomenology goes beyond metaphysics insofar as it gives up the transcendental project in order to allow the development of a finally radical empiricism[17]—finally radical because it is no longer limited to sensible intuition but admits all originarily giving intuition.

This reversal of the a priori principle in favor of the a posteriori immediately entails two determinative theses concerning *ontologia* and ground, respectively. The first follows directly from givenness: the appearance of phenomena is operative without having recourse to Being (at least necessarily and in the first instance). Indeed, here it is a matter of any "intuition" whatsoever, of the fact of its "giving itself," and of "fleshly presence." These three terms suffice to define the perfect phenomenality of the phenomenon without having recourse in any way to Being, to being, and even less to an "objective concept of being." One might legitimately ask whether every phenomenon, inasmuch as it appears, does not at least initially dispense with Being—a phenomenon without Being. Consequently, phenomenology could free itself absolutely not only from all *metaphysica generalis* (*ontologia*),[18] but also from the question of Being (*Seinsfrage*).[19] Phenomenology's relief of the metaphysical and ontological concepts is marked by clearly identifiable transpositions. Let us cite the principal ones.

(1) Henceforth, actuality is replaced by possibility, in the sense that Heidegger ("Higher than actuality stands possibility") reverses Aristotle's fundamental thesis that "the act [ενεργεια] is thus prior to potentiality [δυναμις] according to genesis and time," as well as according to ουσια."[20] (2) Evidence replaces certainty as the privileged mode of truth. The fact of the givenness of the phenomenon in itself replaces what the ego defines according to the limits of what it sees (*certus, cernere*), according to the phenomenon's own requirements. (3) ουσια, as the privileged meaning of being, which is thus the owner of its own goods (according to the primary—landowning—sense of the Greek term), is replaced by the given of Being, which straightaway defines every being as a being-given.[21] The being-given designates being such that its Being does not first amount to possessing its own funds (ουσια) but to receiving itself in Being, to receiving Being or, rather, to receiving the opportunity to be. In all of these cases, one would have to extend the status of a beyond of beingness (επεκεινα της ουσιας) to every being-given, something Plato reserved solely for the "idea of the good (ιδεα του αγαθου)."[22] General metaphysics, as *ontologia*, thus would have to yield to a general phenomenology of the givenness of any being-given, of which the *Seinsfrage* possibly would constitute only a simple region or a particular case. The relief of metaphysics (here, of general metaphysics) by phenomenology goes all the way to this radical point.

5

Thus I come to the second thesis that follows from the "principle of principles." This one concerns the *metaphysica specialis* in its more specifically theological function. Following Heidegger but also the facts of the history of philosophy, we admitted that in metaphysics "God" has, in essence, the function of ultimate ground, of "highest Reason," *causa sui*. It is not a matter here of arguing whether this interpretation of the divine function is suitable or even whether the concept of ground offers a sufficiently divine figure of God according to a renewed problematic of the divine names. At issue is simply whether the connections between "God" and all other beings, or—what amounts to the same thing—with being in general, can be understood and realized as a ground, or even according to an efficient causality. One must ask this since the "principle of all principles" has overdetermined the fact and the effect of being by the most original intuitive givenness, such that being in effect (and thus calling for a grounding cause) is replaced by the being-given (being inasmuch as given). If intuition of itself and by itself alone offers not only the fact of being-given but above all its "source of right," why would this phenomenon still seek the rights of its occurrence in a cause, which would interpret it as an effect? Moreover, would givenness have to be thought starting from the effect or, on the contrary, would the effect have to be received as an impoverished figure of givenness? Precisely inasmuch as it is being-given, the phenomenon itself does not have any "Why?" and therefore does not call for any. In phenomenology, the ground is not so much criticized or refuted (as is essentially still the case in Nietzsche, who undoubtedly never truly reaches his "third metamorphosis"),[23] as it is stricken with theoretical uselessness. "God" cannot be thought as the ground of being as soon as originary givenness delivers (sends, gives) being as a being-given and therefore delivers (frees) it of any requirement of a ground. Consequently, no longer capable of being thought *ad extra* under the figure of the ground, "God" can also no longer be thought *ad intra* under the figure of the *causa sui*. Thus the relief of the *metaphysica generalis* of being as grounded effect by the phenomenological givenness of being-given inevitably entails the relief of the *metaphysica specialis* of the foundation by the phenomenological "source of right" recognized in being-given.

The denunciation—more virulent than argued—of a supposed transposition of special metaphysics into phenomenology or even of a theological highjacking of phenomenology betrays, above all, a deviation that is rather too positivistic in its approach to the phenomenological method. But it conveys, without thematizing it, a fundamental error concerning phenomenology. To stigmatize a return of special metaphysics into phenomenology presupposes that such a return is phenomenologically *possible*. Yet by definition it proves to be impossible, since the requirement of the ground is in principle no longer operative. One might respond, perhaps, that this transposition has in fact taken place, thus proving that certain supposed phenomenologists no longer merit the title—which is precisely what one wanted to show. But this reasoning, in turn, is open to several objections. First, it implies that an essential and often distinguished part of what has always been recognized as belonging to the domain of phenomenological method has in fact ceaselessly betrayed it. This remains to be demonstrated conceptually and in detail—an immense and delicate task. Yet such an undertaking would quickly become dogmatic, since it would presuppose not only that there is a phenomenological method that is unique and that precedes all doctrines but, further, that this method has not evolved since Husserl's idealist and constitutive moment between 1913 and 1929. None of these points is self-evident, especially insofar as it belongs essentially to phenomenology that the a posteriori render it possible and therefore that no a priori prohibition pre-determine it. If there is a philosophy that works with an open method and bare thought, it is indeed phenomenology. Against metaphysics, it won the right to make use of the "Return to the things themselves!" which one might gloss "Prohibiting is prohibited!"[24] The sole criterion in phenomenology issues from the facts: from the phenomena that an analysis manages to display, from what the analysis renders visible. What shows itself justifies itself by that very fact.

But if a reestablishment of the *metaphysica specialis* in phenomenology appears to be a pure methodological contradiction, this nevertheless does not imply that phenomenology remains unfamiliar with what the *metaphysica specialis* treated at the metaphysical level. Could not the already-established relief of the *metaphysica generalis* by phenomenology also be repeated with respect to what the *metaphysica specialis* treated in the onto-theo-logical mode? This question does not aim at any restoration—I have just highlighted the absurdity of this—but a relief: to return to the things themselves, and possibly to the same things, in order to let them appear no longer according to the figure of ground but according to that of giv-enness, in this case no longer according to efficiency (being effect, *causa sui*) but according to the being-given. The three beings that were privileged by the *metaphysica specialis*, namely, the world (*cosmologia ratio-nalis*), the finite mind (*psychologia rationalis*), and "God" (*theologia rationalis*) demand, in the capacity of "thing itself," that we test the possibility (or impossibility) of their phenomenal apparition and therefore of the intuition that could (or not) inscribe them in the being-given. For none of the cases can this requirement be challenged, since it results directly from the phenomenological reduction, namely, to suspend all transcendence precisely in order to measure what is thus given in immanence. Moreover, the phenomenological relief of what was treated by the *metaphysica specialis* already has a long history, going back to Husserl.

A few results can be assumed today as established facts. First, concerning the world: the early Husserl relieves the classical metaphysical aporia (Descartes, Kant) of the necessity, indeed, of the impossibility, of demonstrating the existence of the external "world." Intentionality (and then Heidegger's *In-der-Welt-sein*) directly sets consciousness ecstatically into the world without the screen of representation. It finds the world always already given because it is originarily given to the world more essentially. The relation of constitution between consciousness and its objects will exploit intentionality so far as to put it in danger, but the late Husserl will bring the noetico-noematic relation back under the firm control of the "principle of correlation." The question of the world hence definitely quits the horizon of objectivation for that of the being-given, as *the being-given as a whole*. Next, concerning the finite mind: obsession with the Cartesian ego still keeps Husserl and even Heidegger from giving up on interpreting it. This is, if not still theoretical, at least still constitutive, if only through "anticipatory resoluteness." From this followed the disappearance of ethics or its subordination to theory. It is to the decisive credit of Emmanuel Levinas to have established, in a Copernican revolution, that ontology, even fundamental ontology, cannot reach the ground because that ground belongs to the domain not of theoretical philosophy but of ethics. Not only does ethics thus become first philosophy (*philosophia prima*), which by itself would still remain an arrangement of metaphysics) but it decenters the ego toward the always already open, offered, and abandoned face of the other [*d'autrui*] and thus toward the being-given of the other. The ego no longer ensures any foundation by representing (itself); it finds itself always already preceded by the being-given of the other, whose unobjectifiable counter-intentionality it suffers. Along this line, the passage from the ego to what I call the "interlocuted" [*interloqué*] presents no difficulty: one must simply generalize the reversed intentionality to other being-givens.[25] According to the rule of givenness, the ego thus attains a secondariness[26] that is, nevertheless, more phenomenal than any representational primacy. Put in second place, the ego discovers the other as *the closest being-given*.

The question of "God" remains, which for obvious reasons has remained the question least approached by phenomenology. These obvious reasons spring from different but convergent reservations on the part of Husserl and Heidegger. Husserl clearly indicated (although without returning to the matter, even in his final texts) that the assumption of any "God" whatsoever fell under the blow of the reduction and that "God," transcendent in every sense, therefore did not appear.[27] When Heidegger marks God with the seal of the *causa sui*,[28] he is always and explicitly dealing with the "God" of metaphysics. Can phenomenology go no further than these denials or these warnings?[29] Some would like to leave a choice only between philosophical silence and faith without reason. Such an alternative often clearly has the sole intention of dwelling serenely in silence while banishing reason. Yet outside of revealed theology there is no reason to prohibit reason—here, philosophy in its phenomenological bearing—from pushing reason to its end, that is, to itself, without admitting any other limits than those of phenomenality. The question then becomes: What (if any) phenomenal face can the "God of the philosophers and the scholars" assume? More precisely, what phenomenon could claim to offer a luminous shadow of this "God" so as to correspond to the being-given's relief of being? Does one not, perhaps inevitably, have to answer the being-given with a giver, indeed a being-giver [*étant-donateur*]? And in that case, how could one distinguish that being-giver from a founding being or *causa sui*,[30] and how could one not stigmatize in this long operation a simple restoration of the most metaphysical *theologia rationalis*?

However lucid it may appear to be, this objection remains convincing only if one ignores two arguments. (1) On the hypothesis in which a giver would indeed correspond to the being-given, the giver would be equivalent to a (metaphysical) ground only by maintaining the status of a being and only if the givenness of the being-given given by the giver were still comprehended within the horizon of causality understood as efficiency. Yet neither of these assumptions is self-evident. On the contrary, it could be that givenness can arise only once causality has been radically surpassed, in a mode whose own rationality causality does not even suspect. It could be that givenness obeys requirements that are infinitely more complex and powerful than the resources of efficient causality. Moreover even in the history of metaphysics, the sudden appearance of efficient causality in the field of "God" marks more the *decline* than the consecration of *theologia rationalis*; Leibniz was the equally lucid and powerless witness to this. The objection thus betrays that it depends on metaphysics much more than does the thesis that it contests, since it cannot prevent itself from understanding that thesis hastily and from the outset in a metaphysical fashion. (2) A second argument, however, renders these precautions useless. The answer to the being-given does not assume the figure of the giver but that of the being-given par excellence. If the world can be defined as what appears as the being-given as a whole, if *I/me* can be designated as what appears as the closest being-given, then "God" would be determined as the being-given par excellence. That excellence indicates neither sufficiency, nor efficiency, nor principality, but it attests to the fact that "God" is given and allows to be given more than any other being-given. In short, with "God" it is a question of the *being-abandoned* [l'étant-abandonné].[31]

The phenomenological figure of "God" as the being-given par excellence, hence as the abandoned, can be outlined by following the guiding thread of givenness itself. As the given par excellence, "God" is given without restriction, without reserve, without restraint. "God" is given not at all partially, following this or that outline, like a constituted object that nevertheless offers to the intentional gaze only a specific side of its sensible visibility, leaving to appresentation the duty of giving further what does not give itself. Instead "God" is given absolutely, without the least reserve of any outline, with every side open, in the manner of the objects whose dimensions cubist painting caused to explode, in order that all aspects might be juxtaposed, despite the constraints of perspective. "God" is found given without reserve or restraint. This evidence displays itself in the atonal tonality of bedazzlement. It follows that God diffuses—what God diffuses remains Godself: the Good diffuses itself and therefore what it diffuses still remains itself, perhaps in the way that the modes in which the Spinozist *substantia* expresses itself still remain that *substantia* itself. The givenness par excellence implies an ecstasy outside of self where the ecstatic self remains all the more itself. While the *causa sui* can only fold efficiency back upon itself, the givenness that "God" accomplishes can remain equal to itself (givenness as gift). If the "God" of metaphysics, according to Malebranche, acts only for itself, then the "God" of phenomenology, exactly to the contrary, acts only for what does not remain (in) "God."

This givenness par excellence entails another consequence: the absolute mode of presence that follows from it saturates any horizon, all horizons, with a dazzling evidence. Now, such a presence without limit (without horizon), which alone suits givenness without reserve, cannot present itself as a necessarily limited object. Consequently, it occupies no space, fixes no attention, attracts no gaze. In this very bedazzlement, "God" shines by absence. *Evidence evoids*[32]—it voids the saturated horizons of any definable, visible thing. The absence or unknowability of "God" does not contradict givenness but on the contrary attests to the excellence of that givenness. "God" becomes invisible not in spite of givenness but by virtue of that givenness. One needs a rather weak estimation of transcendence, or even an already militant refusal, to be scandalized by its invisibility. If we saw it, then it would not be "God."

Givenness par excellence can thus turn immediately into givenness by *abandon*. The being-given that is absolutely without restraint exerts a phenomenology such that, due to its intrinsic invisibility, its status as phenomenon might never be acknowledged. The phenomenon par excellence on account of that very excellence lays itself open to not appearing—to remaining in a state of abandon. Indeed, most other phenomena become available to the gaze that sees them, delimits them, and manipulates them. Here, on the contrary, a radical unavailability exposes "God" to the risk of being denied the right to phenomenality precisely because most of the time and at first glance our gaze only desires and only wants to see objects. Givenness par excellence thus turns toward abandon. And this is confirmed every time that one fails to acknowledge givenness under the pretext that given without return or retreat, it is abandoned to the point of disappearing as an object one could possess, handle, encircle. Givenness par excellence actually lays itself open to seeming to disappear (by defect) precisely because it gives itself without reserve (by excess). A strange but inevitable paradox.

6

Of course, although decidedly opposed to the metaphysical figure of a *causa sui*, "God," the figure of "God" in phenomenology that we have just outlined, nevertheless still concerns the "God of the philosophers and the scholars," and in no way the "God of Abraham, of Isaac, and of Jacob."[33] One could also say that the figure of "God" in phenomenology is hardly distinguishable from this latter. The being-given par excellence in fact bears the characteristics of a very precise type of manifestation, namely, that of the saturated phenomenon, or, more precisely, that of the saturated phenomenon typical of revelation.[34] Would one not again have to fear a confusion between phenomenology and revealed theology here?

It seems to me that such a confusion can be avoided through two clear distinctions. (1) On its own, phenomenology can identify the saturated phenomenon of the being-given par excellence only as a possibility: not only a possibility as opposed to actuality but, above all, as a possibility of givenness itself. The characteristics of the being-given imply that it gives itself without prediction, without measure, without analogy, without repetition; in short, it remains unavailable. Its phenomenological analysis therefore bears only on its re-presentation, its "essence," and not directly on its being-given in fact. More than phenomenological analysis, the intuitive realization of that being-given requires the real experience of its givenness, which falls to revealed theology. Between phenomenology and theology, the border passes between revelation as possibility and Revelation as historicity. There can be no danger of confusion between these domains.[35] (2) To be sure, phenomenology can describe and construct the being-given and even the being-given par excellence, but it certainly does not fall to phenomenology to approach the givenness that is identified with and in a face. Or rather, even if it can make the face one of its privileged themes in a strict sense, it cannot and must not understand that face as a face of charity. When the being-given turns to charity (the loved or loving being, the lover in the strict sense), phenomenology yields to revealed theology exactly as the second order, according to Pascal, yields to the third. Here again, no confusion could creep in.

Quite obviously, these theses cannot be adequately developed here. They nevertheless will suffice to indicate what new path phenomenology shows to philosophy, beyond the metaphysics that it relieves—and without returning to *metaphysica specialis*. And on that path, the rational thought of God, which philosophy cannot forget without losing its own dignity or even its mere possibility, finds at least a certain coherence.

—*Translated by Thomas A. Carlson*

"Christian Philosophy"

Hermeneutic or Heuristic?

1

Concepts are mortal too. They can die of insignificance or at least become pure aporias. Is the concept of "Christian philosophy" not undergoing this fate today, pointing only to a way that no longer leads anywhere, an abandoned yard, a dead discipline? But do we have to renounce "Christian philosophy" on the simple pretext that we can no longer think it? Should we not, instead, increase our efforts to think it anew?

Before I go any further, let me recall the principal aporia that still characterizes "Christian philosophy" today. It appeared during a debate provoked between 1927 and 1931 by the position taken by the excellent French historian and philosopher Émile Bréhier. His thesis can be summarized as follows: Christianity has often used very diverse philosophies, but has never created or assimilated any of them, because there is an "incompatibility," or at least a radical "separation," between clear and distinct reason and the mystery of a relationship between God and the human person.[1] Both excessive and provocative, this position nonetheless legitimately once again required clarification of the relation between philosophy and Christian theology—is it an incompatibility, a partial stand-off, or a continuity? One might have expected that Catholics (if not all Christians) would uphold the theoretical legitimacy and historical reality of such a "Christian philosophy" against Bréhier, leaving the task of challenging it to nonbelievers. Yet the distribution of roles was more complex.

Some Catholics held that, "in the sense in which we usually understand it, there is no *Catholic philosophy*, any more than there is a *Catholic science*";[2] this thesis (which was typical of the school of Louvain, for whom Aristotelian Thomism imposes itself on Catholics not because of its Christianity but because of its strict truth) recalled Jacques Maritain's initial position, that only an extrinsic relation exists between the faith and the philosophy of a Christian thinker.[3] Even better, this position also agrees with Maurice Blondel's non-Thomistic and non-Scholastic thought: "this term 'Christian philosophy' does not exist any more than Christian physics does."[4] In this way Catholic thinkers managed to reject "Christian philosophy" by using the argument of its non-Christian opponents, from Feuerbach to Heidegger: this is a contradictory syntagma, a "square circle," an "iron-wood."[5] From this it follows that the concept of "Christian philosophy" can appear as problematic to believers (non-Thomistic as well as Thomistic) as to nonbelievers. The question remains entirely open, because the responses do not depend on the theological options. Should one give it up?

These uncertainties notwithstanding, one formal definition upheld the use of this concept, due to Étienne Gilson's almost solitary initiative: "I call 'Christian philosophy' all philosophy that, while formally distinguishing between the two orders, considers Christian revelation to be an indispensable auxiliary of reason."[6] This definition can be understood to have two meanings. Gilson, for his part, often explained that "Christian philosophy" exists whenever revelation makes suggestions to reason, without substituting itself for reason or modifying reason's requirements, in order to broach themes rationally that reason could not handle by itself or even suspect. He gave the concept of creation as an example. Yet from this point of view one might as well have suggested the concepts of the Eucharist, which became a philosophical theme for Descartes and Leibniz, of grace for Malebranche or Leibniz, of the inspiration of the Scriptures for Spinoza, or of Christology as a whole for Hegel and Schelling. Even more, should one not also qualify as "Christian philosophy" any philosophy that opposes itself to Christian revelation yet does not stop calling upon revelation as upon an "indispensable auxiliary of reason" precisely in order to criticize it in detail? Is this not essentially the case with Feuerbach and Nietzsche, who at least methodologically are no different from the medievals, insofar as they apply reason to the given that is revealed?

It is clear that Gilson intended his definition to have a much more restricted meaning: Christian revelation intervenes as an "auxiliary," not because it would offer themes to reason that otherwise would be unreachable, but because it offers a radically original interpretation of them, that of the revelation of Christ. In other words: in Gilson's best-known thesis, "the metaphysics of Exodus," "Christian philosophy" contends that the quasi-Aristotelian concept of *actus purus essendi* is equivalent to a purely theological and biblical statement, *Sum qui sum* (Exod. 3:14). Let me admit this equivalence as a hypothesis. Yet allow me to question the operation that is accomplished by "Christian philosophy" in this very privileged case. It consists in interpreting a philosopheme as a divine name (and as the first). Yet this philosopheme would remain intelligible, and endowed with its meaning, even if it were not interpreted as an equivalent to such a theological theme. It would be possible for *actus purus essendi not* to interpret the God of Exodus, and it has indeed not denoted it for all non-Thomistic Aristotelians, whether medieval or modern. Inversely, "Christian philosophy" also could *not* interpret the *esse* as the first of divine names (and replace it with a simple concept, as Scotus did), or privilege other transcendentals, such as the *bonum* (according to the prevalent tradition until St. Bonaventure). In short, the assistance from which "Christian philosophy" benefits consists in a theological interpretation of purely philosophical concepts, an interpretation that is possible but not necessary.

Of course, there are plenty of examples of this kind of "Christian philosophy" that originate in a Christian interpretation of philosophical theses: St. Augustine built his entire doctrine of the images of the Trinity within us on the possibility of interpreting the faculties of the soul, *memoria/intellectus/amor*, as Trinitarian indications. To support the vision of ideas in the Word, Malebranche interprets Cartesian innation in theological terms as innation in the Creator. The Christian interpretations of Platonism, stoicism, skepticism, and even Epicureanism are sufficiently well known to make it unnecessary to demonstrate how the Gilsonian definition of "Christian philosophy" also applies to them. Depending on the talent of the interpreter, the *preparatio evangelica*, initially reserved for Platonism, can be generalized to all philosophy. Such has historically been the case. Maurice Blondel must be regarded as one of the most perfect examples of this process when he claims always to be able to read transcendence within immanence ("the immanent affirmation of transcendence"[7]) and to extricate the supernatural "necessarily" from nature: "I feel more and more drawn toward the design of showing . . . the natural necessity of the supernatural and the supernatural reality of the natural itself."[8] Furthermore, theology itself made the method of immanence its own in one of the richest trends of this century and hence appropriated the hermeneutics that defines "Christian philosophy" according to Gilson. Indeed, this was at least the tacit presupposition of the dispute about

Henri de Lubac's *Supernatural* (should natural desire be interpreted as a real capacity to see God?), of analogy according to Erich Przywara (Should the *analogia entis* be interpreted as a Trinitarian determination?), and, above all, of Karl Rahner's theology (Should the passage from finite being to infinite being be interpreted as the theoretical place of Christology? Should the nonbeliever be interpreted as "anonymous Christian"? Does the evolution of "terrestrial realities" allow their interpretation as "signs of the times," heralding the coming of the kingdom of God?). If we retain Gilson's definition that "all philosophy that, while formally distinguishing the two orders, considers Christian revelation as an indispensable auxiliary of reason," these few quickly enumerated but very significant examples show sufficiently that "Christian philosophy" is neither fragile nor marginal in our century. On the contrary, it appears to be the privileged method of a dominant part of Christian and Catholic thought. From de Lubac to Rahner, from Gilson to Blondel, up to Lonergan and Moltmann, Mascall and Tracy, even Ricoeur—our century has been that of "Christian philosophy" as hermeneutic par excellence.

2

As impressive as its partisans are, as important as its results may appear, and as venerable as the method of *preparatio evangelica*, which it continues, remains, this definition of "Christian philosophy" as hermeneutical nevertheless remains highly controversial. I see at least three arguments that bring it into question.

(1) If from the point of view of the revelation of concepts and thus of (supposed) realities already acquired by strict philosophy, "Christian philosophy" can be reduced to a hermeneutic, then it remains secondary, derivative, even elective in comparison with one instance, philosophy, the only original and inventive one. *Actus purus essendi* can also be thought without its interpretation as *Sum qui sum*, since that was the way Aristotle thought it. The triad *memoria/intellectus/amor* can be thought without its Trinitarian interpretation, since that was the way Plotinus thought it. The strictly interpretative definition of "Christian philosophy," therefore, responds to Bréhier's objection only by conceding the essential to it. This supposed "philosophy" limits itself to commentary and merely repeats the results of strict philosophy, which is not Christian. To reduce "Christian philosophy" to a hermeneutic amounts to denying it the level of philosophy.

(2) If, even (and mainly) from the point of view of Christian revelation, "Christian philosophy" is limited to a hermeneutic, it becomes subject to

the suspicions that weigh on all hermeneutics. Two principles are involved. (a) Why privilege the interpretation based on Christian revelation, when others are possible? Marx made this point brutally and forcefully: poverty can be interpreted as an evangelical virtue, but also as an economic phenomenon linked to the capitalist conditions of production. Why select one interpretation over the other? Why deny the second in the name of the first? The objection is so strong that a good part of Christian theology and the accompanying "Christian philosophy" are still in the process of responding to it a century after Marx. (b) Why take the interpretation based on Christian revelation for what it pretends to be? Every interpretation obeys reasons that differ or may differ in an essential way from those it invokes knowingly. These masked reasons for the interpretation may be due to unconscious desire (Freud), from the "will to truth," that is, the "will to power" (Nietzsche), ideology (Marx), etc. Only the result is important: an interpretation cannot be justified by what it says about itself, but usually by what it does not say. Nietzsche summarized this suspicion in the following principle: "There are no moral phenomena, there is only a moral interpretation of these phenomena."[9] This applies to the hermeneutics of "Christian philosophy" in the sense that there is no Christian philosophy, merely a Christian interpretation of philosophy, which then has to justify itself, not because of what it says about itself, but because of what it does not say. Through this a counter-hermeneutics becomes possible, which reverses the hermeneutics of "Christian philosophy" point by point. Two examples will suffice: (a) The philosophical definition of "God" as "moral God" (Kant, Fichte) can be interpreted as an image of the Christian God or, on the contrary, as what leads to the "death of God" (which is the way Feuerbach, Bauer, Marx, and Nietzsche understood it). (b) The definition of "God" as *causa sui* (Descartes) can be interpreted as an image of the Christian God or, on the contrary, as his metaphysical idol par excellence (Heidegger). Such a counter-hermeneutics results directly from the modern critique of all hermeneutics, on the one hand, and, on the other, from the definition of "Christian philosophy" as one hermeneutic among others. As a result, the "auxiliary" of revelation is no longer insurmountable. In other words, reducing "Christian philosophy" to a hermeneutic leads to branding it as arbitrary.

(3) According to Gilson, the hermeneutic definition of "Christian philosophy" must "formally distinguish the two orders" of philosophy and theology, of nature and grace, the known and the revealed. But can it do this? For the interpretation of one in the light of the other to remain possible, must one not already suppose that certain specifically Christian truths are at least already powerfully and *in nuce* within the statements of

strict philosophy (or are "natural," if one can use that term)? How far can this preestablished affinity go? Throughout the history of philosophy, the quarrel about the supernatural has never ceased to reappear every time the hermeneutic of "Christian philosophy" succeeds *too well*: on the topic of double beatitude, the rectitude of free will, the disinterested love of God, the intelligibility of divine ends, the meaning of history, etc. In each case, the danger consisted in taking revelation to be a simple implication of nature and thus of philosophy. To reduce "Christian philosophy" to a hermeneutic thus exposes it to missing the specificity of creation and no less that of revelation—by locking faith in its *preambula*.

This triple result does not automatically lead to a renunciation of all of "Christian philosophy," not even to the definition proposed by Gilson, but it does force us to dispute that "Christian philosophy" be defined exclusively as a hermeneutic.

3

How else can one define it? When taking more precisely into account the "auxiliary" that distinguishes it absolutely from any other kind of philosophy, Gilson without further precision calls it "Christian revelation." Yet this revelation is summarized in Christ. Now by his teaching and finally by his judgment ("He interpreted to them the things about himself in all the Scriptures [διερμηνευσεν αυτοις εν πασαις ταις γραφαις τα περι εαυτου]"; Luke 24:27), Christ exercises a hermeneutic on the world and its wisdom. But he accomplishes it only because of an entirely different characteristic: its radical newness, its unsurpassable innovation. "He introduced all newness by introducing himself [*Omnem novitatem attulit, seipsum afferens*]."[10] If Christ reveals what has always been hidden (the mystery of God) and makes all things new ("Now I am making the whole of creation new"; Revelation 21:5), it is because he himself constitutes all newness, because he comes from God's bosom, from absolutely beyond the world, which for that very reason "did not know him" (John 1:10). His revelation introduced realities and phenomena into the world that never had been seen or known there before him. Without his newness even the sketches of the Old Covenant would have remained unintelligible—sanctity, forgiveness, resurrection, communion, etc. With Christ, a newness lives in the world that is not of the world—"the new heavens and the new earth" (2 Peter 3:13). Revelation interprets only in the context of Christ's Trinitarian innovation.

In what does Christ's innovation consist? He makes manifest that "God is love" (1 John 4:18). This opening, absolutely without parallel among previous representations of divinity, determines charity as the domain of theology. Charity deploys itself immediately in the character of Christ, where it appears carnally, mediately in the Trinity, from which it deduces its interpersonal depth, and as a derivative in the Church, where the Son of the Father recapitulates human beings in the Spirit as his adopted brothers and sisters. These are *revelata* in the strict sense, which belong only to theology and which philosophy need not discuss, even when it is supposed to be "Christian."

However, apart from its theological use, charity has purely theoretical effects on the horizon of rationality. As a new theoretical continent to be explored, it opens up what Pascal called the "order of charity,"[11] in opposition to the order of "carnal grandeurs" (all the powers of bodies, politics, economics, the imagination, etc.). The order of charity, which concerns love in all its facets, dominates the other two and for that reason remains less visible and less known than they do. Indeed, according to an essential paradox, no order can know or see a superior order (even if an order knows itself and can see all inferior orders). Charity, the supreme order, thus remains invisible to the flesh and to the spirit, to powers and to sciences. The result is that charity opens a field of new phenomena to knowledge, but this field remains invisible to natural reason alone. That is why philosophy needs the "indispensable auxiliary" of revelation in order to gain access to it: because it is revelation, as the revelation *of charity*, that offers perfectly rational phenomena to philosophy, although they belong to charity and are as new as it is. One finds here again Gilson's definition of "Christian philosophy," but with a radically new meaning: all philosophy that, while formally distinguishing the differences between the orders (in Pascal's sense), considers Christian Revelation (understood as revelation of charity, thus the third order) to be an indispensable auxiliary of reason. But from now on, the "auxiliary" brought by Revelation not only assists in providing a new interpretation of phenomena that are already visible but also makes visible phenomena that would have remained invisible without it. "Christian philosophy" is not practiced as a simple, possibly ideological, hermeneutic of a natural "given" already accessible to rationality without Revelation, in short, as an interpretive supplement under strange command. It offers entirely new natural phenomena to reason, which reason discovers because Revelation invents them for it and shows them to it. Reason is therefore practiced as heuristic. Gilson's proposed definition of "Christian philosophy" thus can be understood a second time not only as hermeneutic but as heuristic. And, because Gilson did not clearly distinguish the two possible meanings of his thesis or their profound difference, I will suppose that in going from one to the other I will remain under the patronage of this great philosopher.

4

As a matter of fact, the heuristic definition of "Christian philosophy" brings up a difficulty that Gilson often discussed: that Revelation—that is, the revelation of charity—would contribute to the appearance of phenomena, which are new and visible only through charity, thus invisible without it. Charity nevertheless would entrust them not only to theology (the science of the *revelata*), but also to a philosophy, that is, to knowledge ruled only by natural light. In short, the heuristic of charity would provide phenomena uncovered by Revelation to a purely natural philosophy. In consequence, between theology (supernatural) and philosophy (natural), "Christian philosophy" would introduce a mix: a knowledge that would discuss with natural light facts discovered under supernatural light. All the difficulties of this paradox are concentrated into one: the mix of natural and supernatural, or of revelation and philosophy, does not respect the distinction between the orders. "Christian philosophy" compromises theology as much as it does philosophy, because its concept is in the end contradictory.

It is, of course, impossible here to give a complete response, but it is possible to give a few examples. Because the question of entitlement to the borders between the disciplines may be reduced to questions of rights regarding the real objects of these disciplines, can one justify "Christian philosophy" by its formal object? One would be able to do so if one were to succeed in describing one or several phenomena given *in* natural experience and not *by* it, but by the "order of charity" or its revelation. The most convincing example relates not to God or the world but to the human person—in other words, the phenomenon of the human being, that is, of human natural visibility, which is concentrated in the face. One would not deny that this is a phenomenon in its own right, accessible by natural experience to natural reason. But it is not sufficient merely to look at a face in order to see the other who is exposed in it, since one can see the face of a slave without being able to recognize the other in his or her own right. One can also face another face and coldly kill it; we can use our own faces to dissimulate ourselves under masks and hide them from visibility; we even can expose our faces only to lie, hurt, or destroy. In short, the face can objectivize itself, hide itself, or not appear. This is why it was not sufficient for ancient thought to settle on the (theatrical or juridical) term *persona* in order to obtain access to the concept of person: In this particular case it lacked the discovery of the primacy of relation over substantiality, as only Trinitarian theology captured it. The face really becomes the phenomenon of a human being when it makes a person appear who is essentially defined as the crux and the origin of his or her relationships. If seeing a face implies reading a net of relationships in it, I will see it only if I experience "an idea of the infinite" (Levinas), that is, this center of relationships, which cannot be objectivized or reduced to me. Experiencing the infinite in the face of the other cannot be expressed in a formula. It is a behavior that is experimentally verifiable: facing a face disfigured (by poverty, sickness, pain, etc.) or reduced to its extreme shapes (prenatal life, coma, agony, etc.), I either cannot see it or am no longer able to recognize another for myself in it and continue on my way. Or I still can *see* in it what I do not see in it naturally—the absolute phenomenon of another center in the world, where my lookalike lives and whose look upon me allows me to live, thanks to him or her. But in this case, to *see* this invisible face, I must *love* it. Love, however, comes from charity. In consequence, one must hold that the natural phenomenon of the face of the other cannot be discovered except through the light of charity, that is, through the "auxiliary" of Revelation. Without the revelation of the transcendence of love, the phenomenon of the face, and thus of the other, simply cannot be seen. This is an exemplary case of "Christian philosophy."

In this way, I have attempted to justify the paradox of "Christian philosophy" through its formal object, one of its own phenomena, in order to solve through a factual answer a question of right (the possibility of an intermediary between philosophy and theology). It is conceivable that the legitimacy of such a "Christian philosophy" will be guaranteed only by the new phenomena that it would, all by itself, be able to add to the phenomena already treated in philosophy. In consequence, "Christian philosophy" would remain acceptable only so long as it invents—in the sense of both discovering and constructing—heretofore unseen phenomena. In short, "Christian philosophy" dies if it repeats, defends, and preserves something acquired that is already known, and remains alive only if it discovers what would remain hidden in philosophy without it.

5

Even if one admits that only a heuristic theory of charity can invent concepts such as "person" or "face," one must still examine several legitimate objections to this image of "Christian philosophy." I do not intend to resolve them thoroughly in this essay, but I will at least identify them and outline some responses. First objection: the above example of "person" or "face" does not prove anything more than a simple tautology. The heuristic that starts with charity of course discovers some phenomena of charity; but charity only keeps finding itself under other names, and this is why the distance between charity and love matters very little. The heuristic of charity would arrive at real philosophical validity only if it were to produce concepts of phenomena other than itself. This objection deserves all the more attention when we consider that the response allows us to confirm the heuristic scope of charity. To do this, let me examine three of the many concepts and phenomena that charity has invented in philosophy.

(a) First, history, that is to say, not only linear and nonrepetitive temporality, which innovates continually by determining irremediable facts forever, but also a temporality free from any fate, where every individual or collective action makes manifest the will of its actor, who thus judges him- or herself in the face of his or her time, the future, and God. Understood in this way, one can venture to say that history is born as a concept through St. Augustine, who discovers a history in the non-Christian world that until then had been ignored by philosophy and was unthought as such by starting from the history of salvation of Christian revelation.

(b) Second, the icon, starting with the revelation of Christ as "icon of the invisible God [εικων του θεου του αυρατου]" (Col. 1:10), and by derivation the methods Western as well as Eastern painters and sculptors used to represent his elaborated face. By beginning with this icon, the Christian tradition attempted to think and show the paradox of a gaze, in itself as invisible as any gaze, which would not be reduced to the level of an observed object but would in turn envisage the one looking at him or her. This dialogue of two invisible gazes in the visible allows us, then, not only to see prayer but to enter into it. At issue is hence the experience of a counter-gaze crossing mine. By beginning with this paradigm, I was able to introduce a concept into phenomenology that was as unknown to Husserl as it was to Heidegger and whose absence precludes the phenomenology of intersubjectivity or of counter-intentionality almost entirely. The intentionality of the *I* can only know objects and objectivize the other, thus missing him or her. In order for the other to appear as other, that is to say, as a nonobject, the other must be seen as another intentionality, weighing on me. And this counter-intentionality is thought from the icon, the only concept we have to define it. The icon of the gaze of the other thus becomes an intelligible phenomenon starting with the invention of Christ as icon.

(c) As a final example for a heuristic of charity, I shall rely on the authority of Kant, uncontested on the matter of rationalism. Defining belief

(*Glaube*) as "the moral way of thinking of reason in its assent to what is inaccessible to theoretical knowledge," in this case, belief in "what it is necessary to presuppose as a condition for the possibility of the final supreme goal," he adds a note:

> The word *fides* expresses this already; but the introduction of this expression and this particular idea in moral philosophy could seem suspect, because they were first introduced by Christianity, and to imitate them could seem to be a flattering imitation of its language. But this is not a unique case, because this beautiful religion, in the supreme simplicity of its style, has enriched philosophy with moral concepts much more determined and much purer than those that [philosophy] had been able to produce until then; and these concepts, since they are there now, are *freely* approved by reason and admitted as concepts that it could have and should have discovered and introduced by itself.[12]

Nothing needs to be added to this admirable text except to correct its last sentence: it is exactly because it "should have" rather than "could have" invented these concepts that philosophy had to receive them from the Christian religion, through the intermediary of what I dare to call a heuristic of charity.

Second objection: On the supposition that certain phenomena and concepts become accessible to reason only through the "indispensable auxiliary" of Revelation, do they really belong to philosophy, or rather to Revelation? The response is obvious: concepts and phenomena obtained in the light of Revelation remain acquired by philosophy in the strict sense to the extent that once they have been discovered they are accessible to reason as such. The concepts of "face," "person," "history," "faith," etc. function philosophically even without the Christian convictions of their user. And this is why they may find themselves turned against their origin by non-Christian thoughts. The heuristic of charity itself is charitable: what it finds, it gives without reserve. And in this sense, the whole of philosophy could be called "Christian philosophy," so much is it saturated with concepts and phenomena that directly or indirectly were introduced in it by revelation. In this sense, Heidegger, Nietzsche, Marx, and Feuerbach practice "Christian philosophy" as much as Leibniz, Hegel, Schelling, and Husserl do. Recognizing the imprint of Christian revelation on philosophy, and thus the heuristic function of "Christian philosophy" in it, does not depend on a subjective believing or atheistic conviction: it is about facts that any competent historian of philosophy knows thoroughly. One could almost sustain the paradox that the possibility of a "Christian philosophy" almost comes naturally, while a philosophy that has absolutely no connection to Christian revelation seems highly problematic in our historical situation. In short, how could a philosopher who really thinks about the major problems of philosophy not practice "Christian philosophy" (if only to criticize it)?

Third objection: How does this new situation given to "Christian philosophy" respect the formal distinction between natural and supernatural orders? The first answer is that the Incarnation questions this distinction, which henceforth becomes more abstract than real. Yet the distinction must be maintained, at least in regard to the disciplines. Here no confusion is possible. (a) Theology deploys the discourse of charity from and about the *revelata* in the strict sense, that is, truths that only faith can reach. (b) Philosophy discusses facts, phenomena, and statements accessible to reason and its workings. (c) "Christian philosophy" (or whatever one wants to call it) finds and invents, in the natural sphere ruled by reason, phenomena and concepts that fall within the order of charity and that simple reason cannot see or discover. After having formalized them, "Christian philosophy" introduces them into philosophy and abandons them to it. This distinction between the roles demands only one presupposition: that charity, as grace, could be at the same time both natural (created) and supernatural (uncreated). Theologians accept this presupposition, whereas pure philosophy cannot forbid a priori what may be proven experimentally.

Fourth objection: Does the heuristic determination of "Christian philosophy" reject its more common hermeneutic definition entirely? At this point one sees very clearly that the two are not opposed to each other; on the contrary, the heuristic definition often legitimizes the hermeneutic one. Indeed, the major objection to the hermeneutic definition stems from the fact that the proposed Christian interpretation of "terrestrial realities" is arbitrary: Why give them a Christian meaning rather than any other? The heuristic definition, by contrast, makes possible this response: giving a meaning to "terrestrial realities" through charity is justified because charity discovers and introduces new phenomena into the world itself and into the conceptual universe that are saturated with meaning and glory, which order and possibly save this world. Charity does not interpret through and as an ideology, because it gives to the world greater reality and grandeur than the world claims to have by itself. Gilson's statement can be recovered here precisely, but by basing it on a more complete determination of revelation as charity that invents, discovers, works. Thus, it becomes clear that this double function of charity (hermeneutic and heuristic) presumes its most radical execution: charity first must give in order to give to reflection. This implies doing charitable work and contemplating charity in prayer. It is only in this sense that "Christian philosophy" presupposes faith in Christ.

6

These answers to a few objections of course cannot suffice to establish a definition of "Christian philosophy" as a heuristic of charity. In this discussion it was my modest intention merely to contribute a new meditation on Gilson's formula. It is possible that another point of departure may be preferable—even if this one has the advantage of linking to a discussion that in its time was very widespread and serious (and still is today). It is possible that the term *Christian philosophy* may turn out to be more of a handicap than an opportunity in the current state of the debate. In conclusion, I would like to suggest two arguments that seem to me to argue in favor of its maintenance.

As I understand it, "Christian philosophy" is done by introducing concepts and discovering phenomena that come from charity, inasmuch as charity comes from revelation but inscribes itself in creation. "Ever since the creation of the world God's eternal power and divine nature, invisible though they are, have been understood and seen through the things he has made" (Romans 1:20). Consequently, "Christian philosophy" contends that, in a mode not directly theological, philosophy relates to charity, which will from now on be considered as an order, a sphere, or a supplementary (and superior) level of things, and thus of rationality. The world can be read in terms of extension (matter, etc.), of spirit (essence, sciences, logic, etc.), and also of charity (love, grace, and their negative correlatives). Supposing one accepts this situation of "Christian philosophy," what would be its relationship in the dominant and traditional definition of philosophy as metaphysics (science of being as being), or even as phenomenology of being as such, after the "destruction of the history of ontology" undertaken by Heidegger? Of course, "Christian philosophy" does not at all subscribe to metaphysics, or not entirely (in the case of the Thomists). But this irreducibility should not be considered an aberration or weakness, since nowadays metaphysics recognizes its limits by undergoing the "end of metaphysics," while phenomenology claims to manifest the "other than being" [*"autrement qu'être"*] in its multiple modes. By privileging charity beyond being as the final scene, where the most decisive phenomena manifest themselves, "Christian philosophy" not only could be inscribed in the most renovating developments of contemporary philosophy but could also contribute in a decisive fashion to the overcoming of the end of metaphysics and to the deployment of phenomenology as such.[13]

A second argument comes from the age and rigor of the purely Christian uses of the term *philosophy*. Indeed, the Pauline mistrust—"Make sure that no one traps you and deprives you of your freedom by some secondhand, empty, rational philosophy based on the principles of this world instead of on Christ [φιλοσοφιας και κενης απατης]" (Col. 2:8)—has prevented neither the most ancient Christian authors (Tatian, Clement of Alexandria, Justin "philosopher and martyr") nor more recent ones (from Gregory of Nyssa to Erasmus) from strongly claiming this term and even the consecrated syntagma "Christian philosophy." Of course, their interpretation was very different from that of modern authors: it is not about a science of the world (not even from the Christian point of view) but about the wisdom that Christ gives by means of a life radically different from the wisdom of the world, namely, attaining life in God. Among many examples, Justin says: "Philosophy is really a great thing to possess and the most precious for God, God toward whom it alone leads us and with whom it unites us; and those who apply their spirit to philosophy are in reality saints."[14] In this sense, "philosophy" unites with Christ and sanctifies. Without a doubt, this salvific ambition attributed to philosophy in a Christian context finds no echo in recent uses of the term. It is not, however, disqualified, because it is one of the most evident shortcomings of modern philosophy to have lost almost completely one of the original dimensions of ancient pagan philosophy, from Socrates to Iamblichus. One ought to do philosophy in order to attain the highest good, beatitude, even the immortality of the gods. Except for some rare exceptions, metaphysics has renounced this ambition, at the risk of losing one of the primordial justifications for philosophy. When "Christian philosophy" restores the principle that it knows not only from Christ but also in order to attain him and beatitude, rather than turn away from philosophy as it has done, it rediscovers, after the long meandering of metaphysics, the awareness that original philosophy had of its purpose. At a time of nihilism, "Christian philosophy," taken as a heuristic of charity, would call any thought that would want to constitute itself as philosophy back to its forgotten ambition of loving wisdom. Beyond other arguments, it is for these two reasons that I would suggest that the concept of "Christian philosophy" today may be neither obsolete nor contradictory—nor without a future.[15]

[Original translator unknown.]

Sketch of a Phenomenological Concept of the Gift

1

Is it not astonishing that the question of the "gift" comes to the forefront when we deal with philosophy of religion? Of course, the two issues are formally distinct, and there is nothing to be gained by confusing them. Nevertheless, two lines of analysis provide essential links between them. The first link derives from revelation itself. In contrast to the common-law phenomenon, whose poverty in intuition (and its limitation in meaning) permits objective knowledge, production, predication, and reproduction, the phenomenon of revelation (if it exists) is characterized by its excess of intuition, which saturates all meaning and which, due to this saturation, provokes an event whose unpredictability escapes any production or reproduction. This phenomenon thus takes on the status of a gift, appearing to emerge freely and suddenly out of itself. The phenomenon of revelation therefore is revealed from itself and appears in the mode of what gives itself. In a word, revelation only appears as a gift.[1]

The second link between revelation and gift derives directly from phenomenology. Indeed, at least since the "principle of principles," phenomenology thinks through all phenomenality from the starting point of the "giving" intuition: a phenomenon must be able to give itself in order to appear. Moreover, this radical demand goes beyond intuition alone, since Husserl argues for the extension of givenness to certain meanings and essences, right up to considering the constitution of objects to be a givenness of meanings (*Sinngebung*). Givenness, therefore, is not limited to the very restricted case of the phenomena of revelation but defines all phenomenality in a universal fashion.[2] Therefore, rather than reflection abandoning revelation when it considers the gift, on the contrary, it may be that revelation traces the only possible path toward it: givenness as the first level of all phenomenality, the gift as the final trait of every phenomenon revealing itself. But if one must pass through the gift in order to reach a concept of revelation, one must have access to the concept of the gift itself. The central question therefore becomes: "Do we have an appropriate, if not a specific, concept of the gift?"

2

The gift could be understood in a strictly metaphysical sense as a particular case of causal relation. The giver, under the title of active efficient cause, would then produce the gift, considered as an effect, for the benefit of the passive gift-recipient. Despite appearances it is not easy to break with this schema for a simple reason: the criticism itself can easily remain limited to the ground of metaphysics. In this context the habitual recourse to the gratuity of the gift risks only modifying the framework of efficiency, without in any way either suppressing or displacing it: to produce "for nothing" remains, all the same, "to produce" and is hence still tied to efficiency. Moreover, gratuitous efficiency makes this even more obvious. The question that really must be asked is: "Can one attain a concept of the gift or does an essential aporia affect it?"

Because he did not fear to confront this last question, Jacques Derrida was able to define what one could call the paradox of the gift. Pursuing a very convincing analysis, Derrida penetrates the aporia of the gift and also of the act of givenness. I will follow this analysis, both because of its own merits and in order to find there perhaps the means to establish the paradox even beyond criticism. Derrida begins by setting forth the whole conceptual chain of givenness, of which "all the anthropologies, indeed all of metaphysics" make a "system." From the metaphysical point of view—from which it is clearly a question of "departing in a preemptory and distinct fashion"[3]—givenness is linked together by a giver, a given gift, and a gift-recipient. These three are in principle tied together by a link of reciprocity, since the gratuity on the part of the giver claims some restitution on the part of the recipient, albeit tacitly. Let me underline more than Derrida does that this schema, which dominates all the anthropologies of the gift (first among them that of Mauss) remains entirely metaphysical: the giver gives the gift as an efficient cause, uses a formal cause and a material cause (corresponding to the gift), following a final cause (the good of the recipient and/or the glory of the giver). These four causes permit givenness to satisfy the principle of sufficient reason. Reciprocity repeats this sufficient reason right up to the perfect application of the principle of identity in bringing the gift back to itself. It is also by reference to this model that one can measure all the apparently extreme or aberrant forms of givenness, which never really put anything into question. Thinking through givenness always comes down to thinking about the system of exchange, regulated by the terms of causality and the principles of metaphysics. Now as Derrida firmly demonstrates, this model not only enters into self-contradiction with each of its elements, but it actually succeeds in making givenness disappear entirely. The very phenomenon of givenness collapses before our eyes.

The first argument is as follows: "For there to be a gift, there can be no reciprocity."[4] It should have seemed absolutely evident that the gift (or, more exactly, givenness) disappears as soon as reciprocity transforms it into a system of exchange. The fact that this exchange repeats givenness implicitly (and not explicitly, as in commerce) changes nothing. To offer something (an invitation, a service, etc.) still means to offer something, and thus to enter into an economy: the counter-gift follows on the gift, payment on the debt, reimbursement on the loan. As soon as the economy absorbs the gift, it turns givenness into economy. By annexing givenness, the economy dispenses with it. In its place it immediately substitutes calculation, interest, utility, measure, etc. No moral consideration must interfere here with a pure difference between the regimes of different phenomena: if there is givenness, it must break completely with the principle of sufficient reason, that of identity and of quadriform causality, which the economy follows in its metaphysical regime.

The second argument follows immediately: "For there to be a gift, *it is necessary* that the recipient does not give back, amortize, reimburse, acquit himself, enter into a contract, and never have contracted a debt."[5] This refusal must not be understood as simply a subjective ingratitude—ingratitude that intervenes only in the midst of an economy of exchange and reciprocity—but rather as the "non-consciousness" of the recipient, who neither sees nor knows that a gift comes to him or her. The recipient benefits from a gift—pure gratuity—only if he does not immediately interpret it as a gift that has to be returned, a debt to be reimbursed as soon as possible. Moreover, an authentic gift may exceed any knowledge about it by its recipient, thus dispensing him from recognizing what he does not know. In many cases—the most significant ones, in fact—the gift remains unknown. Such are the gifts of life (and perhaps also that of death) and of love (sometimes of hatred). The slogan "If you knew the gift of God" may here serve as a paradigm (but not a theological one in this case) for every phenomenology of givenness: the recipient does not know and does not have to know what gift comes to her, precisely because a gift can and must surpass all clear consciousness. The unconsciousness of the gift—that is, the bracketing of the recipient in givenness—has, moreover, at least two irreplaceable functions: to permit the recipient to support its excess (because a gift scarcely known remains perfectly given) and to permit the gift not to depend on the recipient (because a mishandled gift remains a perfectly given gift). Givenness supposes, therefore, the επoχη of the recipient.

The third argument may be stated thus: "Forgetting [of the gift] must be radical not only on the part of the recipient, but first of all . . . on the part of the donor." The disappearance of the recipient implies reciprocally that of the giver. In effect, the simple awareness of giving awakens the consciousness of one's self as giving, thus "the gratifying image of goodness or of generosity, of the giving-being who, knowing itself to be such, recognizes itself in a circular, specular fashion, in a sort of self-recognition, self-approval, and narcissistic gratitude."[6] The best illustration of this narcissistic return of the giver on himself is taken from Descartes. The *Passions of the Soul* demonstrates, in what Descartes considered an absolutely positive sense, that generosity, taken as self-esteem and as a good use of one's free will, not only provokes the passion of self-contentment but repeats in the ethical order the self-certainty achieved by the *ego cogito* in the metaphysical order.[7] To consider oneself as gift-giver, a fortiori as the giver poorly known by the recipient, is sufficient to produce a self-consciousness and thus to reestablish an economic exchange: in exchange for my poorly known gift, I receive—from myself?—the certain consciousness of my generosity. In losing my gift, I give to myself, or rather, I refind myself in exchange for my lost gift. Loss becomes gain par excellence—the best business possible, because I gain from it infinitely more than I lose: my very self against a simple gift, which was worth less than I. Givenness, therefore, becomes thinkable only if one succeeds in liberating it from the metaphysical thesis par excellence: the ego's preeminence in it (and in respect to the gift) as the transcendental and constituting *I*. The obstacle to arriving at a givenness free of itself is not tied to some theological excess but to a much more certain, absolutely known, and supremely solid foundation—the *inconcussum quid*, which Descartes inaugurated in metaphysics and which still guides us. As long as the ego remains, givenness ceases. It only appears when the ego is bracketed.

After reciprocity, the final implication of the framework of giver, recipient, and givenness is putting the given gift itself aside. This paradox can be supported if one returns to the reason for the displacement of the giver and the recipient: this results from the gift, which, by immobilizing itself in exchange, freezes the economy and therefore makes the giver and the recipient appear to be the agents of the gift. Thus, "the subject and object are arrested effects of the gift."[8] The economic interpretation of givenness as a system of exchange, as the agents froze it, rests upon the gaze that the agents fix upon the gift, seeing it as an object of exchange. Therefore, it is the appearance of the gift, reifying givenness in its objectivity, that provokes the system of exchange and that forbids givenness as such. The consequence immediately arises: "*At the limit, the gift as gift* ought *not to appear as gift: neither to the recipient nor to the donor.*"[9] The appearance or the entrance of the gift into objective phenomenality thus prepares it for economic exchange and logically removes it from givenness. Derrida therefore recovers "the phenomenology of the unapparent," without any theological turn, simply by criticizing the supposed evidence of the gift. It is "supposed" because it is in fact taken into the system of economic exchange. The nonappearance of the gift, however, does not imply any renunciation of phenomenology. First, if it were to appear—and most of the time it appears quite massively—then it would be necessary to renounce the sought-for phenomenology of givenness: the gift does not appear so that givenness as such may appear. Next, the nonappearance of the gift does not imply a renunciation of phenomenology because the reason for such a nonappearance remains phenomenological: if the gift becomes a phenomenon of exchange, it is frozen in presence in the most metaphysical sense. "If he [the recipient] recognizes it *as* gift, if the gift *appears to him as such*, if the present is present to him *as present*, this simple recognition suffices to annul the gift."[10]

What forbids the gift to remain within givenness by leading it back to the rank of an object of exchange only consists—this is the right word —in presence, understood to be the permanent subsistence in itself of beingness. If presence undoes the present (the gift in givenness), it is then necessary, in order to reach the present, to shield it from presence. This perfect paradox definitely echoes the fourth argument: "if the present is present to him *as present*, this simple recognition suffices to annul the gift." Similarly, "It cannot be gift as gift except by not being present as gift." Or, "If it presents itself, it no longer presents itself."[11] This is a disturbing result. One must leave the path toward givenness in suppressing access to the gift by a double impossibility: either the gift presents itself in presence and it disappears from givenness in order to embed itself in the economic system of exchange, or the gift does not present itself and no longer appears, thus closing all phenomenality of givenness.

3

Still, this is perhaps not the obligatory result of this fourth argument (even if that appears to be Derrida's conclusion), but only one of the possible readings left open by its paradox. Does the incompatibility between the gift thought as such, according to givenness, and presence as permanence in subsistence mean that the gift absolutely cannot be thought and appear, or does it mean that it can only do so outside the (deeply metaphysical) horizon of presence? If appearance implies fixation in one's subsistence, then obviously the gift disappears as the given gift as soon as it appears in its presence. This means that it is lost and never offered to the giver, never possessed, and always only conceded to the recipient. It loses itself in this way: it loses a manner of being—subsistence, exchange, economy—that contradicts its very possibility of giving itself. In losing presence, the gift does not lose *itself* but loses that which neither conforms to it nor returns to it. Or rather, it *loses* itself—in the sense in which it finally disconnects from self, abandons itself outside of self—outside of *self*—in order to fulfill its loss, fulfill itself as loss, but not in pure loss. Or rather, exactly as in pure loss, as a *pure* loss that, in order to give itself, must in effect disappear and hence appears at the price of pure disappearance of any subsistence within it. This reversal can be explained in another way: if the gift is not present, so that it can never appear in and as presence, one may obviously conclude that it is not or that it does not *have* to be, namely "to be" according to presence, in order to give itself. The gift gives itself precisely to the strict degree to which it renounces being, is excluded from presence, and is undone from itself by undoing subsistence within it. Derrida's paradox (the present cannot be present in presence) may thus yield another paradox: *the present gives itself without presence.* If the one paradox hides the other, this is related to the very ambiguity of the other name of the gift: *present.* To make a present is by definition not the equivalent of producing a *present* (at least not always, not even nearly always). The *parousia* obviously regulates *presence* but does not control the *present.* The present owes nothing to presence, or at least can very well owe nothing to it. The question of givenness is not closed when presence contradicts the gift; on the contrary, it opens to the possibility of the present without presence—outside of being.

The remarkable fecundity of Derrida's analysis of the gift is manifest not only in its explicit result but also in the counter-interpretation that it supports and even urges. With an exceptional rigor it leads to an enigmatic formula, which I will use here as a paradigm: "Let us go to the limit: The truth of the gift . . . suffices to annul the gift. The truth of the gift is equivalent to the non-gift or to the non-truth of the gift."[12] How should one understand this game of negations? Formally, two meanings could be distinguished here: (1) if *or* has conjunctive value, one has "non-gift" equals "non-truth"; therefore, as the negations annul each other, "gift" equals "truth"; (2) if *or* has disjunctive value, one has "non-truth" or "non-gift"; therefore, as the negations annul each other, the result is "either gift or truth." Thus, the formula can be understood either as the equivalence between gift and truth or as the reciprocal exclusion of the two.

If it were necessary to choose, Derrida would probably support the second interpretation. I do not prefer the first, although it is possible, because the point resides in the very ambiguity of the formula, namely, that truth is equivalent to gift but also contradicts it. It is not surprising that it would contradict the gift: Derrida has demonstrated that its emergence in presence abolishes the gift as such. More astonishing, on the contrary, is the possibility that truth is proper to the gift. In such a case the most elegant solution would ask that one distinguish between the two meanings of gift, one equivalent to and the other the contrary of truth. Despite its artificiality, let me borrow this last path. From Derrida's viewpoint, does such a distinction have any meaning? Up until now the answer has been "no," because the gift always disappears in its truth. However, this thesis is not his last word: he clearly envisions that the gift is split (although this remains at the level of a mere suggestion): "There would be, *on the one hand*, the gift that gives something determinate (a given, a present in whatever form it may be . . .); and, *on the other hand*, the gift that gives not a given but the *condition* of a present given in general, that gives therefore the element of the given in general." The first sense corresponds exactly to the gift whose presence annuls its status as present, the gift taken into the system of exchange and economy. One need not return to this. The second sense remains: it introduces nothing less than a gift that gives, a gift elevated in power, a gift beyond gift. But, since this strange gift gives nothing (nothing real, not a thing), it frees itself in order to give the condition of the given, "the condition of any given in general."[13] It would be at work, for example, in the case of "giving time," "giving life," "giving death," etc. In any case, this advance is not sufficient for my purpose. It is not sufficient, first, because it recognizes that the new gift gives at least one "condition"; now any condition whatsoever and as such remains a typical metaphysical function, that of foundation. Moreover, this foundation here is a ground of a "present in general," which one may suspect is in presence, even identified with it. Next, this advance is not sufficient because the modification of the object of the gift (from "given" to the "condition of given") neither permits the passage of the gift to givenness as such nor frees givenness from the economic model of exchange. Finally, it is not sufficient because the doubling of a concept rarely indicates that we have deepened it. Very often, we simply juxtapose the elements of a contradiction in order to soften it. Still, such a doubling of gift might place us upon the path of givenness.

The two interpretations of the formula "the truth of the gift is equivalent to the non-gift or to the non-truth of the gift," as well as the two senses of gift (giving a given or a condition) give a premonition of a border, whose crossing would lead to an entirely different determination of the gift than that pushed to contradiction by Derrida. If the gift as such, as present, disappears as soon as it enters into presence; if presence defines the manner of being of subsistence in itself, as metaphysics has privileged it; if truth, taken in its unique metaphysical meaning, only lets the present appear in presence; then one must conclude that the gift, if it is ever to be thought through, must come about (first of all, to itself) outside of presence, outside of self-subsistence, and outside of truth.

If truth is indeed sufficient to annul the gift, then the gift only comes about in being dispensed from *this* truth. If the subsistence of the gift is sufficient to annul it in exchange, then the gift will only occur by being freed from this very subsistence. If the present as presence is sufficient to annul the gift, then the gift is performed only by being liberated from this presence. But, one might object, can the gift assume this "duty," or is this a question of a chimerical attempt? How can this be understood, if the "conditions of the possibility of the gift . . . simultaneously designate the conditions of the impossibility of the gift?"[14] Quite simply, one can note that this objection contains its own refutation: it only establishes the conditions under which the gift becomes impossible. In no way does it establish that what thus becomes impossible merits the name of gift. I respond, therefore, that the conditions of impossibility only prove that what was studied does *not* merit the title of gift and that, if there is to be a gift, it will necessarily have other conditions of possibility than this, namely, conditions of impossibility. Positively, this means that the gift is not given in the system of exchange maintained by the reciprocity that links giver and recipient: in this supposed economy of gift, it is the letter of the gift that one saves [*fait l'économie*] by transforming it into a subsistent being, permanently present, accorded value (of use and/or exchange) and finality (useful, without end, etc.), produced or destroyed by efficiency and calculation, shut in by the stranglehold of its causes, in short, by transforming it into a common being. Such a common being can never appear as a gift, not because the concept of gift is contradictory but precisely because this being in no way gives rise to a gift. Any effort that tries to begin with an already obvious and settled concept of "gift" in order to reach the gift never analyzes anything other than a common being under this name. Hypothetically, it should not therefore be possible to reach the least gift.

What is missing here? One must renounce the economic horizon of exchange in order to interpret the gift from the horizon of givenness itself. First, one must break with the metaphysical interpretation of the given as the effect of an efficient cause, that is to say, counter the exemplary metaphysician Spinoza, who claims that "ipsius rei datam sive actuosam essentiam"[15]—literally: the essence of a thing, if and because it is given, is never active as such but is precisely given. The gift comes about as a given, thus from and within givenness. Now it remains to describe givenness no longer according to what it rejects but as such, if such an *as such* is still suitable for it.

4

Describing this givenness is a question of thinking through the gift under the rubric of givenness itself, without referring it to economy, because the impossibility just noted does not concern the gift as such but rather its economic interpretation. Such economy actually destroys givenness. First, this economy defines a permanent circuit with the recipient and the giver interpreted as conscious agents, which generally authorizes not so much the gift without calculation but chiefly the return on the gift—that is to say, exchange. From here the permanent circuit permits the repetition of exchange, thus bringing about reciprocity, which might then take the twist of commerce. At this point the gift has already lost its gratuity; it disappears as such. Next, this exchange also confirms the gift in its status as an object: in order to be able to be repeated, to be exchanged, and to appreciate, the gift must acquire the consistency of objectivity, and thus also the visibility and the permanence that make it accessible to all the potential partners of economic exchange. Now accessible to all potential givers and recipients, the gift becomes indifferent to the terms of its givenness. Stripped of its own secret by its objectivity, it also destroys the possible secret of the partners who put it into action.

If, therefore, the economy of the gift only makes economy of the gift, the gift becomes itself only by breaking away from economy, in order to let itself be thought along the lines of givenness. Therefore, one must lead the gift away from economy and toward givenness. Taking it back to givenness means reducing it. How can we reduce the gift to givenness without falling either into tautology (Is the gift not equivalent to givenness?)

or into contradiction (Does givenness not necessarily imply some transcendence?). If we must have reduction, it could only occur, even in the case of a possible reduction to givenness, in the manner in which reduction always operates in phenomenology: by bracketing all transcendence of whatever type. Reducing the gift to givenness thus means: thinking the gift as gift, abstracting from the triple transcendence that affected it until now—by bracketing the transcendence of the giver, the transcendence of the recipient, and the transcendence of the objectivity of the exchanged object. If one can manage to practice εποχη on the gift, it will be practiced by liberating the gift from the terms and the status of object, from any notion of transcendence or of economic exchange. Thus, it will lead the gift back to pure and simple givenness, at least if such a givenness can occur.

In this operation, the reduction of the gift to givenness does not come about *despite* the triple objection raised against the gift by Derrida but quite clearly *because* of it: the alleged "conditions of the impossibility of gift" (neither recipient nor giver nor gift) would actually become the conditions for the possibility of the gift's reduction to pure givenness, by εποχη of the transcendent conditions of economic exchange. The objection would then become its own response: the gift is reduced to givenness once the recipient, the giver, and the objectivity of the gift are bracketed, in order thus to extract the gift outside of economy and to manifest it according to pure givenness. But can such a reduction of the gift to givenness in fact occur? Once liberated from its transcendent conditions, does the gift remain identifiable as such or does it collapse into a vague cloud, the last breath of a fading concept?

Reducing the gift to itself, that is to say, to pure and simple givenness, implies no longer to thinking it in the economy of exchange, where it would simply transfer as an object between the giver and the recipient, but thinking it as such, as a pure given. Can one nevertheless think the gift as gift without referring it to the terms of exchange? Would it not immediately disappear, not only as gift, but also as object? In order to attempt to respond to this, let me outline this reduction.

5

When a gift occurs, what, exactly, is given to me? In other words, in order to be able to speak of a gift, what lived experience of consciousness is required? It is, of course, necessary to distinguish here between the lived experiences of the gift affecting a consciousness in someone playing the role of giver and those affecting a consciousness in someone in the role of recipient. Let me consider both of these respective situations. First, the viewpoint of the giver: when and how does a gift give itself (to consciousness)? Obviously, when the giver gives it. But what, exactly, does it mean for the giver to give a gift? Would it be a transfer of a piece of property to another? Despite appearances, the answer is undoubtedly "no": First, the transfer does not always take the shape of ceding an item of property (it could be a loan or a lease, etc.), nor does it always assume some juridical status (it could involve a private agreement or a tacit accord, etc.). Second, such control would be sufficient to threaten the very status of the gift by leading it back, as we have already seen, to the status of exchange. Finally, the gift sometimes does not consist in any object at all: in cases involving a promise, a reconciliation, a blessing (or a curse), a friendship, a love (or a hatred), the gift is not identical to an object but emerges only at the moment of its occurrence. Far from becoming confused with the gift, the object becomes a simple occasional support, interchangeable and optional (evidence, promise, memory, etc.), for what is truly at stake in the gift, far more precious and serious than the object that makes it visible. Moreover, the more a gift provides an immense richness, the less it can become visible in an object, or the less does the object rendering it visible correspond to the gift in fact. Thus, giving up power involves, in the final analysis, giving up the insignia of power (the *pallium*, the crown, the pectoral cross, etc.), but the surrendered insignia precisely do not give power, they only symbolize it. Power is not given with an object or objects, because—itself giving the sum of all objects—it is neither an object nor in the mode of objects. To give back power, and thus to give power, is never equivalent to making a gift of an object but rather to giving, on the occasion of an object, the gift of power over objects. Even more, to give oneself to another obviously does not coincide with the gift of some object. The only object that perhaps might prove this gift, because it makes it visible, is the ring worn on the finger: it indicates that another has given himself or herself to me by giving me this ring. But this ring does not attest to the gift made by another, because it is not costly enough either to pay for my own commitment (as if this golden ring were worth my life, my fidelity, my own gift) or to confirm materially what the other has given me in self-giving. On the contrary, the ring attests to the gift I have become not by equaling it but by giving the gift a symbolic support, without any parity with what it nonetheless shows. The gift hence does not coincide with the object of the gift. Moreover, one can suggest the following fundamental rule: the more a gift reveals itself to be precious, the less it is accomplished as an object, or what amounts to the same thing, the more the object is reduced to the abstract role of support, decoration, symbol. Reciprocally, the gifts that give the most give literally *nothing*—no thing, no object, not because they disappoint expectations but because what they give belongs neither to reality nor to objectivity.

But if the gift, from the perspective of the giver, does not coincide with an object, just what is it made of? In order to see it, it is sufficient to consider how the object gradually becomes the object of a gift: it does not become such at the moment when the giver transmits it, transfers it or transports it to the recipient, but rather at the moment when the giver him- or herself considers it for the first time to be a gift or, more exactly, to be givable. If the object becomes givable, it does not owe this status to some intrinsic property or to a real predicate—the object stays the same, whether it is givable or not—but rather to the possible giver's gaze upon it. Thus, in an extreme situation the giver might accomplish this transformation into something givable even without real support in some object (if he gives his faith, if she gives herself, etc.). The gift is not accomplished when it is given but rather when givability arises. Givability arises around the potential giver when she, first of all in relation to herself alone, recognizes that the principle "I owe no one anything" may (and must) admit at least one exception.

The gift begins and in fact ends as soon as the giver envisions that he owes something to someone, when he admits that he could be a debtor, and thus a recipient. The gift begins when the potential giver suspects that another gift has already preceded her, to which she owes something, to which she owes herself to respond. Not only does the gift reside in the decision to give, accepted by the potential giver, but the giver can only decide inasmuch as he recognizes that another gift has already obliged him. The gift decides itself—which means first of all that the gift comes about by the decision, by the giver, to give, but which also means that this decision implies that the giver feels herself obliged, and hence obligated by an anterior gift, which confirms in advance the decision to give. The adage "I owe no one anything" suffers an exception only inasmuch as I already recognize myself, in advance, as the beneficiary of a gift—and am thus obligated toward a givenness. The obligation to give hence results directly from the obligation to an anterior gift. The decision to make a gift implies, first of all, the decision to make onself a giver; but making oneself a giver cannot be decided without the obligation (weighing upon the giver) of the gift that he has first received. The gift decides the giver. The gift itself decides: it resides in the decision of the giver, but this decision rests upon the obligation motivated by an anterior gift. Thus, I will conclude that, in the context of reduction, the lived experience of consciousness where the gift is given consists in the decision of the gift—the decision of the giver to give the gift, but especially the decision of the gift itself in deciding the giver. The gift gives *itself* by giving its giving.

6

Does this paradox find confirmation when we move from the perspective of the giver to that of the recipient, in order to define the lived experience of consciousness of the gift in the context of reduction? What exactly does it mean for the recipient to receive a gift? Would it be the transfer of an object of property from someone else to the recipient? Undoubtedly the answer is "no," despite appearances. First, because such a transfer does not properly concern the gift: it first defines exchange and its economy, where it marks selling and buying. Next, because so many gifts occur without property transfer, because they do not derive their reality from an object: the receiving of life, death, forgiveness, confidence, love, or friendship from another is neither said nor done in terms of property or in terms of disappropriation, because it lacks any object, outside of some possible symbols.

Most importantly, for an obvious reason the act of receiving a gift resides neither in the transfer of property nor in the object received: it resides in the act of acceptance. Two circumstances illustrate this point perfectly: ignorance and refusal. Let me assume a case involving a gift perfect in all of its reality—an object intentionally proposed by a giver. Now, although made within the rules, this gift could effectively cease to be a gift. First, it would be enough for no one to recognize the gift as such, either by purely and simply ignoring it (i.e., by walking by without seeing or taking it) or by treating it in terms of economic exchange (i.e., by paying for it, selling it, stealing it). In such a case, the gift could not fulfill itself perfectly, although it does fulfill the real conditions of givability (objectivity, availability, etc.). What is it missing? It is missing acceptance, that is to say, the recipient's decision to receive it. Next, let me suppose that the gift truly fulfilled and recognized as such nonetheless meets with refusal: either through contempt (it is "too little"), through mistrust ("Just what is it?"), through fear (of those bearing gifts [*et dona ferentes*]), or simply through malice ("That would give you too much pleasure"). In all these cases the gift finds itself dismissed or despised. What is it missing? Obviously, nothing real—everything, everything that has the rank of a thing, has clearly already been given—but here again the gift does not coincide with anything real. What it is missing is not anything real either: it is a question here of its acceptance pure and simple; that is to say, it is a question of the recipient deciding to receive it.

The gift fulfills itself perfectly when as the recipient I make up my mind to receive it. The performance of the gift is linked more to my decision to accept it than to its own availability. Moreover, it is often my decision that decides that something finds itself accepted. If we reflect on the call, for example, the reception of the call (the recognition that there has clearly been a call for me) and the response by me become the strongest confirmation of the availability of this call—which perhaps no one else has heard, to which no one (undoubtedly) has responded in the same manner as I have.[16] If we reflect upon the business of love, it often happens that acceptance provokes the availability of the gift; acceptance does not always hinge on the banal duplicity of seduction, but often on the evidence that I, I alone and more than another, affirm the capacity to let myself be seduced and freely consent to this seduction, like a call inverting the usual chronology. I consent to the possibility of a gift of this person and not of another to me, thus provoking his or her availability. From the perspective of the recipient, the gift consists ultimately in the fact of self-decision, exactly as from the perspective of the giver.

7

One should not object that deciding to give differs radically from deciding to receive, because there is nothing easier than the latter (who does not wish to receive?) and there is nothing more difficult than the former (who wishes to give?), so that the two decisions can be neither compared nor assimilated to each other. Yet there is actually nothing easy even about deciding to receive. First, because receiving might imply receiving what one did not expect or what one did not want, even what one feared the most (what is specific to a gift [*don*] is the fact that often "it is not a present [*cadeau*]"). Next, in order to decide to receive, one must have more than the desire to possess or the search for one's own interest, but one must clearly renounce the independence that permits oneself to be convinced that "I owe no one anything."

To decide to receive a gift implies that I accept owing something to someone due to this gift. The gratuity of the gift is paid for with the recognition—of the gift and of its very gratuity. Note that this is not primarily a question of a recognition of debt toward the giver, such that one would be led back from gift according to givenness to gift according to economy; because the recognition of depending upon a giving gratuity remains even if the giver remains unknown or absolutely missing (such as absent parents, nature, even the state, etc.). It is even possible that this recognition deepens inasmuch as it cannot be fixed upon any identifiable partner, because such a gratuity places in question nothing less than the autarky of the self and its pretension to auto-sufficiency. To decide to receive the gift amounts to deciding to become obligated by the gift. The decision between the potential givenness and the gift does not operate so much from the giver to the gift as from the gift to the giver; the gift, by its own allure and prestige, decides the giver to decide himself for it—that is to say, determines him to sacrifice his own autarky, the autarky of what is his own, in order to receive it. The gift decides about its own acceptance by deciding about its recipient. Thus, I will conclude that, in the regime of reduction, the lived experience of consciousness in which the gift gives itself consists in the decision of the gift—the decision to receive the gift by the recipient but especially the decision to decide the recipient of the gift by the gift itself. The gift gives *itself* by giving its reception.

The gift reduced to givenness gives itself to consciousness as that which gives *itself* from itself, as much from the viewpoint of the giver as from the viewpoint of the recipient, one and the other being decided by it. This first determination has nothing paradoxical or tautological about it. It indicates, in effect, that the gift remains impossible as long as one is not devoted or given over to it [*s'y adonne*], either in giving it or in accepting it. The gift only exists from the moment when its protagonists recognize it in a being, an object, even in the absence of being and object, and an immediate relationship between them. So recognizing the gift implies a strict and specific phenomenological gaze: one that, faced with the fact (object, being, immediate relation), sees it as a gift. One could say that it is a question of hermeneutics, but of a hermeneutics that gives meaning less than it receives meaning, precisely in seeing a gift. It involves less a gift of meaning than the meaning of gift—coming from the gift, or rather, seeing the fact as a gift, because it is envisioned from the starting point of givenness. Seeing the gift implies seeing it from the starting point of givenness. If the gift decides *itself*, it decides from the power of givenness, which weighs equally upon the giver and the recipient. Both only devote themselves [*s'adonnent*] to the gift inasmuch as they yield to the moment of givenness. The instant power of givenness makes the gift determine *itself* as gift through the double consent of the giver and of the recipient, who are less often agents of the gift and are more often acted upon by givenness.

From this, one reaches two conclusions. The first is that the gift, as that which decides *itself* by itself, supposes nothing other than the moment of givenness. Thus it does not belong to the economy of exchange but is accomplished even and mainly in a regimen of reduction. The second conclusion is that this gift, reduced to what decides *itself*, takes its character of the given from givenness alone, that is to say, from itself, without depending on any extrinsic relation—neither upon exchange nor upon the giver nor upon the recipient. The gift gives "itself" intrinsically in its *self*-giving.

8

The gift finds itself thus reduced to what decides *itself* by and for itself. It appears in the horizon of givenness, where it properly (by itself) gives (as all phenomena give) as what (par excellence) gives *itself*. Such a reduction, however, could only have been conducted through the axis of the object taken in exchange, whose bracketing has placed into relief the gift as such. One must still confirm this reduction from the perspective of the two terms of exchange: Is it possible to reduce the gift to pure givenness by bracketing the recipient and the giver? Obviously, it is not a question here of eliminating them but rather of establishing that the gift occurs even if they find themselves suspended and, thus, that they must be thought about from the starting point of the gift—reduced according to givenness—which is quite different from the supposition that the gift depends upon them in order to give itself. Only a positive result would authorize us to speak of a perfect reduction of the gift in all its dimensions to what decides *itself*, thus a reduction to pure givenness.

May one bracket the recipient in the gift without suspending the gift itself? In fact, the bracketing of the recipient belongs intrinsically to the possibility of the gift. It actually manifests itself as being linked to the gift in a manner that is respectively indispensable, possible, and preferable: (a) the bracketing of the recipient belongs necessarily to the gift, since the gift would simply and purely disappear if the recipient remained. Indeed if the recipient preceded the gift and remained independent of its occurrence, he or she could condition, provoke, or even return it. Then the gift would regress to the level of an exchange, wherein reciprocity (actual or desired) reestablishes a pure and simple commerce. The gift would lose all gratuity and hence also all grace if it were given to a recipient liable to "return" it. "If you do good to those who do good to you, what credit is that to you? [ποια υμιν χαρις εστιν]" (Luke 6:33).

The love of enemies might appear, at first glance, to be an extreme and untenable paradox, a simple pedagogical method for marking the logic of love of one's neighbor. Yet loving one's neighbor, even if he or she is demonstrably pleasant or even affectionate, already presents such a difficult task, so far beyond simple reciprocal sociability, that the love of one's enemies seems the height of impossibility. In fact it is quite different for a phenomenology of the gift. If one understands *loving* as *giving* in a privileged sense, this gift can only remain itself inasmuch as it does not diminish itself in an exchange, wherein reciprocity would annul gratuity. In order to give itself, the gift requires that it decide *itself* as a gift beginning with itself alone, and that it give without return, without response or reimbursement. The recipient must not be able to "offer recompense," or at least the hope of some recompense cannot enter into the consideration by which the gift decides *itself.* The "enemy" precisely defines such a recipient, who is identifiable as the beneficiary of the gift but not capable of returning it: the one who does not love in return and therefore permits one to love freely (in other words, without reservation) permits the gift to occur. The enemy places the gift in evidence precisely by his refusal of reciprocity—by contrast to friends, who "return in equal measure [απο-λαβωσιν τα ισα]" (Luke 6:34) and who downgrade the gift to the status of a loan with interest. The enemy thus becomes the ally of the gift, and the friend becomes the enemy of the gift. The enemy represents the reduced recipient, who receives the gift without returning it. The psychological paradox manifests a phenomenological necessity: the gift requires the bracketing of the recipient.

Yet, one will object, does not such a bracketing of the recipient render the gift impossible, even if it appears necessary to the reduction of the gift? If the recipient (the enemy) does not recompense the gift, that is first because he refuses it (he does not want to be loved). Does a refused gift remain a gift in the fullest sense? In other words, does not the enemy annul the gift at the very moment that he permits the gift to occur? In order to respond to this question, it is sufficient to show that a refused gift clearly remains a full gift. One must show that the bracketing of the recipient is not only (a) necessary but also (b) possible. So, what actually remains of a gift refused (seen and rejected, seen and criticized) or even ignored (not singled out, silently overlooked)? First, the given gift remains, as an act of abandon, with or without objective support, where the gift definitively decides *itself.* The gift that is accomplished with neither return nor regret persists with neither recognition nor reception. The simple fact that a gift is abandoned does not destroy it; on the contrary, it confirms it in its character of givenness—with no reciprocity whatsoever, not even the acknowledgment of this gift, which would corrode its pure gratuity. The abandon indicates that the gift not only surpasses every counter-gift but even every possible acceptance. The abandoned gift manifests its givenness by its excess. Nonetheless, in the context of an abandoned gift that is without a recipient, another phenomenon becomes visible: the missing recipient appears in the very figure of its lapse, namely, as ingratitude. "If you knew the gift of God" (John 4:10). It is possible that the recipient does not know it and therefore disdains it. This contempt, theologically as inevitable as it is sinful, still remains phenomenologically fertile, since it permits us to designate the recipient at the very same time as he or she fails to fulfill this role.

The failure of the recipient, necessary for the occurrence of the gift, does not suppress the gift and its appearance. On the contrary, it makes the recipient appear in a figure perfectly suitable for givenness: no longer the one who would return the gift and destroy it (the friend), nor the one who would simply deny it (the enemy), but the one who does not support it (an ungrateful person). An ungrateful person, in fact, is not defined as one who does not want to or is not able to return like for like. Instead it is one who simply does not support duty—not the duty of returning but the duty of receiving, accepting, or even offering a gift. The ungrateful person suffers from the principle and the very possibility that a gift might affect and come to him or her. He does not refuse this or that gift with this or that objective support; he refuses the debt, or rather, the self-avowal of being indebted. In his obstinate effort to reestablish the principle that "I owe no one anything," he thus confirms *a contrario* the sudden appearance of the gift, which decides itself from itself and which places this principle in question. By this principle, the ungrateful person reveals negatively the gift reduced to givenness in all of its purity. Through the same gesture, he thus determines the figure of the reduced recipient, absolutely governed by the pure givenness of the gift.

From here on, one can better understand why the bracketing of the recipient might finally appear (c) desirable. The recipient masks herself under the appearance of the enemy and the ungrateful one, whose negations permit the gift to manifest itself according to its pure givenness, without either return or reciprocity of exchange. But this bracketing of the recipient does not necessarily imply a similar negation of the gift. It can also occur with the reception of the gift. The situation finds its perfect illustration in one of the eschatological parables: when Christ will return at the end of time, he will separate the just from the evil according to the criteria of the gifts they will have made to him on earth—thus situating himself in the position of the recipient. But the elect, like the damned, will be astonished to have never seen, met, or identified as hungry, thirsty, homeless, naked, ill, and imprisoned the recipient they have (or have not) nourished, refreshed, housed, clothed, healed, and visited. No one has ever seen the recipient—in this case, Christ. "Then they will respond to him and tell him: 'Lord, when have we seen you?'" (Matt. 25:37, 44).

This invisibility manifests the bracketing of the recipient without dispute. Nevertheless, far from forbidding or weakening the gift, this invisibility doubles it by universalizing it: every human being may discern the face of the recipient precisely because this face remains invisible—"Truly I tell you, just as you did it to one of the least of these my brothers, you did it to me" (Matt. 25:40). The impossibility of identifying the recipient par excellence, Christ, permits us to let the gift emerge on every other human face; Christ's withdrawal permits the "least of his brothers" to rise and offer himself to the gift as a recipient's face. Thus universalized by the absence of the recipient, or rather, by his withdrawal, which sets up the place for universalization of the function of the recipient, the gift, which reduces the recipient, acquires its perfect freedom: it gives without making distinctions between people, in complete indifference to the recipient's merit or demerit, in perfect ignorance of any possible reciprocity (in other words, in complete conformity with the gratuity of givenness). So I will conclude that the recipient may and must be bracketed; this indispensable operation, possible and preferable, in a way reduces the gift to pure givenness.

9

Now I must consider the second part of the question. It asks, "Is it possible to bracket the giver in the gift without suspending this gift itself?" In order to respond, one needs to bring about such an authentic bracketing, as in the case of a gift whose giver remains unknown or unknowable—in other words, an anonymous gift. Does the gift remain in such a case? Yes, it remains.

The gift remains, first, because the absence or anonymity of the giver permits the recipient to exercise full responsibility in deciding whether there is a gift or not: it thus reserves for him the full exercise of his function of interpreter ("Is this a gift?") and of his decision concerning recognition ("Am I its designated recipient, and, therefore, am I under obligation?"). The inquiry involved in searching for the absent benefactor permits the giver to execute the logic of the gift perfectly reduced to givenness without reservation, because it does not obliterate the preliminary evidence of the designated recipient from a possible recognition or recompense. The regression to an economy of exchange remains impossible from the moment that one of the two terms is missing. Far from forbidding the gift, the bracketing of the recipient powerfully contributes to reducing the gift to givenness—that is, to itself.

But it is necessary to go beyond this. In the case of an absent, un-known, or undecided giver, I find myself, as recipient, in the situation where returning the gift is, in principle, impossible, whatever my inten-tion may be (even if I am among the best intentioned). This impossibility reinforces the evidence of givenness on two levels: first, it marks the fact that the gift gives *itself* here without limit, without return, outside of com-merce. It marks the fact that here it is precisely a question of a gift and not of a loan (thus of a future return). The giver who gives according to the mode of givenness does not know what he gives: "When you give alms, your left [hand] should ignore [μη γνωστω η αριστερα] what your right [hand] does" (Matt. 6:3). Perhaps he does not even know if he is giving. Most importantly, he does not want to know if the possible recipient knows that he is giving. He gives not in order to know or to make it known or to make himself seen—but rather in order to give. If the gift only absolutely gives (itself) by giving itself to the point of loss, the loss of the giver also contributes to the occurrence of the gift. Far from marking the impossibility of the gift, the absence of the giver manifests the reduction of the gift to givenness. But the impossibility, in principle, of "making a return" also manifests the reduction of the recipient to giv-enness: not being able to "return," he understands himself as definitively in debt. The debt is not simply added here to an already self-confident consciousness, in the way the consciousness of some object becomes in-scribed in a consciousness that is originally self-consciousness. It is in rec-ognizing its debt that consciousness becomes conscious of itself, because the debt precedes all consciousness and defines the self: the self, as such, the self of consciousness, receives *itself* right away as a gift (given) without giver (giving).

The debt brings about the self so that the self discovers itself already there—that is, as a fact and thus as given. The consciousness of knowing that one is indebted to the absent giver brings about an exact coincidence among the self, the debt, and the consciousness of the debt and the self. The recipient discovers himself primordially and definitively insolvent—not only by his lack of will for reimbursement or by lack of methods for reimbursement or even by the recipient's ignorance but, in the first place, by the irremediable anteriority of the debt before any response. The debt here does not designate an act or a situation of the self, but rather its state, its definition—possibly, its manner of being.[17] The debt exercises *différance*: the absence of the recipient precedes everything that it gives, so that even the consciousness of self-reception by the gift (self-conscious-ness) and of obligation as a given gift (consciousness of debt) definitively makes a late entrance in regard to indebting givenness. Any recognition of debt, and thus all recognition of the absent giver, confirms rather than eliminates différance. But such différance, if it is exercised with the debt, ultimately makes manifest givenness itself: the consciousness of debt defines the mode of manifestation of the recipient when it finds itself bracketed—that is to say, reduced in the horizon to the function of pure givenness.

I have reduced the gift to givenness in order to expose the fact that beyond all objective support and any economy of exchange, *the gift intrinsically gives itself from its self-giving*. I also bracketed, first, the recipient in the figure of the *enemy* (of the ungrateful and the anonymous one) and then the giver, in the figure of the unsolvable *debt*. This yields the following paradox: *the gift, reduced to givenness, decides to give* itself *as an unsolvable debt given to an enemy*. Thus, one may suppose to have reduced gift, recipient, and giver also to givenness. This triple reduction obviously does not aim to abolish the gift, the recipient, and the giver. On the contrary, it makes them play freely according to the mode of pure givenness.

10

From the outset, I recognized phenomenology's narrow link between the questions of givenness (as a dimension of any phenomenon) and revelation (as a particular case of phenomenality). I have just sketched a reduction of the gift to itself and thus to pure givenness. Does this analysis illuminate my starting point? It does so without a doubt, because it establishes the possibility of a gift reduced to pure givenness by describing the gift without making it depend upon a cause or inscribing it within an exchange. Appearing in the manner of a gift does not depend on a possibly efficient giver (or even on a receptive recipient) but rather on the very mode of appearing in terms of what decides itself as a gift. The character of gift—givenness—intrinsically belongs to the gift and to its mode of appearance rather than to the process whereby givenness defines itself extrinsically in relationship to a giver, to a cause, or to a certain efficiency. Givenness is in no way equivalent to production, but it is tied to the phenomenality of what appears only by deciding itself from itself. Among all phenomena, it is the particular prerogative of the phenomenon of revelation to accomplish the most radically this emergence from self and not from a cause. This is because, for revelation, appearance is ceaselessly exhausted in givenness, because it gives itself in the strict sense—it abandons itself. But with this abandon, another question opens up.

—*Translated by John Conley, S.J., and Danielle Poe*

What Cannot Be Said

Apophasis and the Discourse of Love

1

What we (wrongly, as we shall see) call "negative theology" inspires in us both fascination and unease. In it, we actually encounter a mode of language or even a language game that claims (perhaps deservedly) to express what cannot be experienced. It fascinates us, first, because it claims to express an event, or better an ineffable advent. But it also makes us uneasy with its assurance that the inexpressible can really be experienced according to the frequently attested paradox: "What no eye has seen, nor ear heard, nor the human heart conceived" is, Paul announces, precisely "what God has prepared for those who love him."[1] In short, this language game occurs only in circumstances where "what had not been told them they shall see, and what they had not heard they shall contemplate" (Isaiah 52:15). Hence it is something unseen, unheard of, ungraspable. To give an extreme but unavoidable example, at stake is the paradox of seeing in human flesh him "whom no one has ever seen" (John 1:18), for "no one shall see me and live" (Exodus 33:20).

The language game of what is called "negative theology" all too quickly claims not only to speak the unspeakable but to phenomenalize it, to experience what cannot be experienced and to express it inasmuch as it remains inexpressible. In philosophical terms, one can thus say (as did Descartes) that "in effect, the idea of the infinite, in order to be true, must in no way be comprehended, for incomprehensibility itself is contained in the formal reasoning of infinity [*idea enim infiniti, ut sit vera, nullo modo debet comprehendi, quoniam ipsa incomprehensibilitas in ratione formali infiniti continetur*]."[2] In more theological terms, one can say of God that "we thus call him . . . the inexpressible, the inconceivable, the invisible, and the incomprehensible, he who vanquishes the power of human language and surpasses the comprehension of human thought" (John Chrysostom).[3] Since the two conditions of this speech exercise are unambiguously extreme (to experience what cannot be experienced, to express the inexpressible) one can hardly avoid looking for an alternative, when faced with such claims. On the one hand, one could simply challenge all "negative theology" as a language game that is both impractical (after all, one cannot experience what one cannot experience) and contradictory (one cannot, after all, express what one cannot express). In this case one chooses to respect the double prohibitions by Kant ("by means of principles to show the specific limits [of reason])"[4] and by Wittgenstein ("Whereof one cannot speak [*sprechen*], thereof one must be silent").[5] On the other hand, one could accept "negative theology" but restrict it to the domain in which it claims its validity, that of the purest and most extreme religious experience, the domain attributed to the "mystical." This acceptance would amount to a marginalization, since this domain remains inaccessible to most of us—certainly to most philosophers. Even if admitted in principle, "mystical theology" would thus remain an unfrequented territory, willingly abandoned by those who attempt to ignore it to those who are willing to lose themselves there, at the risk of irrationality. This refusal in principle is thus reiterated by a refusal in fact. Metaphysics has amply confirmed these two attitudes, as is proven indisputably by its modern history—which can be described as a rejection (indeed, a tenacious elimination from thought) of what cannot be comprehended as one of its objects.

Or rather, this situation has preceded us, for modernity itself has found its limits and is attempting to identify them. Thus the theme of "negative theology" has resurfaced in philosophy in recent years, at least in a vague manner. Among other indications, one can cite Heidegger, who was unable to avoid "comparing" the step back of the thought of presence toward that of giving (*Geben*) "with the method of negative theology."[6] Or Wittgenstein, who states, with a different accentuation: "There is the ineffable [*es gibt allerdings Unaussprechliches*]. It *shows itself*. It is the mystical."[7] It remains simpler, however, to rely on the most explicit testimony—Derrida's arguments (which, moreover, were elaborated in response to my own publications), for a new pertinence for "negative theology" in the forum of contemporary philosophy.[8] As we know, Derrida revived this theme in order to subject the apophatic moment of "negative theology" to deconstruction. He did so by establishing that it inverts itself and, in the end, achieves a second-order kataphasis so as to reestablish the metaphysical primacy of presence, a goal that was in fact never abandoned by theology. To say of God that he is and then that he is not in the long run would aim only at thinking of this nonbeing as the ultimate and finally unchanging figure of his being—a being beyond being. Because, having undergone the ordeal of its negation, the being of God is thus able to prevail not only in transcendence but in presence over the being of all other beings: "apophasis has always represented a kind of paradoxical hyperbole."[9] In this way, the "metaphysics of presence" annexes "negative theology" without any other form of trial, reducing it to the ranks of a pure and simple auxiliary of metaphysics without too much circumspection. Hence deconstruction finally triumphs, by getting rid of a possible rival that is all the more dangerous in having preceded it and having come from elsewhere. One can nonetheless show that this interpretation deals a double blow—and the more violence it exerts, the more fragile it becomes.

(a) First, it denies the patience and suffering of the apophatic negation, without taking into account the seriousness and the work of the theologians involved. One need only think of a very explicit remark made by John Scotus Eriugena on the irremediable nature of negation, which can be neither abolished nor mitigated by a final naming:

> For, when we declare "God is super essential," we imply nothing other than a negation of essence. Whoever declares "God is super essential" explicitly negates that God is essence. Consequently, although the negation is not found in the words themselves, its meaning does not escape the understanding of those who think about it seriously. In this way, in my opinion, I am constrained to admit that the divine names enumerated below, though at first they seem to imply no negation, belong more to the negative part of theology than to the positive part.[10]

In fact, the negation remains as radical and definitive for language as kenosis does for its referent.

(b) But in order to bring everything back to the "metaphysics of presence," this attempt to reduce apophasis to kataphasis must also cancel the third path, often called the path of eminence. How is one to understand, in effect, that everything is predicated of God while at the same time nothing is predicated of him—other than by recognizing that a third path surpasses the first two and only thus does away with the contradiction?

Of course, it remains to be seen whether there is a language game that could dispense with affirmation and negation like this, and thus dispense with truth and falsity. Would we still be dealing with a meaningful assertion and, more particularly, with a predication? Without a doubt, but as Aristotle foresaw, not all assertions refer to truth and falsity following the model of predication: "Prayer [is] certainly a discourse [λογος], but it is neither true nor false."[11]

Even before answering these questions, one can already point to evidence in this direction: First, the phrase "negative theology" does not describe the situation we are dealing with correctly, for the moment of negation (admittedly with variable positions) is inscribed within a triple determination that articulates discourse into (i) *via affirmativa*, (ii) *via negativa*, and, especially, (iii) *via eminentiae*, radically other and hyperbolic. It does not mirror the negation with another superior affirmation (whether disguised or admitted), but tears discourse away from predication altogether, and thus away from the alternative of truth or falsity. Two consequences follow. First, I will no longer say "negative theology," but rather, following the nomenclature of the Dionysian *corpus*, "mystical theology." And second, one will come to realize that "mystical theology" (when it claims to be following the third path) no longer has the ambition of making constative use of language; its ambition is, rather, to be freed from such use. But what type of language use can replace it? I have suggested that it involves moving from a constative (and predicative) use of language toward a strictly pragmatic usage.[12] This has yet to be proven. What follows is an attempt to do just that.

2

But, just as "negative theology" is finally not really negative, it is also possible that it cannot be confined to the theological—at least understood in the narrowest sense. Indeed, one must not exclude the possibility that the pragmatic system used by mystical theology extends to other states of affairs and to other utterances. Nor can one exclude that these other uses may allow us to establish with greater clarity the true function of the third path, which is neither affirmative nor negative. I will thus choose a privileged case of pragmatic language outside of theology, one that illustrates the third path indubitably. I propose considering the erotic event and its corresponding utterance: "I love you!" The question then becomes that of determining what it is one says when one says "I love you!" supposing that one says anything at all. Let me take a famous example from *The Charterhouse of Parma*, when Clélia meets up with Fabrice after years of separation: "'It's me,' a dear voice told him, 'I've come to tell you I love you, and to ask you whether you will obey me.'"[13] Are we dealing with a constative utterance here? Is Clélia really saying something? And is she saying something about something? And in this case, is it a predicate of herself or of Fabrice? I will attempt to respond to these complex questions by emphasizing successive difficulties.

One can first reduce her utterance to its central nucleus, "I love you," and ask what "I love you" says. If, first hypothesis, one reads the formula as it stands, it falls in the domain of pure private language: neither Fabrice nor anyone else can understand what Clélia is saying. Of course, if I were to make an analogy with my personal experience, I could conjecture that she is describing her subjective attachment to the person of Fabrice. Yet one cannot exclude that she may be pretending or lying, either to Fabrice (to seduce him), to a possible witness (to embrace her standing), or even to herself (to love loving, without loving anyone in particular). In order to defend the constative character of Clélia's utterance, one can also reduce her sentence, "I've come to tell you that I love you" to a quasi-predicative proposition in the style "Someone exists—X, me, Clélia—such that she is in love with another—Y, you, Fabrice" (let me allow for the moment that the identification of X and Y with Clélia and Fabrice is not problematic). What signification does this utterance offer? One that is revealed by its method of verification. Here two possibilities open up.

(a) "I love you" could perhaps be verified by precise interactions between things and actors (to approach, to speak to, to watch, to take care of, to serve, etc.). Yet can one locate them, and then establish which and how many are sufficient to give a meaning to the predication "X is in love with Y"? Clélia undoubtedly invests herself—"It is I who have come to tell you," just as she has undoubtedly given sufficient proof of her devotion in the past, helping Fabrice in prison, helping him escape, thinking of him, etc. Yet one cannot say that "I love you!" exactly signifies "I helped you in prison, I helped you escape, I abandoned myself to you, I thought of you," etc. Not only because all of this is far from proving "I love you" (a lot is missing here), but also because one can oppose to these facts other, at least equivalent, facts: Clélia has in the meantime married someone else (Count Crescenzi), she has promised the Virgin never to see Fabrice in the light of day, she has avoided meeting him, etc. Thus, reduced to behaviors and states of affairs, the declaration "I love you!" remains ambiguous, precisely because it doesn't describe anything with precision.

(b) A second possibility remains: since the reduction of "I love you" to a predicative proposition does not guarantee its verification, it remains possible to trust in Clélia's sincerity by considering that the meta-narrative "It is I who have come to tell you" guarantees what she says in the phrase "I love you." But how is one to recognize and prove this sincerity? All the facts and actions that one could inventory belong to the world. They cannot say anything, nor can they determine the validity of someone's sincerity, which in principle remains both out of this world and absolutely foreign to things. At its best, sincerity pertains to the private sphere and thus cannot be described or verified any more than lying can. One cannot even invoke private language in this situation, because the private sphere is precisely deprived of it. What is more, as soon as someone claims to speak and prove his or her sincerity by speaking utterances of the type "I am sincere," "you can trust me," experience has taught us that we should rather hear an indication of deceit, such that the utterance "I am lying" would suggest that I am in fact not lying. Thus Clélia is saying nothing about nothing to Fabrice when she says "I love you!"

Another interpretation is possible, however. Even if Clélia says nothing to Fabrice, she speaks to him as herself. "I love you" perhaps states nothing concerning any state of affairs and predicates nothing at all, but this utterance nonetheless speaks this nothing *to* someone, Fabrice, and it speaks it *on behalf of* someone else. Let me look once more at the example: "'It is I,' a dear voice told him, 'who have come to tell you that I love you, and to ask whether you will obey me.'" Especially if Stendhal is saying nothing about nothing, it is clear that he insists on the speaker and the person spoken to, to the point of saturation: first the speaker, for she says "it is I," "I have come to tell you," "I love you"; then the person spoken to, for he hears "tell *you*," "love *you*," "ask *you*." Clearly, predication and proposition fade away, leaving the naked intrigue of the two speakers, that is to say, the interlocutors, in the foreground. Could we not describe "I love you!" as a strict dialogue, without an object but perfectly intersubjective?

Several arguments compromise this position: (a) Understood in this way, Clélia's declaration to Fabrice is in effect reduced to a pure dialogue between "I" and "you," in other words, between two pronouns labeled personal and thus, properly speaking, both impersonal and improper. Not only could Clélia rightfully make the same declaration to someone other than Fabrice (and what proves that she has not done just that or that she will not do so?), but Fabrice could equally well receive it from someone else (why not from Sanséverina or from "little Annetta Marini," who faithfully listens to his sermons?). The roles could also be reversed. Yet, most importantly, anyone (not only Clélia and Fabrice) can take on these two roles, like characters in a play, or on the spontaneous stage of everyday life. In "I love you!" "I" and "you" remain empty terms, which essentially produce occasional expressions (occasionally significant) and nothing more.[14] Simple pronouns, they suffice neither to bind people, nor to attribute names, nor to create lovers out of them. Thus Clélia does not speak herself to Fabrice, for purely logical reasons. (b) What is more, if "I love you!" is not sufficient to establish a true signification or even the identity of the person one thus claims to love, that is not only because I can love anyone but especially because I can love someone who is not present or who remains anonymous. In fact, the more I sincerely love (or think I love, which amounts to the same for me), the less the identity of the presence of the loved one is required. I can love a woman or a man whom I know only superficially, or whom I do not know at all (based on his or her name or reputation), or even about whom I know nothing. I can love someone who is absent most of the time and who will probably always remain thus, and I can even love someone absent who has never yet been present, not even for a moment. I can love a woman whom I have lost or whom I have left. I can love someone dead out of loyalty and a child not yet born out of hope. Because I love, what I am in love with does not have to *be* at all, and can thus dispense altogether with maintaining the status of a being. Not only does this absence not stop us from loving and desiring, it reinforces this desire. For the loved one, the person to whom "I love you!" is spoken, it is no longer about being or not being, or about being or not being this or that, but only about the fact that one is loved. Thus (and this time for motives that are not only logical, but also erotic), what Clélia says to Fabrice does not designate Fabrice and is not even addressed to him. "I love you," then, neither produces a proposition with a reference (a signification), nor does it predicate a meaning, nor does it even mobilize identifiable interlocutors. It thus does not constitute a locutionary act.[15]

3

And yet, even if it is not a locutionary act, "I love you" remains a speech act. To see this, we can consider a second hypothesis: that "I love you!" constitutes an illocutionary act, in other words, a performative. By pronouncing "I love you!" the speaker does not in effect say anything (neither meaning nor reference), but accomplishes what he says, puts it into practice simply by saying it; the force of the utterance enforces what is said.[16] This hypothesis, one must admit, seems convincing. It would justify the fact that, strictly speaking, "I love you!" offers neither meaning nor reference, without, for all that, saying nothing, since in saying "I love you!" it is not a matter of communicating information or making a predication but of loving in act and in force. So when I say "I love you!" to someone, or when I hear it spoken by someone else, an act is accomplished immediately: whether my lover and I rejoice (as occurs with Clélia and Fabrice) or are worried (like Phaedra and Hippolytus in another context) is due to the fact that this love, simply because I declared it, becomes an effective and unquestionable fact, which modifies intersubjective reality and which one must, from now on, take into account. One can add to this: because this illocutionary act is a performance, it intervenes in a precise time and place and thus attaches a precise and identifiable signification and precise, identifiable speakers to what hitherto remained an essentially occasional expression: here and now, it is a question of Clélia accomplishing this speech act once and for all and definitively for the benefit of Fabrice and for no one else except her and him. In the same way, the "I don't know what inexplicable and fatal force" that seals the friendship between Michel de Montaigne and Étienne de la Boétie (as if according to a performative) identifies them absolutely and determines the reference to them: the famous but difficult utterance "because it was him; because it was me" thus eliminates at least the danger of an essentially occasional expression and ensures that we are dealing with them, in Bordeaux and in 1554, and no one else, nowhere else.[17]

However, the speech act "I love you!" cannot be analyzed as a performative or illocutionary type. Moreover, so far as I know, neither Austin nor Searle mentions it among the latter (in fact, they seem to ignore it entirely, no matter what heading one gives to it). To understand this impossibility, one need only address Austin's conditions for all illocutionary acts and measure whether or not "I love you!" satisfies the requirements under each heading.

(1) "There must exist a conventional procedure having a certain conventional effect, a procedure that includes the utterance of certain words by certain people in certain circumstances." If by such a conventional procedure one is to understand a ceremony, whether public (marriage, contract, social pact, etc.) or private (engagement, marriage proposal), then "I love you" is not appropriate: I can say it or hear it in all circumstances, sometimes even in a semi-unconsciousness (pleasure, sleep, etc.), even almost in silence. (2) "What is more, the particular people and circumstances in a given case must be suitable to invoke the particular procedure they would invoke." "I love you" satisfies this criterion so long as it implies two people capable of communicating and possessing at least a certain freedom of feeling. But it does not comply, inasmuch as it ignores all

"particular procedures" and can be performed in all circumstances and in all language games. (3) "The procedure must be executed by all participants both correctly and" (4) "completely." But "I love you" can very well remain unilateral (this situation is all too common) and thus does not necessitate that "all" (the protagonists of the action) satisfy this requirement: one is more than enough. As for the requirement of a "completely" executed "procedure," it has no pertinence, not only because in this case no "procedure" is required but especially because a "complete" utterance either would change nothing, or by changing something would weaken "I love you!" rather than reinforce it: to add to "I love you!" something like "a lot" or "very much," amounts to saying much less than simply "I love you!" and even insinuates that "I don't love you!"

Let me look at the two remaining conditions: First, (5) "when, as is often the case, the procedure is meant to be used by people having certain thoughts and feelings, or to trigger a certain behavior having consequences for any one of the participants, then a person who participates in this procedure and claims to have certain thoughts and feelings must in fact have them, and the participants must have the intention to behave accordingly; what is more" (6) "they must in the future so behave."[18] It is clear that "I love you" can satisfy these last two requirements even less than the preceding ones. First, as Stanley Cavell has judiciously remarked,[19] I cannot say "I love you" unless motivated by passion, or at least from a passion. Yet no one can verify this passion, not even (or rather especially not) the person who is supposed to benefit from it. Thus my "intention" remains utterly unverifiable. Here one finds the aporia of sincerity: it is a totally private mood, ineffable in everyday language. Thus to say "I love you" guarantees my sincerity no more than it presumes the acceptance (or refusal) of the other or, for that matter, his or her own sincerity. Following Cavell once more, one must next recognize that the freedom and fragility of "I love you" have no ambition to be of any value for anything other than "now," certainly not "in the future": How can I guarantee to someone that I love him or her, if I myself have no certitude? One could answer that I can very well promise to love someone in the future, in spite of the fickleness of my heart and my moods. Of course, but then one is dealing with a promise ("I promise to love you"), and thus with a completely different speech act from "I love you!" The promise is, in fact, the perfect illocutionary act, even the epitome of the performative, satisfying all the enumerated conditions, precisely those that "I love you!" does not satisfy (conventional procedure and effect, fixed circumstances, formal and complete fulfillment, guarantee of reciprocity and the future, etc.).[20] Thus, the promise differs essentially from "I love you!"; it can only be added on, and this supplement confirms that by saying "I love you!" I do not perform an illocutionary speech act.

4

Admittedly, then, "I love you" cannot be considered an illocutionary act, since it respects neither the conventions nor the conditions of such an act. However, the one who pronounces these words does indeed accomplish an act, even if it is not the act of actualizing what he or she says. One does not do what one says by saying it, but in saying it one nonetheless does do something. What can it be? By saying "I love you!" I do not thereby factually or actually love, but I nonetheless radically modify the intersubjective relation between me and my interlocutor; from now on nothing will be the same, for better or for worse. Wherein lies the difficulty, then? Perhaps in this: whereas the illocutionary act effectively accomplishes what it says (to promise, condemn, curse, bless, etc.), the act that says "I love you!" accomplishes something other than what it says: for example, to be fond of someone without sincerely loving him or her, or to admit to holding someone in affection without hoping for the return of that affection, or else to satisfy a preliminary request or to gain a moral advantage by virtue of my sincerity, etc. When I pronounce "I love you!" I do not prove that I love (as with an illocutionary act), but I nonetheless always produce an effect on my interlocutor: returned love, saddened or fearful refusal, placing the other in a position of power over me, fear, gratitude, surprise, etc. The act therefore does not accomplish what it says, but it says what it says in order to have on the interlocutor an effect that is other than what it says—even if it is simply to draw his or her attention and to constitute the other as my interlocutor in an erotic dialogue.

Now this is exactly what is called a perlocutionary act, as defined by Austin: "an act that we instigate or accomplish by saying something: to convince, persuade, frighten, etc."[21] Searle usefully specifies: "If we consider the concept of the illocutionary act, we must also consider the consequences, the effects that such acts have on the actions, thoughts, or beliefs of the *listeners*, etc." That is, by saying something, we elicit a different effect: to persuade, convince, but also frighten, make aware of, lead to act in a certain way, etc.[22] Cavell gives us a perfect example: "the [perlocutionary] effect [brought about by Iago] of helping to drive someone [Othello] mad with jealousy."[23] When I say "I love you!" I try (and in fact always manage) not necessarily to perform the love that I speak but to move, to influence, and, at the very least, to summon my listener to consider my declaration. I declare my love as one declares war: it is not yet to engage in it, but already to oblige my adversary to mobilize him- or herself, and thus to determine him- or herself in relation to me. The declaration of Clélia, if we understand it as a perlocutionary act, must be reorganized: the sequence "to tell you that I love you" must be understood in terms of the sequence that precedes it—"I have come to"— because together they try to produce another effect than that of the declaration itself, an effect that Clélia renders perfectly explicit: "to ask you to obey me." By saying "I love you!" I do not love for all that, but I in effect ask the other to love me or at least to answer me sincerely. I thus accomplish neither a locutionary act nor an illocutionary act, but rather a perlocutionary act.[24]

In fact, other characteristics of this type of act fit what I do when I say "I love you!" (a) The perlocutionary act produces its effect by saying something, but this effect acts, beyond the *dictum*, on the other speaker or the speakers thus provoked; to be more precise, it "produces certain effects on the feelings, thoughts, and actions of the listeners, the speaker, or *other persons*; and it can be done with the goal, the intention or the will to produce them."[25] Instead of doing what I say, I say *in order to* do something to someone, in the same sense in which, in everyday French, as in English, "faire quelque chose à quelqu'un"—"to do something to someone"—means to provoke, to intrigue, to move, to overwhelm, and possibly to seduce someone. Instead of saying something about something, or bringing about what I say, it is rather, for me, about saying *to* someone, not necessarily what I say, since I mean for my listener to understand something *other* than what I say, but that I am here, that I am speaking to him or her, imposing my will or having his or her will imposed on me. Contrary to the illocutionary act, the perlocutionary does not involve itself so much with the utterance as with the person spoken to, and the speaker always takes the initiative: "The speaker is on his or her own to create the desired effect."[26] (b) Perlocutionary acts prove to be nonconventional, or at least "it is difficult to say where convention begins and ends."[27] We have seen that "I love you!" dispenses with almost all conventions proper to locutionary acts, in particular that of reciprocity. This does not signify the disappearance of such conventions in principle, but that in this case they belong neither exclusively nor primarily to logic or language theory, although they do come within the scope of such theory: they arise out of the space of dialogue itself and from the pragmatics that ensue. To sum up, if there must be conventions, they will first depend on the originary fact of the other. In this way, when I say "I love you!" what I say produces an effect that depends not so much on the obvious meaning of my utterance as on the identity, the situation, even the state of mind of my interlocutor. And I can predict this effect, because my interlocutor's moods follow from language conventions: for example, Don Giovanni plays better than Leporello, when it is a question of speaking to Elvira in particular and to women in general. (c) Indeed, in the perlocutionary act what essentially matters is not what I say (the intention and the meaning) but to whom I say it (others, an audience, or a specific someone); the listener is thus privileged over the speaker. Hence the pedagogical rule of thumb that, to teach math to Pierre, one must know mathematics, and above all Pierre. The decisive factor, according to Cavell, consists in the fact that "in perlocutionary acts, the 'you' comes essentially into the picture,"[28] while in illocutionary acts, everything depends on my capacity, as the speaking "I," to perform what I say. And of course, with "I love you!" more than in any other act, what takes center stage is called "you," which constitutes the perlocutionary act par excellence. (d) One last point, decisive for my inquiry, must be addressed: because one is dealing here not with what I utter but rather with the "responses" to it, hence the effects produced when "I have an effect" on my interlocutor, these effects (emotions, thoughts, reactions, etc.) taken in themselves "can be accomplished additionally or entirely by non-locutionary means." In short, there is nothing contradictory or unthinkable about a "non-verbal response."[29] Not only do perlocutionary acts accomplish intersubjective effects (which lie outside the particular utterance) and contradict what is said, but what is more, the responses arrived at in this way can be given in silence (outside of language). Who does not see that "I love you!" can, once its effect is produced, receive a response all the more satisfying in that it remains silent? It could even be that silence constitutes, if not the best response, at least always the first, and that, without this first silence, the following verbalization would not be convincing. Since all these characteristics are reunited in the utterance "I love you!" one can thus conclude that one is dealing with a performative of the perlocutionary type. And, granting it this status, I am justifying, against its omission by Austin and Searle, what Cavell specifically calls a "passionate utterance."[30]

5

It has now become possible to describe the perlocutionary act that I accomplish when I say "I love you!" or at least to trace a sketch. It is a matter of acting in which not only the fact *that* I speak is more important than *what* I say but in which the fact *that* it is spoken has an effect on *the person to whom* I said it. This characteristic, which goes beyond the field of language [*langue*] and its use [*langage*] to give preponderance to individual speech [*parole*], establishes a structure that is essentially pragmatic, and in this case dialogic. This act speaks inasmuch as it calls out. This call elicits a response and possibly a response to the response, without there necessarily being an end in sight. Thus erotic discourse unfolds according to a call, a response, and a counter-call that can be seen as following three paths.

Let me consider the first and affirmative path. How can I make an affirmation if I am, strictly speaking, not saying anything when I say "I love you!"? As we have seen, this proposition does not offer any reference that can be verified, either by myself (I promise nothing—it is not an illocutionary act) or by the person to whom I am speaking (I can lie, and even if I don't lie, he or she does not know the difference—it is not a locutionary act). It also does not offer a precise meaning (to love can mean to possess like an object, to desire, or, on the contrary, to want the best for and even to sacrifice oneself for someone).[31] Yet as a perlocutionary act, "I love you!" does affirm something: the effect that it produces as a speech act. But this effect is split. First, by affirming to someone that I love him, I choose him as my interlocutor; not only do I distinguish him from the crowd of others who remain anonymous or at least indifferent but, by placing him in a prominent singularity, I individualize him, name and compromise him along with myself, whether he wants this or not: I identify myself through him by identifying him with me. Then, in the dialogical space that has thus been opened, I impose upon my interlocutor a decision regarding whether or not he loves me in return. This decision comprises two questions: Does he accept that I love him, or does he refuse to accept it? but also Does he love me in return, or does he hate me? Even a refusal to answer one or the other of these questions would be equivalent to a response (negative in this case). No affirmation can impose itself as powerfully as "I love you!" but, paradoxically, it imposes itself as a question whose contours are almost impossible to trace, as the most radical question that one can perhaps ever ask. Put otherwise, if my affirmation *that* I love him neither promises nor teaches him anything, it nonetheless forces him to answer a question, a question that is formulated from my point of view as "Does he love me?" while he hears it as "Do you love me?" It follows that the initial affirmation "I love you!" as categorical and affirmative as it remains, ends up producing the effect of a "Do you love me?"—a question that leaves room for doubt, for choice, and for a possible refusal. Affirmation thus elicits negation in and of itself; kataphasis becomes apophasis.

One must thus examine the second and negative path. However, can one really consider the question "Do you love me?" to be an apophasis?

This assimilation certainly seems paradoxical, but paradoxes are themselves imperative. Let me try to conceive this. To do so, one must remember that, in the case of a perlocutionary act, one does not consider *what* is said but the fact *that* it is said, the effect it has on the listener; but this effect belongs unambiguously to apophasis. By telling her "I love you!" I expect to hear (and to elicit) that she loves me, thus what I want to say is "Do you love me?" and I await confirmation. By this means I find myself in the exact same position as my listener, who, hearing my "I love you!" asks herself and me if I am telling the truth (in other words, if my thoughts concur and if my conduct will reflect what I think and say); she thus asks me as well, in words or in silence, "Do you love me?" Is it possible to give a categorical answer (affirmative or positive) to this double and yet unique "Do you love me"? If it is a question of deciding whether or not (referentially) I am sincere, or whether or not I understand (semantically) what "to love" means, neither she nor I know anything at the moment of the declaration—hence the apophasis. One might answer that what is at stake is not our sincerity but our concrete behavior and coherence: each of us will learn more about the intention of the other over time, which means that if I ask "Do you love me?" at a particular moment t_1, I can hope to obtain the beginning of an answer at moment t_2 or t_3, etc. This, in its turn, implies that the answer to the question is reached, in the best of cases, only in the moment that follows after. Yet if precisely only the *following* moment can affirm something in response to what I asked only the moment *before*, the temporal gap between doubt and confirmation cannot be abolished and will extend from question to response, endlessly. Thus, even in the case of a happy confirmation, the temporal delay and lateness maintain a différance.

With all other questions about states of affairs or objects that are in principle characterized by a certain permanence, this différance does not seriously compromise the answer. But in the case of the erotic relation, where the fickleness of the heart holds sway even with no intention of lying (and this is precisely why I cannot stop asking "Do you love me?"), différance disqualifies the answer, even when it is positive. One need only think of the common experience of receiving a letter in which the sender reassures me, "I love you too!" This answer can never definitively get rid of my anxiety (I who just said "I love you!" and am waiting for a confirmation today), precisely because it was written and posted several days ago, and I know nothing of what the other was thinking during that time, such that today, now, at the exact moment when I read it, it is too late and still leaves me unsatisfied. "Do you love me?" thus remains decidedly apophatic. This is emphasized from the point of view of the speaking I, for whom doubt goes even further (and not, as one might too quickly assume, less far), for by saying "I love you!" I know that I provoke another question in return as the perlocutionary effect: "Do you love me?" And I also know that there is no way for me to respond to this question and that, on the contrary, I have every reason in the world not to know anything about it. Even if I am sincere in the moment, I know very little about my motivations (desire, the vanity of seduction, fear of solitude, moral altruism?) or about their future (for how long?), such that if I confirm, by answering, "Yes, I love you!" I know only one thing—that I am stepping out of bounds and that, at bottom, as far as the moment to come is concerned, I know nothing. The question "Do you love me?" thus effectively establishes an apophasis.

And yet, despite this apophasis, the erotic dialogue is no less persistent. How is this possible? By means of a third path, a hyperbolic redoubling, a sort of eminence. I can really only repeat "I love you!" precisely because the other repeats ceaselessly "Do you love me?"; and for her, it is the same. She and I, we repeat "I love you!" only because her first enunciation (kataphasis) could not avoid giving rise to the apophatic "Do you love me?" And this repetition is prolonged without foreseeable end, because the confirmation always arrives too late for the question. In the same way, we repeat "Do you love me?" although we know that we cannot obtain a definitive response and although we undergo an insurmountable apophasis on its account, because we do not want to renounce the declaration of love that we can never truly promise or act. It follows that the other and I repeat "I love you!" (over and over again) because it cannot be verified. We repeat "Do you love me?" because we do not want to resign ourselves to invalidating it. I keep saying and *repeating* "I love you!" precisely because, on the one hand, I cannot guarantee it, *and*, on the other hand, I cannot give up trying. Short of answering the question, "Do you love me?" I repeat the perlocutionary act that instigates it, "I love you!" It is a question neither of kataphasis nor of apophasis but rather of a temporalizing language strategy, a repetition that affirms nothing, negates nothing, but that keeps alive a dialogic situation.[32] What the present tense sees as impossible (an affirmation cancelled by a negation), and constative language as contradictory (a kataphasis that gives rise to an apophasis), repetition and the future it conquers makes possible, but in a pragmatic, more precisely perlocutionary, sense. I reach the other and the other reaches me because "I love you!" and "Do you love me?" continually provoke a (perlocutionary) effect in us, or to be more exact, incite each of us for and by the other. We tell each other nothing in a certain (constative) sense, yet by speaking this nothing, or rather, these nothings, we place ourselves (pragmatically) face to face, each receptive to the (perlocutionary) effect of the other, in the distance that both separates and unites us. Constative and predicative (locutionary) or even active (illocutionary) speech definitively gives way to a radical pragmatic (perlocutionary) use: neither saying nor denying anything about anything, but acting on the other and allowing the other to act on me.

6

If we accept the conclusion toward which these analyses have been leading, a few remarks are in order. First, pragmatic usage (which elsewhere I have attributed to mystical theology in order to gain a better understanding of the third and last path) finds a lateral confirmation in the perlocutions of erotic discourse. In both cases there is a pragmatic use of language, in the form of three privileged perlocutions (and all of their variations, which could be itemized): "I love you!" and "Do you love me?" and their repetition, corresponding to kataphasis, apophasis, and hyperbole. In this sense, mystical theology would no longer constitute a marginal and insignificant exception in language theory but, on the contrary, would indicate a much more central and vast domain, where pragmatics, perlocutions, and what they render utterable unfold, among other things. It is no longer a question of a discourse about beings and objects, about the world and its states of affairs, but rather the speech shared by those who discourse about these things when they no longer discourse about them but speak to one another. The suspicion that modern philosophy has bred of the encounter with theology in general and mystical theology in particular differs little from its disinheritance of the question of love in all its forms. One could then interrogate the dimensions of this encounter between erotic discourse and mystical theology. Are we dealing with a formal similitude, limited to linguistics, or a deeper univocity? I cannot answer such a question in this context. I am already satisfied with having been able to ask it. Two comments, marking a convergence, can nonetheless be made

First of all, the following: just like mystical theology, erotic discourse mobilizes three types of names, to name the beloved in three different ways. (a) I love him and thus affirm him using all possible names, predicates, and metaphors in all registers of all possible languages. Consequently, I do not hesitate to attribute to him not only all appropriate names, but also and especially all inappropriate names, names taken from animals, even obscene or religious names, etc. But these excesses are not perhaps perverse at all, no matter how indecent, because they attempt, awkwardly to be sure but perfectly logically, to reach the very limits of the kataphasis that claims the saturated and exceptional phenomenon that is the other in its eroticized flesh. (b) Yet this uncommon phenomenon ends up exceeding all nomination. It thus becomes appropriate to name it precisely as having no name, as resisting all ownership, all character, and all determination. One then has recourse to minimalist designations, childish, animalistic, or silly names, to pure tautology, to deictics and possessive pronouns, or even onomatopoeias, etc.; offering no meaning, they say nothing and thus manifest a strict apophasis. (c) Yet if the flesh of the other remains definitively her own, and mine, my own, they nevertheless accomplish a single common and reciprocal erotics. In *jouissance*, we still speak to one another and, in a certain sense, still give each other names. But *jouissance* can only speak its own repetition, operating it without syntax and managing its temporality: it is a question of articulating together "I love you!" and at the same time "Do you love me?" using alternately "now" (kataphasis), "again" (apophasis), and "come" (eminence). And one could show without difficulty that at least here one is dealing with an analogy from the path of eminence, or more precisely, from the discourse of praise.

In this context (and this is the second comment) one can also question the episode near the end of the Gospels in which Christ asks Peter three times, "Do you love me?" (John 21:15–7). In response to the first questioning, Peter answers, "Yes Lord, you know that I love you." Why does this categorical response not satisfy the initial question? First, because Christ already knows and has always known that Peter does not love him, or at least that at the decisive moment he did not love him as much as he had promised, betraying him (Mark 14:66–72) instead of risking his own death (Mark 14:30). Peter's kataphasis thus actually signifies an apophasis. He denied, in other words, "negated" (Mark 14:68, 69) Jesus' name and even "swore 'I don't know this man *you* are talking about'" (Mark 14:66). He refused even to say the man's name, so that he put the responsibility for uttering it on others. Thus when Christ repeats the question "a second time" (John 21:16), one can assume that Peter hears an allusion to this past lie, also spoken "a second time" (Mark 14:70). Thus he utters his love a second time, as if to compensate for his second denial: this latent confession thus accomplishes the apophasis. Speaking in this way, he either supposes that a locutionary act is expected of him (to inform Jesus of his love and to confirm this information), the stupidity of which is immediately apparent, since Christ knows everything, including this, or else he thinks that by repeating himself it will "sink in" and convince Jesus that today at least he truly loves him. Such an illocutionary act in fact performs nothing, and it is not enough to prove Peter's sincerity. Or else perhaps he finally understands what the third questioning asks of him: it is not about what Peter says about things (first questioning), nor is it about his behaving in all sincerity (second questioning), for Peter knows that Christ knows he knows ("Lord, You know everything, You know [thus also] that I love you"; John 21:17), but rather it is about the perlocutionary effect that Christ expects to have on him: "Tend my sheep." Christ expects neither that Peter should admit not loving him nor that he pretend to love him, but that out of love of Jesus he love the other believers, present and to come. These three stages within a single utterance follow the three paths of mystical theology and of erotic discourse. Is this so surprising, inasmuch as between God and humans everything remains ambiguous except, precisely, love? We repeatedly say, despite all the impossibilities that prohibit it, "The word that resounds even to the heavens, the word, the word of gods and men: 'I love you!' "[33]

—Translated by Arianne Conty

The Banality of Saturation

I sometimes see within a banal theater.

—Baudelaire, "The Irreparable"

1

In several steps and not without some stumbling and a few retractions, I proposed a new concept for phenomenology: the saturated phenomenon. This concept will pose the question for my reflections in this essay. The innovation I proposed should be understood cautiously. Formally, at least, it does not mark a revolution but merely a development of one of the possibilities that is by right already inscribed within the commonly accepted definition of the phenomenon. By "commonly accepted definition" I mean that of Kant and Husserl. If not alone, then at least as the first in modernity these two philosophers have saved the phenomenon by according it the right to appear unreservedly.[1] For them, a phenomenon is a representation that ceases to refer, like a symptom, only to its subject (like an inadequate idea in Spinoza) and instead gives access to a thing placed facing it (possibly an object), because some actually given intuition in general (sensible or not, the question remains open) finds itself assumed, framed, and controlled by a concept, playing the role of a category. On these two conditions, the representation is modeled after its objective, concentrated on it and absorbed in it, such that the representation becomes the direct presentation of its objective; its semblance passes through to this object and becomes its appearance. Intuition can then become objectively intentional (like an appearance, no longer a mere semblance) in and through the concept that actively fixes it (according to the spontaneity of the understanding). But reciprocally, the concept becomes objectively intentional (and plays the role of a category) only in and through the intuition that fills it from the outside, by virtue of the passivity that it transmits to it (according to intuition). Without underestimating the no doubt significant differences in how each philosopher states his case, I therefore assume the compatibility, indeed the equivalence, of Kant's and Husserl's definitions of the phenomenon.

There are then two variations of this initial formulation, according to how one considers the two relations that the two constitutive elements can maintain. Kant and Husserl each traced one variation. On the one hand, truth is accomplished in perfect evidence when intuition completely fills the concept, thereby validating it without remainder; this is the paradigmatic situation, and for that reason the least frequent. On the other hand, we have the partial validation of a concept by an intuition that does not fulfill it totally but is enough to certify it or verify it; this is the more ordinary situation (truth in the common sense of verification, validation, confirmation), even though it can seem unsatisfying. My innovation intervenes in the wake of these two: it consists only in paying attention to a third possible relation between intuition and concept—that in which intuition would surpass the concept (in multiple senses) by inverting the common situation where the concept exceeds intuition and the exceptional situation of an equality between them. In other words, it concerns the situation in which intuition would not only validate all that for which the concept assures intelligibility but would also add a given (sensations, experiences, information, it matters little) that this concept would no longer be able to constitute as an object or render objectively intelligible. Such an excess of intuition over and above the concept would invert the common situation without, however, abandoning phenomenality (or the terms of its definition), since the two elements of the phenomenon are still operative. The ideal norm of evidence (equality between intuition and the concept) is no longer threatened only and as usual by a shortage of intuition, but by its excess. I named and explained this phenomenon by excess as the (intuitively) saturated phenomenon.

I have not only formally identified this new determination of the phenomenon. I have also tried to apply it to the task of offering reasons for a type of phenomenon that has hitherto been left in the margins of ordinary phenomenality—indeed, has been excluded by it. Or rather, not to offer reasons, since what is at issue is liberating a phenomenon from the requirement of the principle of (sufficient) reason, but to offer it *its own* reason, so as to give it a rationality against all the objections, the prohibitions, and the conditions that weigh on it in metaphysics (indeed, partially also in phenomenology). What is at stake here is offering legitimacy to nonobjectifiable, even nonbeing phenomena: the event (which exceeds all quantity), the work of art (which exceeds all quality), the flesh (which exceeds all relation), and the face of the other [autrui] (which exceeds all modality). Each of these excesses identifies a type of saturated phenomenon, which functions exactly like a paradox. I then suggested the possibility of combining, on the one hand, some of these types and, on the other hand, all four together in order to describe other, still more complex saturated phenomena. The face of the other [autrui], for example, doubtless combines the transgression of all modality with the surpassing of quantity, quality, and relation.[2] Finally, this combining opens access to a radicalized mode of saturation, one that I designated with the name "phenomenon of revelation." Finally, on the basis of this complexity of saturations, the case of Revelation might possibly become thinkable. But it would no longer fall within phenomenology (which deals only with possibility, not the fact of its phenomenality) to decide about Revelation, which it could admit only formally. For that, one would have to call on theology.

2

As a general rule, one should neither expect nor hope that an innovation be adopted immediately and unreservedly. Especially if by chance it should be borne out, an assertion cannot lay claim to novelty and to success at the same time. If it meets with no resistance, it is doing nothing more than respond to already-established convictions, which amounts to yielding to the (always) dominant ideology. If instead it incites a reaction, that could be because it is innovative (provided that it is not simply mad). Criticism therefore pays homage despite itself to the innovation that it helps to validate. Even if it does not validate more than it invalidates what it challenges, criticism remains inevitable and indispensable because by its very resistance it lays bare the truly symptomatic points of what is thus advanced. Criticism can hence open a royal road to what is at stake. This seems to be the case for objections addressed to the legitimacy of a saturated phenomenon, for they allow me to identify at least two resistances, therefore two questions. To simplify, I will use two particularly clear formulations of these objections, ones that sum up all the others. The first questions the terms in which the saturated phenomenon is defined; the other, its principle. Although aware of the "appalling uselessness of explaining anything whatever to anyone whatever,"[3] in examining these objections I will try to answer their assault, but above all I will try to extend their lines of attack so as to reach through them once again to the heart of the question.

The first objection points to two contradictions, which lead to two impasses. First, the hypothesis of the saturated phenomenon pretends to go "beyond what canonical phenomenology has recognized as the possibility of *experience* itself," all the while pretending "to be inscribed within an experience."[4] What is more: because "there is no 'pure experience,'" especially not of "full transcendence [and] its pure alterity," it follows that "no Revelation, with a capital R, can be given within phenomenality."[5] In short, we do not have any experience of what passes beyond the conditions for the possibility of experience; yet by its very definition the so-called saturated phenomenon passes beyond the limits of experience; therefore we have absolutely no experience of it. And there is no discussion concerning what cannot (and therefore should not) be thought. Yet who cannot see that this objection, without critiquing or even admitting it, presupposes that experience has only one meaning and that this meaning is the one suited to the experience of objects? In short, who does not see that the objection presupposes the univocity of experience and of objectivity? Now, the entire question of the saturated phenomenon concerns solely and specifically the possibility that certain phenomena do not manifest themselves in the mode of objects and yet still do manifest themselves. The difficulty is to describe what could manifest itself without our being able to constitute (or synthesize) it as an object (by a concept or an intentionality adequate to its intuition). From the outset, by its simple formulation the objection misses the sole and central question, substituting for it a pure and simple fiction—the fiction of a "pure experience," a "full transcendence [and] its pure alterity"—whose absurdity is easy to show. Not only does the description of the saturated phenomenon never use such pompous and deceptive formulations, but it does not even speak willingly of experience (except in the mode of counter-experience). That is, under the guise of modest showiness, the very notion of experience already presupposes too much, namely, nothing less than a subject, whose measure and anteriority define from the start the conditions of experience and therefore of objectification. Consequently, if one wants to contest the horizon of the object in order to do justice to the possibility of the saturated phenomenon, one must also contest the conditions for the subject of experience and therefore the univocal notion of experience itself.

To this first invented contradiction a second is added. Even if one can rigorously admit an experience without object, one cannot think "an experience without a subject."[6] This is why, even if it pretends to stick to an "entirely empty, passive, seized upon, affected, powerless and so on" subject,[7] the saturated phenomenon should maintain intact its role within phenomenality: "yet its function (which is to allow the appearing of phenomena) remains unchanged . . .; the character of subjectivity is maintained throughout and . . . the promised dispossession or dismissal has not taken place." Thus, I "reestablish, without admitting it, what [I] claim to have dismissed."[8] This contradiction supposes that the (in principle) criticized subject coincides exactly with the (in fact) maintained subject; in other words, it rests on the univocity of the concept of subject. Yet how can one feign not to know that the entire question—and the entire difficulty—consists in seeing whether "subject" cannot and should not be understood in many senses or, in other words, if the critique of the transcendental subject does not free another sense of "subject," or more exactly, of who comes after the subject (to take up a helpful phrase from Jean-Luc Nancy)?[9] I can hardly see why such an equivocity should be dismissed, given that phenomenology has already broached it—if only in passing from Husserl (the transcendental subject) to Heidegger (*Dasein*), indeed, within Heidegger's own thought (from *Dasein* to what succeeds it), not to mention the questioning of the subject who is master of experience in Sartre, Merleau-Ponty, Levinas, and Henry. Anyway, why should the "subject" or whoever comes after it disappear without remainder if it no longer plays any role within the process of phenomenalization except that of response and "resistance" to what gives itself, then of screen where what gives itself would show itself? Why should the "subject" or whoever comes after it be abolished simply because it has lost the activity of the understanding in favor of a more originary receptivity, the spontaneity of representation (or intentionality) to the benefit of a more radical, and perhaps in another mode more powerful, passivity? In not asking these questions, the first criticism betrays an extraordinarily noncritical sense of who comes after the subject—possibly the devoted [*l'adonné*].[10]

The second objection remains. It evidences, at least apparently, a ruthless radicality, since it contests the very principle of the possibility (and therefore the actuality) of a saturated phenomenon: "There remains the (enigmatic, incomprehensible . . .) fact that one could *see otherwise*—that I or the others, we saw otherwise." See what? Saturated phenomena no doubt, but more simply, by a slippage that is as hasty as obsessive, always and already "God." In fact, according to this objection, the one counts for all the others, since in all cases it is a question of denying purely and simply that there is anything whatsoever to see: first, in the saturated phenomenon in general ("one no longer speaks of anything—that is, of nothing that can be assigned"),[11] next, in a phenomenon of revelation in particular ("What will you say to me if I say to you that where you see God, I see nothing?").[12] Indeed, what should I say? Yet the force of the argument can be turned against the one who uses it, for the fact of not comprehending and seeing nothing should not always or even most often disqualify what it is a question of comprehending and seeing, but rather the one who understands nothing and sees only a ruse. Not only does admitting an insurmountable powerlessness to see or comprehend guarantee that something does indeed give itself to be seen and comprehended but the glorious claims of blindness directly and of themselves constitute a theoretical argument against this possibility of seeing or comprehending. To be sure, claiming to see is not sufficient to prove that one saw. Yet the fact or the pretense of not seeing does not prove that there is nothing to see.[13] It can simply suggest that there is indeed something to see, but that in order to see it, it is necessary to learn to see otherwise because it could be a question of a phenomenality different from the one that manifests objects. In phenomenology, where it is a matter only of seeing what manifests itself (and describing how it manifests itself), relying on the authority of one's blindness in order to call a halt to research constitutes the weakest argument possible. Indeed, it is an admission of defeat, to be used only in the last instance. In any case, it is not fitting to flaunt it as a strength, a profound mystery, and a great discovery. After all, blindness can also be explained in the sense that, as Aristotle says, "as the eyes of bats are to the light of the day, so is the reason in our soul to the things that are most visible in all of nature."[14] Until the contrary is proven, it behooves me to persist in making evident what at first appears to offend: "Whether convenient or inconvenient, and even though (because of no matter what prejudices) it may sound monstrous to me, it[15] is *the primal matter of fact to which I must hold fast* [Ursache die ich standhalten muss], which I, as a philosopher, must not disregard for a single instant. For children in philosophy [*philosophische Kinder*], this may be the dark corner haunted by the specters of solipsism and, perhaps, of psychologism, of relativism. The true philosopher, instead of running away, will prefer to fill the dark corner with light."[16]

3

The hypothesis of the saturated phenomenon gave rise to a discussion that is still ongoing, despite or because of my detailed accounts.[17] A serious motive must underlie this refusal or at least skepticism. What is this motive, if not the fear that phenomena are saturated only in the case of "exceptional intuitions"[18] and in a "maximalist" mode?[19] Do saturated phenomena touch us only rarely, in an enchantment that is confused and out of the ordinary?

To address this objection, one must distinguish between the *frequency* and the *banality* of phenomena. Common or poor phenomena appear frequently, and this is a consequence of their very definition. First, their constitution as objects requires only an empty or poor intuition, so that the difficulty of comprehending them consists most of the time only in determining the concept or concepts, not in the ordeal of intuition. It follows that their actual production does not mobilize uncommon experiential resources. They therefore appear frequently. Next, if these phenomena with no or poor intuition assume the status of technically produced objects (which is most frequently the case), their mode of production demands no other intuition than that which gives us their material (a material that itself becomes at once perfectly appropriate to each "concept" and available in an in principle limitless quantity). Hence nothing or very little opposes itself to what their production reproduces according to the needs of consumption, itself without assignable limit. The mode of constitution of available objects (*Vorhandenheit*), namely, production, of itself authorizes their reproduction for use (*Zuhandenheit*). Whence follows a frequency of technical objects and their phenomenality that accumulates day by day. It could even be said that the world is covered with an invasive and highly visible layer of poor phenomena (namely, the technical objects produced and reproduced without end), which ends up eclipsing what it covers over. And what does it cover over, if not other phenomena (e.g., the event, the painting, the flesh, or the other [autrui]), which I proposed naming saturated phenomena? In this specific sense, poor and common phenomenality not only guarantees a higher frequency to technical objects, but it makes this frequency inevitable and irrepressible by virtue of its very definition. In this specific sense, saturated phenomena can appear only in less frequent, therefore exceptional cases.

Banality must be understood in a way entirely different from frequency.[20] In the strict sense, what becomes banal, by political and legal decision, concerns all and is accessible to all: all, that is to say, the vassals and their vassals [*le ban et l'arrière-ban*]—the men the lord can mobilize from his own fiefs and then also, in perilous times, from the fiefs of his men for the purpose of waging a war, by derivation, the men in the force who are of age and then the others, the elders. Calling on vassals and their vassals obviously does not happen frequently; at least, all those concerned in this banality hope it will be as rare as possible. By extension, one speaks of the banalization of a forge, a mill, a field, etc., which means that these facilities, properties of the lord, are either used obligatorily (nobody can use another stove, another mill, etc.) or else are used only by those who need them (a field whose pastures are open to those who do not possess their own). Neither banality (obligatory or gracious) has anything frequent about it: only the lord can grant it and one turns to it only in cases of need. Banality, which is open to all, does not equal frequency; indeed, it sometimes opposes it.

To speak of a banal saturated phenomenon therefore does not imply that it becomes current and frequent nor, *a contrario*, that it must become exceptional and rare and therefore be confined to the margins of common phenomenality, which supposedly fixes the norm. The banality of the saturated phenomenon suggests *that the majority of phenomena, if not all* can undergo saturation by the excess of intuition over the concept or signification in them. In other words, the majority of phenomena that appear at first glance to be poor in intuition could be described not only as objects but also as phenomena that intuition saturates and therefore exceed any univocal concept. Before the majority of phenomena, even the most simple (the majority of objects produced technically and reproduced industrially), opens the possibility of a doubled interpretation, which depends upon the demands of my ever-changing relation to them. Or rather, when the description demands it, I have the possibility of passing from one interpretation to the other, from a poor or common phenomenality to a saturated phenomenality. That is, "those things that are the clearest and the most common are the very things that are most obscure, and understanding them is a novelty [*nova est intentio eorum*]."[21] At least that is what I will try to show.

It seems reasonable not to yield to an antitheological obsession, one that would refuse the hypothesis of saturated phenomena en masse for fear of having to admit one particular and exceptional case (God). In short, it seems reasonable not to hide from what is more evident so as to avoid a consequence less evident, though indisputably possible.[22] I therefore suggest that we provisionally disconnect these two questions so as to avoid a voluntary phenomenological blindness. Or, and this amounts to the same thing, before deciding about the possibility of saturated phenomena and the legitimacy of their appearing, it is appropriate first to examine whether such a thing can be found in fact. In other words, when and why must one resort to the hypothesis of the saturated phenomenon? One must do so each time one admits that it is impossible to subsume an intuition in an adequate concept, something always done in the case of a poor or common-law phenomenon—in other words, each time that one must renounce thinking a phenomenon as an object if one wants to think it as it shows itself.

4

There is no shortage of experiences that would permit us to trace the border between these two phenomenalities; one only has to follow the five senses of perception.

Suppose that I perceive, or rather that I undergo, the sensation of three colors arranged one on top of the other—for example, green, orange, and red, it matters little in what figure (circle, horizontal bands, etc.). This intuition, as simple and primary as it is (after all, the color red is literally primary), opens onto two radically different types of phenomena. In the first case, a concept lets us synthesize the phenomenon in an objective mode, and the intuition is inscribed adequately in this concept, which contains and comprehends it all. This is the case when I assign these three colors to the flag of a nation or the signal that regulates traffic at an intersection. In this case, the concept (either the country at issue, here something like Ethiopia or Guinea, or the authorization or prohibition to cross) grasps the intuition without remainder, and the intuition literally disappears in it—to the point that it becomes insignificant, pointless, and even dangerous to concentrate one's attention on the exact form of the colored spots, their intensity, or their nuances. If one does so, one is distracted from the signification, which alone is important to practical knowledge and therefore to the use of this phenomenon. That is, when it is a question of phenomena produced as signs, their intuitions and their forms pass without remainder into their significations, and they appear as signs, thus in terms of their concepts, only on the condition of disappearing as autonomous intuitions of color. This is why it always remains possible to change the intuited colors (of the flag or the crossing signal) arbitrarily, or else blatantly to dispense with them, replacing their visual intuition with a different type of intuition—for example, by substituting the sounds of a national anthem or an alarm. In these cases, intuition plays only a very minor role in relation to the concept (signification, intention), precisely because the phenomenon does not rest first on intuition or appear in its light but is governed and comprehended through and through by the concept. The concept can possibly even be substituted for the lacking intuition because, giving more, it dispenses with intuition radically. In this way the phenomenon of an object is manifest.

Yet there remains a different way for these three colors to appear. Suppose that they are imposed vertically over one another in three horizontal bands in a rectangular frame, as, for example, on Mark Rothko's canvas *Number 212*.[23] Here the phenomenon (this painting) appears with a manifest conceptual shortage or, if one prefers, an evident intuitive excess. Initially, there is no concept in the sense of form. First, each of the horizontal bands resembles a rectangle only approximately. Second, the very imprecision of their edges (in the sense of an ideal and geometric precision) plays the positive function of making the two contiguous colors vibrate in relation to each other (all the more so as a vague and indistinct strip of yellow comes between the green and the red, then between the green and the orange). Third, the arrangement of the three bands of color resembles nothing at all: it shows nothing other than these very colors and the play among them, without making evident anything else in the world, without producing any object, and without transmitting any information. There is no concept in the sense of a signification, still less of a sign that would refer arbitrarily to a second signification. The painting means nothing that we can comprehend; it is not connected to any signification that would assume it; it is not assumed in anything that would permit coding it by doing away with the intuition of its formless colors.

A painting is distinguished from other visibles (objects) in that no signification can comprehend it or do away with our encountering its intuition. A painting consists first in its intuition, which discourages all the concepts that one can mobilize to comprehend it, indeed, which submerges them, although it nevertheless gives rise to them and nourishes them indefinitely. One always has to go see a painting; the *only* thing one has to do is *see* it, without any other "exceptional" intuition besides that of simply, but truly, seeing it. On condition that one should speak only one meaning, all intuition as such, even the most simple, turns out to be exceptional insofar as it and it alone gives (to see). Before this Rothko painting, no form, no signification, no concept, nothing can relieve us from our vigil over its intuition and from responding to its mute summons. And this intuition to be seen resembles nothing besides itself, refers only to the visible itself, and thus it refers us to it. This saturated phenomenon does not have to be constituted or comprehended as an object; it only has to be confronted and submitted to, as it comes upon me.

One undergoes this gap between the objective phenomenon and the saturated phenomenon (a perfect phenomenological difference) not only in vision but also in all the other senses. Consider hearing: What differences arise between the simple sound, the sound as signal, the sound as voice, and the sound as song? In each case, the acoustic experience remains of the same order, and yet the intuition is enriched and made more complex from moment to moment. When the hostess who greets you in the train station or airport makes an announcement or answers a question, she produces an acoustic effect that is pleasant enough as such (she was chosen precisely for the tone of her voice, articulate and yet reassuring, seductive and yet informative), comparable to that of a jazz singer in Chicago or an alto in the aria of a Bach cantata. And yet one voice differs from another as an object differs from a saturated phenomenon. How do we notice this difference? By the fact that, in order to listen to an announcement at the airport, one must comprehend it—that is to say, reduce it immediately to its signification (or to its meaning), without remaining frozen in the sonic intuition used to communicate it. If, instead, I linger over this sonic intuition as such, I would no longer comprehend the information, either because I succumb to the charm of the voice and the woman that I imagine to proffer it or because I do not comprehend the language she is using. In this case, hearing demands comprehending—that is to say, leaping over the sounds and passing directly to the signification. Hearing becomes (as in many languages) synonymous with comprehending, therefore with *not* hearing. In the case of listening to the voice of an alto, however, I can perfectly well not comprehend the text in her song or aria clearly (it might be in German or Italian) or I can know the words by heart without paying the least attention to them because, in both cases, I am not asked to learn a text or gather information but to enjoy the voice, the pure and simple listening to the sonic intuition that it delivers. I listen to *the* Bergenza, *the* Schwarzkopf, almost without concern for what is sung, but because *she* sings it.[24] When the sound is at stake in such an intuition, no clear and distinct signification can subsume it in the role of concept. I could attempt to explain the pleasure I find in listening, to find arguments to blame or praise the song, to discuss the performance with other listeners, and therefore mobilize an indefinite number of concepts (those of music criticism, musicology, acoustics, etc.), but assuming I am not a philistine, I would never imagine that I could successfully include this sonic intuition within the limits of one or several concepts. Not that it pleases without concept, but rather because it calls for all of them, and calls for them because it saturates them all. Thus one listens to a saturated phenomenon.[25]

One can trace the gap just as clearly in the case of touch; for it happens that one touches in two distinct or even contrary manners. In one sense, to touch means to follow a surface in its twists and its turns in order to gain information about the form of an object—as when one fumbles about in the darkness in order to know where one is located and where objects are found, or, more exactly, what objects are there. In this case, one is not seeking intuition (which a flat or rough, hot or cold, convex or concave surface reveals) so much as a signification, comprehended even without anything being seen. I would like to know whether I have run up against a wall or a door to open, whether I am bumping against the corner of a table or perched on the back of a chair, where the light switch is, etc. In this darkness, I therefore do not first touch surfaces or materials; rather, I recognize objects, which is to say that I touch significations directly. Moreover, as soon as these significations are recognized (the room where I am located, the door through which I pass, the chair in which I sit, etc.), I no longer have to touch them by groping with an intuition that touches. Even in the darkness, I can see them directly and spot them in space. To touch here means to see a signification with closed eyes. With Braille, touching allows meaning to be read, significations to be reached, and objects to be known, with nothing being seen in intuition, therefore without intuition par excellence.

By contrast, when I rest my flesh on another's, one that I love because it does not resist me (a gesture that should not be reduced to the convention of the caress), when I touch the one I desire or the one who suffers and dies, I no longer have any signification to transmit, no information to communicate. Often the other does not want to, indeed, cannot hear any. I do not caress in order to know or to make known, as I grope around in order to orient myself in space and to identify objects. I caress in order to love, therefore in silence, in order to console and soothe, to excite and enjoy, therefore without objective signification, indeed, without identifiable or sayable signification. Thus touch does not manifest an object but a saturated phenomenon: an intuition that no concept will assume adequately but that will demand a multiplicity of them.[26]

We can also oppose two modes of phenomenalization in terms of taste. On the one hand, taste can serve only to distinguish two objects—for example, a poison (cocaine) from a food (sugar)—by limiting intuition to the maximum (one does not want to put oneself in danger by exposing oneself to too much) so as merely to anticipate a difference that is ultimately conceptual (two physical bodies, two chemical compositions) and can be expressed exhaustively by numbers and symbols. In this instance, even taste reaches what Descartes would call a clear and distinct idea: "it is so precise and sharply separated from all other perceptions that it contains within itself only what appears to one who considers it as he should."[27] Thus taste can give the intuition of objects and be exhausted in a concept. On the other hand, taste can be exercised over what escapes any concept: for example, when I taste a wine, especially if I participate in a blind tasting (e.g., in the somewhat silly game of recognizing and thereby distinguishing several wines), it is not a matter of leading a clear and confused intuition as quickly as possible back to a supposedly distinct concept. The definition that a chemist can quickly and accurately fix for it offers no response to the vintner's questions: Is this wine worthy of its name and of which one? To answer this question, one must not pass from intuition to the concept or substitute the latter for the former, but rather prolong the intuition to its maximum and plumb its depths. It is a matter not of making the taste of the wine pass away but of following it in time (Does it have a long finish, does it open out at the end?), in density (Does it have body, tannin, bouquet? etc.). It is even necessary to summon sight (its color) and smell (the aroma) so as to reach a precise and exact identification in the end (this grape, this harvest, this plot of land, this year, this producer), yet one that is nevertheless inexplicable in conceptual terms and not transmittable by information. The support provided by custom or by the oenological guide serves only to make it understood that one has not tasted the wine or, having mistasted it, that one perceived nothing or almost nothing. The vintner knows what he or she has tasted and can discuss it precisely with an equal, though without employing any concept, or else with an endless series of quasi-concepts, which take on meaning only after and only according to the intuition that is the sole and definitive authority. This intuition indicates its privilege in that one can never dispense with it. One must always return to it—from one year to the next, from one wine to another, from one moment of the same wine to another moment, it changes, obliging the description to be resumed, all the metaphors to be rediscovered. What is more, this intuition cannot be shared immediately from one taster to another. Accordingly, only one possibility remains to them: to speak of it endlessly—whence a paradoxical conviviality: that of the incommunicable and through it.[28] At issue is an idea that is at once clear and confused for whoever does not participate in wine culture, but clear and distinct for those in the know. In short, tasted wine has nothing objective about it, but appears according to a saturation of intuition, which incites a plurality of quasi-concepts and approximate significations.[29]

The same goes for smell. When I sense an odor of gas or a solvent, of humidity or fire, I am constrained to approach intuitively what could be described by models and parameters (graphs of temperature, pressure, humidity, etc.), if I had the time and the means. I then immediately transform the intuition into obvious significations (danger of flood, of fire, of an explosion, etc.) on which my attention and my activity are concentrated. I no longer remain with my nose in the air, drinking in the smell for pleasure. In other words, in these cases smell refers to a concept (or even a group of concepts) that is, in principle, able to grasp the intuitive totality. It does not merely refer to it, but disappears in it by letting itself be coded in rational equivalents. It is reducible to information concerning the state of things, objective phenomena. But the sense of smell also smells in an entirely different way: when someone with "a nose" for things takes a whiff, as do the experts whose sense of smell is so refined that they can combine fragrances into new perfumes, it is clear that no univocal concept, no signification, will ever succeed in designating this smell or distinguishing it. And yet if it is a success, the perfume thus produced can provoke an experience recognizable by thousands, to the point that even without a label one can recognize Chanel and distinguish it from Guerlain. Arbitrarily and naïvely alterable, the names that we impose on these perfumes do not identify them like a concept or a definition. On the contrary, only their firm and stable intuitions assure them an identifiable signification, although it never rescues them from the arbitrary. The names signify nothing, for the perfumes do not have a univocal signification any more than a definition. They draw their strength from their intuition, ever to be resumed and impossible to comprehend, which provokes new significations, both necessary and provisional, each time: "Perfumes there are . . . / Green as the prairies, fresh as a child's caress." The uniqueness of smell stems, no doubt, from the fact that it receives at the outset and almost always saturated phenomena, which can only in exceptional cases and after the fact be assigned to a concept. Before making itself sensed, "the myrrh, or musk, or amber" provokes significations without assignable object. They have straightaway "the expansiveness of infinite things."[30] As soon as its vapors rise, perfume makes something other than itself appear, a pure unforeseeable: "Languorous Asia, burning Africa, / And a *far* world, *defunct almost, absent*, / Within your aromatic forest stay! / As other souls on music drift away, / Mine, o my love! still floats upon your scent."[31] Thus the relation between common-law and saturated phenomena is reversed: though the former arise most often and from the outset, the latter, by virtue of their very banality, offer a more originary determination of phenomenality.

Thus considering each of the five senses opens a gap between the phenomenon as object and the phenomenon that "fills the soul beyond its capacity."[32] And in this gap saturated phenomena become visible. Thus the hypothesis of a saturation of the visible by intuition proves to be not only possible but inevitable: first, of course, in order to do justice to "exceptional intuitions" that saturate from the beginning all thinkable significations of certain phenomena that are nonobjective from the outset; but next and especially to do justice to the belated saturation of phenomena at first glance banal, yet more originally irreducible to an objective constitution. This hypothesis therefore has nothing optional about it, since the range of the "everyday banality"[33] that gives itself to appear calls for it and confirms it. Without admitting the hypothesis of saturated phenomena, either one cannot see certain phenomena that nevertheless appear banally, or one has to deny what one nevertheless sees. One impugns it, therefore, only at one's own risk. And is there a greater crime for a phenomenologist than not seeing or, worse, not accepting what one sees—in short, an inflicted or voluntary blindness?[34]

5

The question of fact is thus settled. It remains to consider the question of right: In making an exception to the conditions of common-law phenomenality, does the saturated phenomenon not give up the power to claim the name *phenomenon* legitimately?[35] In wanting to be free from the constraint of every phenomenological a priori, do we not find ourselves in the position of the "light dove" that "cleaving the air in her free flight, and feeling its resistance, might imagine that her flight would be still easier in empty space"?[36] Whoever wants to see too much imagines that he can cross all limits of experience; does he not by that very move abolish the conditions of experience and remain sunk in the illusion of seeing more and better, while in fact he no longer sees anything?

Although repeated by many different voices, this objection is not valid. The hypothesis of saturated phenomena never consisted in annulling or overcoming the conditions for the possibility of experience, but rather sought to examine whether certain phenomena contradict or exceed those conditions yet nevertheless still appear, precisely by exceeding or contradicting them. In other words, the experience of saturated phenomena proves, de facto, that the question is not confined to a choice between, on the one hand, an objective experience (in conformity with the conditions for the possibility of experience) and, on the other, a nonexperience of objects (contradicting all the conditions for the possibility of experience). A third option remains: the genuine and verifiable experience of a nonobjective phenomenon, one that would truly appear while contradicting the conditions for the possibility of objects of experience because it would arise with a nonobjective experience. Or, if one shudders at the formulation of a positively nonobjective experience, one can speak instead of the experience of what, contradicting the conditions of experience, appears in the mode of their saturation in a counter-experience.

This other option can already be detected in Kant's own argument, which is often invoked to deny it. How must conditions for the possibility of experience be understood? Obviously in terms of the famous formulation according to which "the *a priori* conditions of a possible experience in general are at the same time [*zugleich*] conditions for the possibility of *objects* of experience."[37] The first consequence that follows is this: the conditions for the possibility of experience concern only objects and therefore are valid only for phenomena understood as objects. For that matter, one can invoke a priori conditions in general and identify the conditions for experience in particular with those of the objects of experience only by referring to these very objects: namely, to that which alone can admit being thought in advance (by contrast to that which comes upon me without warning and counter to my foresight). But as all phenomena are not reducible to conditioned and foreseeable, produced and reproduced objects, a second consequence follows: contradicting the conditions for the possibility (of the objects) of experience means at the same time contradicting the condition of object for the phenomena in experience. It is therefore not enough to object that one risks contradicting the conditions for the possibility of experience in general by admitting nonobjective phenomena. For by what right can one speak of experience in general, or why should experience admit conditions? In other words, on what condition must experience always submit to conditions? Or if experience in general is identified with certain conditions, *what* experience is meant, and is *this* concept of experience self-evident?

It could be that one can legitimately argue against the so little critiqued use of the concept of experience by highlighting the presuppositions that ground it—the first of which might well be the prevalence of a "subject" (or whatever one wants to call it) supposed to know and always already present, whose priority alone can impose conditions on experience. These conditions are imposed only on condition that we cut experience in general to the measure of what the "subject" can receive. But this condition of all conditions is not self-evident, and here the modest, empirical showiness of the *tabula rasa* quite poorly hides the prideful assumption of a consciousness that, in order to remain empty, nevertheless stays always already in place a priori, so as to keep a transcendental posture even in this arrangement, in fact, *especially* in this arrangement.[38] This transcendental posture governs experience with a certain legitimacy only because it understands how to know solely persisting, certain, and constant objects—in short, present (*vorhanden*) beings whose presence is indisputable. Moreover, when one so quickly and so solemnly calls upon experience to be the judge and the last bastion of defense against other possibilities that phenomenality holds in reserve, one doubtlessly does so only to assure oneself of the enduring presence of being, which constitutes the sole privilege of objects. It could be that this assumption, far from closing the debate, sets its terms and therefore opens it. I ask: Is experience limited to the experience of objects, or does the constitution of objects define only one particular and restricted field of experience, which contradicts the immense banality of the intuitive saturation of phenomenality? Does it go without saying that presence in the present should determine the Being of all beings? Does it even go without saying that all that appears should first be? This empiricism remains thoroughly rooted in the most ponderous metaphysical presuppositions, and it does not dare to question them because it does not even suspect them (whereas Descartes, Kant, and Husserl, to speak only of the greatest, knew perfectly well that the object constitutes only a species, and not even the most usual, of what appears).[39] There is therefore no authority that could legitimate challenge or even dispute the hypothesis of saturated phenomena and the phenomenology of givenness that renders it thinkable. Nothing proves that experience is reducible to the conditions imposed on it by the concern for objectness and objectivity nor that, when I have the experience of what does not appear as an object, I experience nothing or that nothing appears if it does not appear as an object. A third way remains: to experience what contradicts the conditions of objective experience; to experience, at the very least, what this contradiction leaves always accessible and possible for us—the counter-experience itself.

One must, therefore, set out from this decisive point: the notion of experience is equivocal. It does not always aim at an object, nor is it always determined by a transcendental subject. It can also expose an *I* that is nontranscendental (and nonempirical), but given over to [*adonné à*] a phenomenon that cannot be constituted because it is saturated. Do the conditions for the possibility of experience miraculously disappear in this case? In no way. They remain in place, but insofar as they are contradicted and subverted by phenomena that are not limited by them, that do not bow to them, and that are no longer constituted by them as objects. The conditions for experience (of objects) themselves thus become all the more visible and clear as they are more evidently contradicted. Their contradiction does not annul phenomenality as such; it simply testifies that this phenomenality runs up against the finitude of the devoted (of the "subject"), who undergoes it without possessing the power to objectify it. Far from leading to the denial of finitude, the experience of the saturated phenomenon confirms it and attests it perfectly.[40] From the fact that the saturated phenomenon cannot be said univocally or defined adequately, one should not conclude that it is simply lacking—in short, that there are no such phenomena. This lack itself is not at all lacking. Instead, it raises a question that demands a specific response: either the concept is lacking because it simply is not a question of a phenomenon, or the concept is lacking because intuition exceeds it. To be sure, the lacking concept is not enough to prove that a saturated phenomenon rather than nothing gives itself. Yet this lack is enough to demand that one should investigate its status and, subsequently, that of a possible saturated phenomenon.[41] As a result, it is not a question of deciding on a whim if there is, if there must be, or if there can be saturated phenomena in general. When confronted with this phenomenon, it is a question of seeing whether I can describe it as an object (a common-law phenomenon whose intuition is contained within the concept) or whether I must describe it as a saturated phenomenon (whose intuition exceeds the concept). This affair is not decided abstractly and arbitrarily. In each case, attentiveness, discernment, time, and hermeneutics are necessary. But what else is there in philosophy, and are we still philosophers if we refuse this work?

6

A question remains: Even if one admits the legitimacy of such a contradiction of the conditions for experience, what can it still describe, since it no longer describes objects? If it permits the description of nothing, of what phenomenon are we speaking and what phenomenology are we practicing?

Without going back over analyses conducted elsewhere,[42] I would like to recall briefly the chief characteristic of the experience of the saturated phenomenon: it is always a contrary experience, or rather, one that always counteracts. In contradicting the conditions for the experience of an object, such an experience does not contradict itself by forbidding the experience of anything at all. Rather, it does nothing but counteract experience understood in the transcendental sense as the subsuming of intuition under the concept. It is confined to counteracting the counteracting of intuition by the concept. Thus, far from counteracting all experience, it liberates the possibility of an unconditioned experience of giving intuition. Once again, one should not object that an experience without conditions would become impossible and untenable, since it would be a self-contradiction. The issue is precisely to decide whether the conditions for the experience of objects are always and at the same time the conditions for all experience in general, or whether, by contrast, experience can sometimes (indeed, banally) cross the conditions of objectification. In other words, nothing suggests that the possibility of experience should be equivalent to the possibility of experiencing objects or to what a transcendental subject can synthesize, constitute, and maintain in an objective condition. That experience might also contradict the conditions for the possibility of objects means only this: experience does not always or only give access to objects, but also possibly to nonobjective phenomena. That experience is not limited to the field of objectivity does not suggest that it is *self*-contradictory, but only that it contradicts the conditions for the experience of *objects* by a transcendental subject, therefore that it can sometimes (indeed banally) *contradict its transcendental meaning*. According to this hypothesis, experience would unfurl as contrary, or rather as *counteractive*. The counter-experience does not contradict the possibility of experience, but to the contrary frees it insofar as it counteracts its assignation to an object, therefore its subjection to the transcendental subject.

Henceforth the finitude of the transcendental subject (and therefore of its intuition) is not transposed or declined automatically in a finitude of univocally objective experience but is suffered and experienced as such in the contradiction that the excess of intuition imposes on it with each saturated phenomenon. It imposes on the transcendental subject that it must confess itself a devoted. Such a counter-experience can be recognized by several specific characteristics.

(1) Contradicted by the excess of intuition, intentionality can no longer aim at a signification (or a concept) that would permit it to constitute an object. It no longer reaches any intentional "object," because what it reaches no longer has the status of object. Intentionality is therefore turned back on itself, no longer indicating the signification of a definite object but the limits of its own aim, disqualified precisely by intuitive excess. I always see, but what I see no longer attests anything; rather, it measures the range of my disappointed vision. I no longer achieve any vision, but I experience the limits of my sight: "on an island charged by air / not with visions but with sight."[43] As it undergoes the trial of itself inasmuch as refused and rebuked by intuition, the intentional aim less reaches an object to signify or conceptualize than finds itself affected by the rebound off an ungraspable objective, one that no concept permitted it to foresee or foretell. Affected in return by what it intended, intentionality rediscovers itself displaced, beside itself, "moved" (like a rugby scrum by the enemy scrum), in short, *altered*.

(2) Counter-experience is marked by the saturation of every concept by intuition. This saturation can, of course, be translated by a positive bedazzlement,[44] but not always or necessarily. Or rather, bedazzlement can itself be conjugated in *disappointment*: not a shortfall of all significa-tion but the fulfillment of another signification besides that intentionally aimed at, a sort of displaced fulfillment, at an unforeseeable distance from the fulfillment that intention awaited and foresaw; not so much a nothing as an unforeseen signification, a seen not fore-seen by the foresight of any object. Such a disappointment, provoked by no lack but by a displace-ment of overabundant intuition, proposes to fill *another* concept, one not foreseen, indeed, an unknown and not yet identified concept; for what it is worth, this characterizes the scientific attitude (at least in the case of a revolution of scientific paradigms).[45]

(3) Above all, the saturation of the aim by intuition can be signaled by the very perturbation induced by the reception of its excess. In the case of saturated phenomena, I no longer see anything by an excess of light; I no longer hear anything by an excess of sound; I no longer sense, taste, or smell anything by an excess of excitations—at least nothing objectifiable, realizable as a thing other than myself and able to be looked at as placed before me. Here it must be emphasized that these excesses never face the danger of being illusory—for example, of imagining there to be excess of intuition while there is "nothing." This is so, first, because the (supposed) illusion of an intuitive excess becomes at once an intuitive excess of the illusion itself, since I undoubtedly undergo this excess (it alters me, per-turbs me, disappoints me, etc.) as genuine and verifiable. If I believe I see too much light, even if no excess of "objective" light can be found,[46] I do indeed undergo an excess. Second (and the excess is verified precisely for this reason), the ordeal of excess is actually attested by the resistance, pos-sibly the pain, that it imposes on the one who receives it, and this resis-tance can no more be disputed than one can doubt undergoing one's own pain (for we "feel our pain" without any doubt or separation). This *resis-tance* suggests a wholly other sense of objectivity: objectivity would no longer mean access to an objective that is targeted, foreseen, and con-structed according only to the demands and possibilities of intelligibility, such that "object" ends up designating precisely what does *not resist* the cognitive intention but yields to it without offering any resistance whatso-ever, to the point that the object designates the alienation of the thing from itself and its seizure by method. Inversely, counter-experience is an issue of the obstinate resistance of what refuses itself to knowledge that is transparent without remainder, of what withdraws into its obscure origin (the unseen, unheard, untouched, etc.), as is sometimes the case with the

resistance of another gaze to my gaze, which marks the irreducibility of this gaze to my own. What we call "meeting" the gaze of the other [autrui] (maintaining eye contact) is in fact equivalent to deadening the blow, to challenging the other's power to annihilate, and to returning the weight of an aim.[47]

Thus counter-experience can be defined precisely according to the *notae* alteration, disappointment, and resistance. The experience counteracting, or more precisely, the contrariety that the saturated phenomenon imposes on the one who undergoes it *etiam invito*,[48] is not only imposed on the side of the experience of objects but resists the reproach of subjectivism by its very overcoming of objectivity. That is, the devoted verifies itself infinitely more when face to face with a saturated phenomenon than before an object, since it experiences itself as such in the counter-experience that resists it. Resistance can go so far as to expose me to a danger, the danger of seeing too much [*l'oeil en trop*], hearing too much, sensing too much, tasting too much, smelling too much. This resistance imposes itself as suffering, and what does one feel more than one's pain?

7

Such resistance can and should be experienced in a couple of senses. (1) It can be experienced as the ordeal of what gives itself in the encounter with finitude, by a definitive excess of intuition over every concept that I could impose on it. In this case, resistance translates the effect of the phenomenon on whoever sees it without, however, objectifying it. It is a matter of the reverential fear of the finite before what surpasses it, frightening and attracting it at the same time. Respect (for the good use of my free will, for the moral law, for the face of the other [autrui], for holiness, etc.), the sublime, or enjoyment—all these, which are always accompanied by some suffering or humiliation, are described in this way. This resistance recoils by definition before what it glimpses, precisely because it recognizes its excess. (2) The same resistance can take the form of denying what gives itself to sight, not because we see it poorly [*voit mal*] (indistinctly or doubtfully), but precisely because we see it well [*voit bien*] (clearly if not distinctly, indubitably) and this vision pains us [*fait mal*]. In other words, my resistance does not so much undergo as it represses what doubtlessly affects it precisely because this affection becomes an unbearable suffering. In seeing what I see, I also see the obligatory darkness created by the all too clear excess of light. This obligatory darkness spills over the one who sees the truth because it imposes on him a dark obligation: that of re-vising his own self to the (measureless) measure of the saturating excess of intuition. That is, since the saturated phenomenon cannot be reduced to the measure of objectivity, it demands of the one it affects that she see it and admit it in its very excess, without the security of a concept. It therefore demands of the affected that she give herself over [de s'adonner], let herself be (re-)made, (re-)defined, and, so to speak, (un-)measured by the measure of its own excess. Instead of summing up the given within the limits of my own finitude (of my concept), I experience the obscure obligation of letting myself conform to (and by) the excess of intuition over every intention that my gaze could oppose to it. This demand can no longer merely provoke a bedazzlement, a disappointment, or a resistance; rather, it incites a second-order resistance (resistance to the resistance, in order to hide from it or to evade it), to the point of a recoiling, a denial, a refusal. It is possible that the intuitive evidence of the saturated phenomenon might not produce the recognition of its truth or its disclosure, but to the contrary and quite logically, the impossibility of receiving it, therefore the possibility of rejecting it. The disclosure of the saturated phenomenon might forbid its reception because, by dint of excess and bedazzlement, its evidence seems to accuse as well as clarify, challenge as well as illuminate. By dint of accusing the traits of the phenomenon, the truth appears to accuse the one who receives it.

To do justice to this ambivalence, Saint Augustine did not hesitate to offer a radical redefinition of the essence of truth: to its straightforward phenomenality (in the Greek sense), in which the more evidence discloses the thing the more its truth is disclosed, he added and perhaps opposed a counteracting phenomenality, in which the more evidence discloses the thing the more access to it is shut, the more it becomes the object of a refusal, indeed, a scandal. Object? Of course, in the sense of the objective around which denial focuses, the objective to be destroyed precisely because it offers no object but exceeds objectivity and objectness. Here, where the truth concerns the unveiling not of a *common*-law phenomenon (one that is objectifiable within the limits of my finitude) but of a saturated phenomenon, one has to pass from the *veritas lucens*, the truth that shows and demonstrates [*montre et démontre*] in a straightforward fashion, to a *veritas redarguens*, a truth that shows [*montre*] only inasmuch as it remonstrates [*remontre*] with the one who receives it. This "remonstrating" truth inevitably accuses whoever challenges it or whoever excuses him- or herself from it. Thus the criteria for reaching the truth are modified: the love of excess is substituted for the evidence of disclosure. Love (or hate) becomes the manner of truth: "Truth is loved, [but] in such a way that those who love something else would like it if what they love were the truth, and because they do not like to be deceived, they also do not want to be shown that they are deceived. And so they hate the truth for the sake of whatever it is they love instead of the truth. They love the truth insofar as it illuminates [*lucens*], but hate it when it turns its light upon them [*redarguens*]."[49] This text does not concern the demand to love the truth already seen or even the requirement to love the truth in order to see it.[50] Rather, it concerns loving the truth so as to bear it, without faltering or condemning oneself to bear the cruel clarity that its radiance poses and imposes on whoever risks gazing at it and the charge it imposes on him or her, "because glory overwhelms who sees it, when it does not glorify him [*porque la gloria oprime al que la mira cuando nole glorifica*]."[51]

Before any moral or religious sense, it is first of all a matter of a strictly phenomenological necessity. The bedazzlement and the disappointment of intentionality by the saturated phenomenon impose on the aim the necessity of confronting the excess of intuition directly—without the mediation of the concept or the screen of the object that it allows to be constituted. This excess that pours itself out over my gaze without intermediary affects it, constrains it, and wounds it. This can, indeed almost inevitably *must*, lead the gaze to refuse what shows itself [*se montre*] only by remonstrating [*en remontrant*] with this gaze and what gives itself without excuse. This *veritas redarguens* turns its merciless evidence upon and therefore against the one who sees it (or rather can no longer see it). It can therefore be defined as a light counter to my sight, a light that goes up against my (fore-)sight, rendering it confused and me along with it. I become confused before this light, in all senses of the term: My sight loses its clarity and grows blurred; I lose my confidence, my good sense, and my security—to such a degree that this truth that accuses me of untruth can indeed be called a counter-truth. But here counter-truth does not at all mean the contrary of truth or the simple lie that I could oppose to it, but *the truth that counteracts the one whom it affects*, me. It counteracts me; for if I am to see it without danger, it requires of me that I love it and lend myself to its radiance by conforming myself to its purity.

8

It now becomes possible to broach a final difficulty, one that bears on the one whom a saturated phenomenon affects. The objections often challenge the devoted by privileging the "subject" (quite possibly "without subjectivity") or, inversely, "subjectivity" (sometimes "without subject"). Often they consider it a subject less or more transcendental or, inversely, more or less empirical, according to their preference for one or the other title. These approximations indicate the difficulty of thinking "who comes after the subject," if not our powerlessness to do so I will limit myself to two basic remarks.

(1) The distinction between "subject" and "subjectivity," a hazy one at best, loses all pertinence as soon as the phenomenon concerned, by hypothesis, can no longer be constituted as an object. Therefore, if there is a saturated phenomenon, it will not affect a "subject" or a "subjectivity," precisely because both one and the other function only in a metaphysical situation, where it is a question of constituting and not of admitting an affection, a question of constituting objects, phenomena poor in intuition or common-law phenomena. What or whom a saturated phenomenon affects no longer precedes it, conditions it, and constitutes it, and therefore cannot claim any "subjectivity" or any "subject."[52] (2) A fortiori, one cannot play on the opposition between a transcendental "subject" and an empirical "me." This is so first because the givenness of the phenomenon (which renders it nonobjective, but perhaps also determines it even when it seems objective) makes it always come upon me, by its own advent [*arrivage*], before, without, or counter to the conditions for possibility that the transcendental instance would impose on it.[53] In principle, a phenomenology of the given frees (or tries to free) the phenomenon from all transcendental subjection. Furthermore, an empirical "me" has no meaning or legitimacy except in opposition to a transcendental *I* that it balances and whose shadow it extends. If one is lacking, the other disappears. As I observed above, the supposed empiricity of such a "me" remains doubtful so long as the concept of experience that it puts into operation remains essentially burdened by a transcendental pretension: that of receiving the empirical given without also receiving itself in this givenness, hence of waiting for it and preceding it. Consequently, it seems to me to be wiser to renounce hypotheses that are as imprecise as they are metaphysically charged. To the novelty of the hypothesis of the saturated phenomenon must correspond, at least as an attempt, a new determination of what or who it affects.

I suggest that here we consider anew the figure of the *witness*.[54] In order to focus on what is essential, let me restate the paradox: the witness sees the phenomenon, but he does not know what he sees and will not comprehend what he saw. He sees it indisputably, in perfect clarity, with all requisite intuition, often with an intuitive excess that profoundly and enduringly affected him, possibly wounded him. He knows what he saw and knows it so well that he stands ready to witness it again and again, often counter to his immediate interests. Witnessing becomes for him a second nature, a job, and a social function, which can end up rendering him tiresome, if not odious to those who have to deal with his "obligation to remember." And for all that, the witness still does not ever succeed in saying, comprehending, or making us comprehend what he saw. Most of the time, he does not even claim to do so, indeed, he ends up plunging into silence. This is, nevertheless, its own explanation, for what he saw remains withdrawn from the complete comprehension of the event, a comprehension that the concept alone could secure. Yet the witness precisely does not have available the concept or concepts that would be adequate to the intuition unfurling over him. He develops *his* vision of things, *his* story, *his* details, and *his* information—in short, he tells *his* story, which never achieves the rank of history. Most of the time, he is wise enough not to claim to produce a global interpretation and gladly leaves that to the labor of the historians. In short, the witness plays his part in the interval between, on the one hand, the indisputable and incontestable excess of lived intuition and, on the other, the never-compensated lack of the concepts that would render this experience an objective experience—in other words, that would make it an object. The witness, who knows what he saw and that he saw it, does not comprehend it by one or more adequate concepts. As a result, he undergoes an affection of the event and remains forever late with regard to it. Never will he (re-)constitute it, which distinguishes him from the engineer, the inventor, or, to use a more recent term, the "designer," who produces objects because he comprehends them in terms of their concept before turning to any actual intuition, indeed without recourse to it at all. And in *this* sense it could be said that the "designer," by contrast to the witness, accomplishes the "creation of events." This oxymoron becomes thinkable only as the denegation of the saturated phenomenon by the power of technology, which attempts to produce objects even where the event unrolls.

Described in this way, the witness escapes the majority of the criticisms, however contradictory, that are often addressed to what or whom a saturated phenomenon affects. (a) Does it remain sunk in pure passivity, reduced to recording the given and submitting to the monstrous excess of intuition? Obviously not, since the witness does not stop thinking this intuitive excess by having recourse to all the concepts available to her, in a labor that can be called an infinite hermeneutic. Writing the history of the historians, but also constructing her own identity (or that of others) by the narrative of her individual story, implies an ongoing effort that, remaining without an end that concepts could set, requires no less the activity of response—the response by concepts delayed behind the precedence of intuitions. The devoted is in no way passive, since by her response (hermeneutic) to the call (intuitive), she, and she alone, allows what gives itself to become, partially but really, what shows itself.

(b) Does the devoted, by contrast, exercise a spontaneous activity without admitting it, thus betraying the unexamined persistence of the transcendental attitude? Obviously not, since the witness never exercises the transcendental privilege of fixing conditions for experience in advance, by formatting it within the limits of objectivity and objectness. Her activity always remains that of response, determined and even decided by the advent [*arrivage*, event] of intuition. This responsive posture imposes on the witness not only that she receive herself from what she receives, without any advance warning, precaution, or patrimony, but that she remain always in radical dependence on the event that gave her to herself. The figure of the *hostage*, so often criticized as excessive and hyperbolic, here finds its legitimacy: de facto and de jure, the witness is herself only through an other [*un autre*], more interior to herself than the most intimate within her—more her than she herself, and forever because always already.

(c) Does this figure of the witness abandon phenomenological rigor by importing ethical or theological thinking? This reproach raises more questions than it resolves. First, it presupposes that ethics and theology escape strict rationality or are confined to derivative uses of it. Arguing this way, one fails to see that rationality not only holds sway over all domains but often arises or flows forth where thought did not or no longer expects it. What right does one have to rule out the possibility that the model of rationality might migrate from mathematics and physics to biology or information, but also to the poetic word, the ethical demand, or theological revelation? Next, who can fix limits for phenomenology and by what right? One thing is clear: the real phenomenologists, I mean those who actually made visible phenomena heretofore unseen, never stopped crossing these limits, or rather, ignoring them, so that after them phenomenology became, each time, infinitely more powerful than it had been before. It could be that one defends the limits of phenomenology, its orthodoxy, and its past when one has simply given up practicing it. But perhaps involving oneself in phenomenology does not consist in involving oneself in phenomenological doctrines, their history, and their archaeology, but in what phenomenologists themselves are involved in—the things themselves, that is to say, in the phenomena and their description. As for deciding if (and which) saturated phenomena actually give themselves, how could one decide this for someone else? And yet, one could surmise that some such phenomena impose themselves on everyone—above all, the erotic phenomenon.

—*Translated by Jeffrey L. Kosky*

Faith and Reason

What opposition seems more evident than that between faith and reason, between believing and knowing, between believing without certainty and knowing from certain science? If one adds that it is "modern science" facing Christian faith, then the dichotomy imposes itself beyond dispute, ready for all the weekly reports, for all the prefabricated debates and ideological arguments. Yet one must be on one's guard against this evidence, for by a strange reversal the authoritative argument in this banal debate today inevitably is situated on the side of "science," object of the most unwavering faith for its pious, whereas on the other side doubt, a critical sense, and an attitude of research remain the prerogative of "believers" (admittedly at times involuntarily). In fact, as the best philosophers of science have demonstrated, there is nothing more fragile than this opposition. The first task of even a merely honest and informed mind would be to show it to be an unacceptable artifice, for faith has its reasons and scientific reason has its beliefs.

1

First, Christians themselves would have to begin by realizing that their faith cannot and must not in any way do without reason, even less pride itself on any lack of reason. Believing without reason actually comes down to scorning him in whom we claim to believe. This is so, first, because, as St. Peter underlines, we must be "ready to make a defense [απολογια] to anyone who demands an accounting [λογος] for the hope that is in" us (1 Peter 3:15). To believe without knowing how or what does not increase faith but leads it astray, maybe even ridicules it. The point of "giving an account" here actually is not to quarrel with the interlocutor face to face, as in an ideological battle, but to render justice to him in whom we say we believe, in him and in his high reason, for the believer will have to "give an account [αποδωσουσιν λογον] to him who stands ready to judge the living and the dead" (1 Peter 4:5). We will have to answer to Christ for what we will have answered humans on his behalf and "for every careless word you utter, you will have to give an account [αποδω-σουσιν περι αυτου λογον] on the day of judgment" (Matt. 12:36). What we will have said of Christ before humans, Christ will say of us before the Father.

Immediately this raises another question: Why does God expect us to speak of him with arguments, reasons, and rationality? Does God not know better than any of us that we can neither comprehend him nor even reason correctly about him, without taking into consideration our fear before those who do not accept him? Yet if God is God, he knows all that and more; thus if he asks us to speak with reason, without doubt he has good reasons for asking it of us. What do we know about these reasons? We know at least this: Christian religion announces the death and resurrection of a human being who was God and still is. This man Jesus Christ is called the *Logos*, the Word, and hence Reason. Even the paradox of his crucifixion, which contradicts "the wisdom of the world," remains still a *logos*, "the *logos* of the cross," which opposes a different *sophia* to the wisdom of the world, namely, the "wisdom of God" (1 Cor. 1:18–25). When St. Paul debates the Athenians on the Areopagus, it is in the name of the *logos* of him who by right carries the name of *Logos*. And when he announces the foolishness of the Cross against secular Corinthian culture, he still speaks according to a *logos*, because he speaks in the name of the *Logos* and according to the *Logos*. Even and especially when someone faithful to Christ confronts the rationality of the world, he or she confronts it with reasons and for the love of wisdom. "To witness" can designate making an argument as much as giving one's life, to philosophize as much as suffering martyrdom. Thus the first Christian to have claimed the title of "philosopher," Justin, that Palestinian from Nablous who during the second century discussed so serenely with a Jew, Trypho, was also a martyr. Moreover, he carries the admirable title of "philosopher and martyr." And the final giant among the Greek Fathers (but also the most difficult), Maximus the Confessor, who achieved the brilliant Christological and Trinitarian synthesis in the seventh century, which had been in progress since the council of Chalcedon, also suffered martyrdom: in order to silence his arguments, one had to cut out his tongue. Concepts can also bear witness.

The announcement of the Word come to reveal God in his humanity to humanity deploys [*déploie*] a new and superior reason, which can only be spread [*se déployer*] with reasons. The *logos* is not optional for Christians, since he from whom they take their name bears the title of *Logos*. For better or for worse, they must resume the Greeks' acquisition, their *logos*, and hence their philosophy and their sciences (as they will later do with Roman law). Besides, as St. Augustine firmly emphasizes, Christianity flatly refuses comparison with the ancient religions (the *theologia civilis* or the *theologia fabulosa*), accepting comparison only with the *theologia naturalis*, the effort toward a rational knowledge of the divine by the study of celestial motions. And, facing the theological cosmology of the ancients, Augustine claims a true knowledge of divinity for his Christian faith, as the only correct sense of the term *theologia*, which is pagan in origin and thus suspect. Since it is a matter of truth, "it is with the philosophers that the comparison must be made [*cum philosophis est habenda conlatio*]." For us strangely, for him obviously, faith thus seems first a matter of philosophy, since he concludes, "the true philosopher is someone who loves God [*verus philosophus est amator Dei*]."[1] Of course, the ultimate destiny of philosophy, the science of being that later became "metaphysics," makes its identification with the science of God impossible (even though in the formulation of *philosophia christiana* it would last at least until Erasmus). But one thing will not disappear: the duty of Christian theology to rationality—a duty that at times it has fulfilled too well, at the risk of reducing the revealed Word to a system of concepts. Yet this duty has nevertheless permitted the development of a *theo-logy*, a knowledge about God through reasons coming from God. We take this accomplishment for granted, but all things considered, it is achieved *as such* only in the Christian religion. Yet both cases confirm that faith has a duty to reason in regard to itself.

Certainly, one will object, it is not a matter of faith's duty to reason with regard to itself but a matter of its rationality in regard to reason itself, the type of reason deployed in the sciences. And how could one not think of several conflicts that have marked history, from Galileo to Darwin, to stick only with the most legendary cases?

This manner of putting the question calls forth three remarks. (1) First, the most obvious: no conflict could have broken out between this or that science or this or that decision of the common Magisterium of the Church if both had not been situated on a single shared ground, precisely that of reason, to the point that one must sometimes wonder whether this ground was really shared, whether the encounter was even legitimate. Did the Magisterium have to defend a particular cosmology against a different one—and besides, is that really what happened? Did Galileo really contest the rules for the interpretation of the Scriptures—and did he do so in full consciousness? Contemporary history and philosophy of science have made us much more prudent about these questions than our predecessors were, and one can reasonably assume that the two camps themselves were lacking epistemological prudence. (2) A second comment follows from this: the history of the Christian faith stands out less for its omissions than for its often decisive contributions to the birth and growth of the sciences. Without the collection and transmission of ancient texts, the foundation of the universities, the autonomization of the "arts" in these universities as independent from theology, the impetus given in the schools to mathematics, astronomy, and physics, and so forth. The Christian faith, precisely because it first had to apply rationality to itself, could not keep it to itself but extended it into the world and human society. (3) Finally, even the conflicts or at least tensions that today oppose the Magisterium of the Catholic Church to certain developments in biology and the neurosciences have something rational at stake: How is one to reconcile the freedom to beget with the humanity of begetting, how determine the humanity of a biological life, how recognize the end of a human life, how guarantee the identity of the individual against the menace of cloning? These questions are doubtlessly vexing and continue to be divisive, yet who could disregard them and abandon them to irrationalism? To the contrary, they oblige us, rather, to complicate the models and the technical protocols accepted at present, in order to reach a rationality that would be more sophisticated, more flexible, hence higher.

2

A higher reason—what does that mean? If one intends to ask the rationality of contemporary sciences to manage to think about God, that would be an absolutely impossible demand: first, for the sciences, which never claim absolute knowledge of the world or of its possibly divine dimension (at least one reasonably can hope so today); then for faith, since one would thus do harm to the transcendence of God, who is known only by not being known—"such is the summit of human knowledge in regard to God: knowing that it does not know him, for as much as it knows what God is, that even exceeds all that which we understand of him [*illud quod Deus est, omne ipsum quod de eo intelligimus, excedere*]."[2]

But could we think this higher reason in a different sense, one more precise and rigorous? This might be possible by hearing anew one of Nietzsche's rather enigmatic aphorisms: "You say 'I' and you are proud of this word. But greater is what you do not want to believe—your flesh and its reason [*dein Leib und seine grosse Vernunft*], which does not say 'I,' but makes it."[3] This strange formula raises two questions. What is meant by "the flesh"? And how is it partially linked to a "great reason"? Flesh does not mean the body, which, extended in the space of the world, is found there perceived or rather sensed, but it means this other and unique body, mine, which alone senses the bodies of the world. My flesh senses bodies that themselves do not sense. It can do so by virtue of another privilege: it senses everything else only by sensing itself sensing. But how could this flesh possibly surpass the *I* and its reason?

In order to understand this, one must consider what the *I* knows, this "proud" ego of modern metaphysics. It knows with certainty because it remembers from experience only what it can keep of it or foresee in it, abandoning all of the rest as unknowable. Descartes identifies as order and measure what reason can so grasp; today we would call it models and parameters. But only phenomena of extension, of quantity, and hence of exteriority offer such material to certain knowledge. We call "objects" the kind of phenomena for which intuition responds in advance to the expectations of the concept, without filling it to the brim. A method of constitution and of production of objects thus corresponds to each science. And modern rationality is ceaselessly deployed in enlarging the number and the range of such objects. Not only does it constitute them intellectually and realize them experimentally, but it produces and reproduces them technically, in such a way that a new world of technical objects has sprung up under our increasingly less surprised eyes. More and more, this new world covers over and replaces the ancient world of things. This change has defined a new common rationality of reason, which is also extended to nature, of which we have become "masters and possessors."[4]

This success and uninterrupted process (for each crisis of science becomes the occasion for a new technological leap) nevertheless leaves us perplexed, even anxious. We suspect that the world is constituted of objects only from afar, only at a distance, only at a distance in the remote region where objects face us, precisely as the objective of our aim. In effect, we know objects as we produce them—at a distance. But, living among them, we sense them, and in this way, inevitably, we first feel ourselves. This felt immediacy, precisely the flesh, concerns what is closest, whereas the rationality of objects concerns what is furthest away. In the immediacy of feeling, we experience without distance; in that case the distant knowledge of objects no longer helps us: we do not face each other but sense what we are and are what we sense the closest, hence the knowledge of pain and pleasure, death and birth, hunger and thirst, sleep and fatigue, but also of hatred and love, communion and division, justice and violence. We know very clearly that the common rationality of objects knows nothing and can do nothing about what is closest to us.

In *this* sense, Heidegger could legitimately say that "science does not think." He should have added that it has claimed this as its privilege: science does not think; it measures and orders in the form of modeling, of parameter, and of objectivation. Technology produces what is understood in this way and vice versa. By contrast, only the flesh reaches nonobjective phenomena, those where an excess of intuition saturates the limits of the concept already known and always foreseen—for example, it reaches: (a) the event, which occurs, unpredictable despite its supposed impossibility; (b) the idol, which fascinates the gaze while offending it; (c) the flesh of this other who eroticizes mine; (4) the face of any other, who imposes respect upon me and asks me to save him. No one can pretend to ignore such phenomena. Nevertheless, no one can conceive of them according to the rationality of objects. Before them, I cannot simply say *I*, constitute them, foresee them, and hold them at a distance in front of me. To the contrary, they are phenomena saturated with intuition, which make me and unmake me. The flesh exposes me to what *I* cannot constitute as an object. It surpasses my objectifying rationality. It really does point to a "greater reason."

Who can practice such "great reason" today? This is a fair question, except that one should rather ask: Who must practice it and cannot dispense with it? Response: All those for whom the humanity of humans, the naturalness of nature, the justice of the polis, and the truth of knowledge remain absolute requirements. That is to say everyone, or at least all those who believe these things still to be possible—or more exactly, all those of us who still want to believe in them. A second difficulty must be confronted more urgently than this first one (objectivity), one linked to it but cruder: namely, nihilism. One often claims that it is enough to complement the science of objects with a supposed "soul supplement." This is a simplistic illusion, since what is meant by the term *soul* has been rendered inaccessible by objectivity: henceforth, what we can no longer know as a certain object, thus at a distance, can only be thought as a kind of value. Yet in this time of nihilism, the highest values are being devalued. There is no point in "defending" the vanished soul, nor any of the supposed values, for this reverts to recognizing an intrinsic weakness in what it is a matter of defending or attacking, as value, completely dependent on whoever evaluates or devalues it. In any case, nihilism expands its dark sun by insinuating into each of us this disarming question: "What's the use?" What is the point of the humanity of humans, the naturalness of nature, the justice of the polis, and the truth of knowledge? Why not rather their opposites, the dehumanization of humans to improve humanity, the systematic sapping of nature to develop the economy, injustice to render society more efficient, the absolute empire of information-distraction to escape the constraints of the true? These counter-possibilities are no longer a phantasm or a prediction, since the sole program of the ideologies that have dominated history since the beginning of the last century has been to put them into effect. These ideologies ignore all flesh; hence, literally, they no longer sense themselves, and, no longer sensing, they accomplish nihilism without even knowing it.

Reason, as we know it, thus suffers two limitations that are linked to each other and can become real dangers. To reduce experience to objectifiable phenomena and to ignore our flesh can lead to the devaluation of all values and to ceding to ideology. Hence it is today no longer a matter of saving reason from obscurantism or from superstition, but of saving it from its own dangers. It is no longer a matter of giving reason to all things, but of giving reason for rationality. In this situation, one must no longer wait for a miracle or for a "god" to save us (as if he were not already come). It is necessary that all those who can act, that is to say, first, who can think and think otherwise, do so.

3

What can we do in the present situation of reason (for there is only one, communal and not optional)? All who think can contribute to giving explanations for reason [*rendre sa raison à la raison*] in their own way, scientists as well as poets, wise men as well as politicians, the poor as much as the rich, all religious traditions and all cultural heritages, each for its own part, original and indispensable.

What kind of contribution can and should Christians make to this accord? Here, as in any other case, Christians cannot bring anything other than what they have received: Christ. "For I received [παρελαβον] from the Lord what I also handed on [παρεδωκα] to you, that the Lord Jesus on the night when he was betrayed [παρεδιδετο] took a loaf of bread, and when he had given thanks, he broke it and said: 'This is my body [given] for you, do this in remembrance of me'" (1 Cor. 11:23–24). He who gives and delivers himself as our bread belongs to all. Christians do not own Christ as a property, but as first recipients they must in turn hand him on to others, at least to those who really want him (for people do not love God very much). Receiving the glory of Christ, that is the burden and the test for all, not only for "Christianity" understood as the avant-garde of humanity's proletariat; every one of us, without exception and in some manner or other, has had, must, or will have to explain him- or herself to Christ, whether believing in him or not. Not to believe in Christ is already to respond to him. Christians' contribution to "great reason" hence does not come from them, but from him from whom they draw, like a nickname, even their own name. What does Jesus Christ, therefore, deliver to all, everywhere and always?

A nonobjective and saturated phenomenon without equal, one that would remain inaccessible without him—love or the erotic phenomenon: "God is love" (1 John 4:16), and "You shall love the Lord your God with all your heart, and with all your soul, and with all your strength, and with all your mind; and your neighbor as yourself" (Luke 10:27; citing Deut. 6:5 and Lev. 19:18). In this way those who love God live in him, namely, those who love each other (1 John 4:20). This announcement becomes good news for us for innumerable reasons, and all the time in the world would not be suffice to proclaim or to celebrate it.

Among those reasons is this: only this love can give access to the "great reason." The love revealed by the Word, hence by the *Logos*, is deployed as a *logos*, hence as a rationality. And a rationality in full right, because it allows us to reach the closest and the most internal phenomena, those experienced by the flesh which intuition saturates. If the Revelation of Christ had shown only that, namely, that love has its reason, a forceful, original, simple reason, which sees and says what common reason is missing and does not see, it would already have saved, if not humans, at least their reason. But Christ has not only shown the logic of love, he has demonstrated and proven it in facts and acts by his passion and his resurrection. Since the coming and the presence of the *Logos* among us, love has not only found its logic, it has accomplished it "all the way to the end [εἰς τέλος]" (John 13:1). For "grace [*charité*] and truth came through Christ Jesus" (John 1:17), and we have seen him, see him, and will see him, at once and indissociably, "saturated with love and with truth" (John 1:14; trans. modified). Love does not only give itself in truth in the gesture of Christ; one must go to the point of turning this proposition upside down: in Christ, love manifests itself as the final and first truth, the one that makes all the others possible and recapitulates them all at the end of time: "I am the way, the truth" (John 14:6). One can challenge this claim as an illusion without future, denounce it as a presumptuous delusion, or even believe it to be a revolution that corrupts youth. In all these cases, Christians can say nothing other than that, because they have received it as it is.

What kind of reason does the logic of love deploy? Let me limit myself here to indicating some of these laws. (a) First, certainty. Love "excuses all, loves all, hopes all, supports all" (1 Cor. 13:7). This means that love always loves without condition, never on condition, in particular not on the condition of reciprocity. In order to love it does not require return on its investment, because it enjoys an unheard-of privilege in regard to any economy: a love one refuses or scorns, in short, a love that is not returned, remains no less a perfect love accomplished without remainder; a gift refused remains no less a given gift. It only depends on love in fact loving: since the creation, since the cross, this unconditioned and unilateral precedence of love over being. (b) Second, possibility. For love nothing is impossible, especially the ability to love without regard for persons, to the point of loving one's enemy (Luke 6:27–35), precisely because for love only love itself is necessary for loving. God is characterized by the privilege of the impossibility of impossibility; it is even one of his properties, a privilege comparable to no other: "What is impossible for mortals, is not impossible for God; for God all things are possible" (Mark 10:27). Yet Christ adds immediately that the one who believes shares fully in this privilege, provided this belief is by love and in love: "If you are able! All things are possible for the one who believes" (Mark 9:23). The resurrection of Christ proves it, and hence ours becomes possible. (c) Third, the knowledge of self. We have seen that if our *I* wants to found itself on thought, this existence performed by *my* thought is still exposed to two threats: either the illusion of thought ("What thinks in me?") or the suspicion of nihilism ("What's the point?"). Thus, says St. Paul, "anyone who claims to know something does not yet have the necessary knowledge." But how must one know, in order to know oneself assuredly? One must let oneself be known by God, and for that one must love him: "anyone who loves God is known by him" (1 Cor. 8:2). To know oneself by thought, certainly, but not by *my* thought, instead, by that of him who thinks me in loving me and only makes himself known to whoever loves him. One must "have come to know God or rather to be known by God" (Gal. 4:9). Hence the other, who loves me, reveals himself to be more interior to myself than myself. The founding ego because founded. (d) Fourth, alterity. Only love achieves knowledge of the other, because it believes in the other [l'autre] par excellence. Indeed, in order to know what he loves, love has no other need than to represent it to itself, nor to conceptualize it, that is to say, to restore the known to itself. Or rather, what he loves will appear to him in the strict measure in which, in loving it, he will envisage it, and, in envisaging it, it carries him off course in it. Only love can know beyond itself, because it alone is displaced outside of itself and can "know the love of Christ which surpasses all knowledge" (Eph. 3:19). Such a knowledge by transfer into the known, in fact, into the loved, is called communion. It alone reaches the transcendence of love through love.

Hence nothing accomplishes better than love the earnestness, work, patience, and pain of the negative, precisely because only for love is it not a matter of the negative but of kenosis, of the self-emptying and the abandonment that is characteristic of its positive nature. Love hence is in its full and entire right to resume charge of what philosophy, without really already knowing what it wants to say, has set out for these fragile virtues. "The love of truth" (2 Thess. 2:10), in other words, that of the *Logos* become flesh and hence master of all proximity, Christologically resumes philosophy's own definition as the "love of truth."

Faith hence does not lack rationality, at least if it presents itself as it must think itself—as faith in the sovereign and poor power of love. And faith also would not lack assurance: for, as faith in love, it loves *already*, hence deploys the logic of love *already*. It is not faith that is defined as the "shadow of future things" (Heb. 10:1), but the promise of the Law. Faith, itself, attains already "the assurance of things hoped for [πιστις ελπιζο-μενων υποστασις]," because it finds, in its practice, *already* "the conviction of things not seen [ελεγχος or βλεπομενων]" (Heb. 11:1). And what kind of invisible things become certainly accessible by faith in this way? St. Augustine has exhibited them: all the phenomena that are closest to my flesh, like "the will of your friend for you," or rather, "the good faith, by which you believe what you do not see in him," in short, "love of those who love, which we do not see."[5] That one not object that it is a matter here of the knowledge of the other [*d'autrui*], not that of God. For knowing signifies loving and love cannot be divided.

Reason so far has been content with interpreting the world, hence with transforming it into objects that it masters. It is time for it to begin to respect them. Respecting the world means seeing, hence envisioning the face of the other human being. And that is only possible in the figure of love, following its logic and in the light of its glory. Christians have nothing better to propose to the rationality of humans.

Christians, have no fear, be rational! And you, who do not believe in Christ, be reasonable, do not fear his great reason!

—Translated by Christina M. Gschwandtner

Notes

Preface

1. Marion uses the French term *donation*, which since the translation of *Reduction and Givenness* (*Réduction et donation*) has been translated into English as "givenness." Some of the earlier translated versions of essays in this book translated this term as "donation." All these have been changed to "givenness" in the present edition.—Trans.

2. With one exception: the introduction of "being-abandoned [*l'étant abandonné*]," in order to correspond to "being-given as a whole [*l'étant donné en totalité*]" and to "the closest being-given [*l'étant donné le plus proche*]," in section 5 of Chapter 3, "Metaphysics and Phenomenology." The copula "is [*est*]" is at times used too easily. I have abstained from it much more consciously from at least *God Without Being* and *Being Given* on.

1. The Possible and Revelation

1. The inclusion of the essay in *Religionsphilosophie Heute*, ed. A. Halder and K. Kienzler (Düsseldorf: Patmos, 1988).

2. Immanuel Kant, *Kritik der reinen Vernunft*, 2d ed., vol. 3 of *Kants Werke* (1787; Berlin: Walter de Gruyter, 1968); trans. Norman Kemp Smith under the title *Immanuel Kant's Critique of Pure Reason* (London: Macmillan, 1964), A85/ B117. All references to this work will refer to pages in the first and second German editions, given in the margins of the Kemp Smith translation.

3. Immanuel Kant, *Die Religion innerhalb der Grenzen der bloßen Vernunft*, bk. 3, div. 1, § 6, *Kants Gesammelte Schriften, Akademie Ausgabe* (Berlin: Königlich Preußische Akademie der Wissenschaften, 1902–1910), 6:110 G; trans. Theodore M. Greene and Hoyt H. Hudson under the title *Religion Within the Limits of Reason Alone* (New York: Harper & Row, 1960), 100–101.

4. G. W. F. Hegel, *Phänomenologie des Geistes*, ed. W. Bonsiepen and R. Heede, *Gesammelte Werke* (Hamburg: Felix Meiner, 1980), 11:313; trans. A. V. Miller under the title *Phenomenology of Spirit* (Oxford: Oxford University Press, 1977), 459.

5. Aristotle, *Metaphysics*, 8, 1049b5 (see 1051a2–3).

6. Martin Heidegger, *Sein und Zeit*, 10th ed. (Tübingen: Max Niemeyer, 1963), §7, 38; trans. John Macquarrie and Edward Robinson under the title *Being and Time* (New York: Harper & Row, 1962), 62. Given that Heidegger pays homage to Husserl in this statement, one can suppose that in his eyes this reversal between actuality and possibility is due to Husserl.

7. Husserl, *Idee der Phänomenologie*, ed. W. Biemel, vol. 2 of *Husserliana: Edmund Husserl Gesammelte Werke* (The Hague: Martinus Nijhoff, 1950–), henceforth Hua, 74; trans. William P. Alston and George Nakhnikian under the title *The Idea of Phenomenology* (The Hague: Martinus Nijhoff, 1964), 59.

8. Husserl, *Ideen zu einer reinen Phänomenologie und phänomenologischen Philosophie: Erstes Buch, Allgemeine Einführung in die reine Phänomenologie*, §24, ed. W. Biemel (The Hague: Martinus Nijhoff, 1950), Hua 3:74; trans. F. Kersten under the title *Ideas Pertaining to a Pure Phenomenology and to a Phenomenological Philosophy: First Book, General Introduction to a Pure Phenomenology* (The Hague: Martinus Nijhoff, 1982).

9. Respectively, Husserl, *Cartesian Meditations*, V, §46, Hua 1:133, and Heidegger, *Being and Time*, §7, 36/60 (or *Prolegomena zur Geschichte des Zeitbegriffs*), §9, *Gesamtausgabe* (Frankfurt am Main: Vittorio Klostermann, 1976–), 20:119. Here and throughout, where dual page numbers are given, the page in the original language precedes the page in the English translation. The *Gesamtausgabe* will hereafter be cited as *GA*.

10. Heidegger, *Prolegomena*, §32, *GA* 22:423.

11. [Throughout, *l'être/Sein* is translated as "Being" and *l'étant/Seiendes* as "being."—Trans.]

12. Heidegger, Letter to R. Munier, 16 April 1973 (trans. R. Munier), in *M. Heidegger*, ed. M. Haar, Cahiers de l'Herne (Paris: L'Herne, 1983), 112.

13. Heidegger, *Being and Time*, §7, 36/60.

14. Ibid., §7, 35 (see 28 and 31) / 59 (see 50 and 54).

15. See my study on this point in *Réduction et donation: Recherches sur Husserl, Heidegger et la phénoménologie* (Paris: Presses Universitaires de France, 1989); trans. Thomas A. Carlson under the title *Reduction and Givenness: Investigations of Husserl, Heidegger, and Phenomenology* (Evanston, Ill.: Northwestern University Press, 1998), chap. 1.

16. Rudolf Bultmann, "Der Begriff der Offenbarung im Neuen Testament" (1929), in his *Glauben und Verstehen*, vol. 3 (Tübingen: Mohr Siebeck, 1961), respectively 21 and 23. Or also, "There is no possibility for the reader to return behind the sermon, albeit to a "historical Jesus" (ibid., 21). On this text, see my essay "Remarques sur le concept de Révélation chez R. Bultmann," *Résurrection*,

no. 27 (1968): 29–42. A deeper study of the relation of Barth to Husserl is H. J. Adriaanse, *Zur Sachen selbst: Versuch einer Konfrontation der Theologie Barths mit der phänomenologischen Philosophie Edmund Husserls* (The Hague: Mouton, 1974).

17. Heidegger, "Phänomenologie und Theologie" (1927), *Wegmarken, GA*, vol. 9, respectively 52 and 53, trans. Jams G. Hart and John C. Maraldo under the title "Phenomenology and Theology," in *Pathmarks*, ed. William McNeill (Cambridge: Cambridge University Press, 1998), 39–62. One must here remark a very Bultmannian formula: "faith is an appropriation of revelation that co-constitutes the Christian occurrence, that is, the mode of existence that specifies a factical *Dasein*'s Christianness as a particular form of destiny" (ibid., 53f/45).

18. Heidegger, "Brief über den Humanismus," in *Wegmarken, GA* 9:351 (see 326, 331, and 361); trans. Frank A. Capuzzi under the title "Letter on Humanism," in *Pathmarks*, ed. McNeill, 239–67.

19. Ibid., 338f./258. On the interpretation of these texts and, in general, the subordination of the Revelation of God by himself, see my discussion with Jean Beaufret (and F. Fédier), in Jean-Luc Marion, *Dieu sans l'être: Hors-texte* (Paris: Arthème Fayard, 1982); trans. Thomas A. Carlson under the title *God Without Being* (Chicago: University of Chicago Press, 1991), chap. 2, §4–5 and chapter 3, §2–4.

20. Heidegger, "Wozu Dichter?" *Holzwege, GA* 5:270; trans. Julian Young and Kenneth Haynes as "Why Poets?" in *Off the Beaten Track* (Cambridge: Cambridge University Press, 2002), 200–241.

21. Karl Rahner, *Grundkurs des Glaubens: Einführung in den Begriff des Christentums* (Freiburg im Breisgau: Herder, 1976), 127.

22. Ibid., 44, 128, and 127.

23. Husserl, *Logische Untersuchungen: Prolegomena zur reinen Logik* §36 (Tübingen: Max Niemeyer, 1913), 1:117; trans. J. N. Findlay under the title *Logical Investigations: Prolegomena to a Pure Logic* (London: Routledge, 1970), 140; and *Ideen* I, §150, Hua 3:371; trans. W. R. Boyce Gibson under the title *Ideas* I (New York: MacMillan, 1931), 418.

24. Husserl, *Ideas* I, §51, 122/157.

25. Heidegger, "Phenomenology and Theology," 66/53.

26. Michel Henry, *L'essence de la manifestation* (Paris: Presses Universitaires de France, 1963) and *Philosophie et phénoménologie du corps* (Paris: Presses Universitaires de France, 1965).

27. Didier Franck, *Chair et corps: Sur la phénoménologie de Husserl* (Paris: Minuit, 1981) and "La chair et le problème de la constitution temporelle" (1984; rpt. in *Dramatique des phénomènes* [Paris: Presses Universitaires de France, 2001]).

28. Emmanuel Levinas, *La théorie de l'intuition dans la phénoménologie de Husserl* (Paris: Alcan, 1930) and *En découvrant l'existence avec Husserl et Heidegger* (Paris: Vrin, 1949, 1974). See J. Colette's very good clarification, "Lévinas et la phénoménologie husserlienne," in Emmanuel Levinas, *Les cahiers de la nuit surveillée*, ed. Emmanuel Levinas and Jacques Rolland (Lagrasse: Verdier, 1984).

29. Martin Heidegger, *Metaphysische Anfangsgründe der Logik im Ausgang von Leibniz, GA*, 26:117 (see 211).

30. [Marion is here employing aesthetic imagery (especially from painting) for the possible experience of revelation and its transgression of the horizon.—Trans.]

31. Husserl, *Logical Investigations*, §39, 3:122/2:766.

32. Heidegger, *Being and Time*, §43 b, 209–11/193–95.

2. The Saturated Phenomenon

NOTE: This text has profited from several helpful readings. I wish to thank in particular B. Besnier, Natalie Depraz, and Didier Franck for their remarks.

1. Immanuel Kant, *Kritik der reinen Vernunft*, 2d ed., vol. 3 of *Kants Werke* (1787; Berlin: Walter de Gruyter, 1968); trans. Norman Kemp Smith under the title *Immanuel Kant's Critique of Pure Reason* (London: Macmillan, 1964), A218/ B265. All references to this work will refer to pages in the first and second German editions, given in the margins of the Kemp Smith translation.

2. Ibid., A220/B267.

3. Ibid., A219/B266.

4. Leibniz, *Principes de la nature et de la grâce*, ed. A. Robinet (Paris: Presses Universitaires de France, 1954), §7, 45.

5. Leibniz, *Nouveaux Essais*, IV, II, §4, in *Die philosophischen Schriften*, ed. C. Gerhardt (Berlin: Weidmann, 1875–1890), 5:355.

6. Leibniz, Letter 123 to DesBosses (19 August 1715), in *Die philosophischen Schriften*, 2:506.

7. Leibniz, Letter 6 to Des Bosses (17 March 1706), in ibid., 2:306.

8. Edmund Husserl, *Ideen zu einer reinen Phänomenologie und phänomenologischen Philosophie: Erstes Buch, Allgemeine Einführung in die reine Phänomenologie*, vol. 3 of *Husserliana: Edmund Husserl Gesammelte Werke* (The Hague: Martinus Nijhoff, 1950–), 52; hereafter Hua; trans. F. Kersten under the title *Ideas Pertaining to a Pure Phenomenology and to a Phenomenological Philosophy: First Book, General Introduction to a Pure Phenomenology* (The Hague: Martinus Nijhoff, 1982), 44 (trans. modified).

9. On this point, see Michel Henry, "Quatre principes de la phénoménologie," in *Revue de métaphysique et de morale* (1991), n.1, 3–25.

10. Husserl, *Ideas* I, §83, Hua 3:201 / 197 (trans. modified). The connection Husserl makes between the horizon of lived experiences and the Kantian idea will become important for us. Can one object that the horizon is defined solely by lack of intuition? Undoubtedly not, since signification, even without intuition, is given as such.

11. Husserl, *Ideas* I, §82, Hua 3:200 / 196 (trans. modified). See also Edmund Husserl, *Formal and Transcendental Logic*, §99, Hua 17:257.

12. Martin Heidegger, *Sein und Zeit*, 10th ed. (Tübingen: Max Niemeyer, 1963), §7, 38; translated by John Macquarrie and Edward Robinson under the title *Being and Time* (New York: Harper & Row, 1962), 62.

13. Edmund Husserl, *Idee der Phänomenologie*, Hua 2:14; trans. William P. Alson and George Nakhnikian under the title *The Idea of Phenomenology* (The Hague: Martinus Nijhoff, 1964), 11. See Husserl, *Logische Untersuchungen* III, §3: "Appearances [*Erscheinungen*] in the sense of objects appearing [*erscheinenden*] as such, but also with regard to phenomena as experiences in which phenomenal things appear"; and V, §2: "We cannot too sharply stress the equivocation that allows us to characterize as a phenomenon [*Erscheinung*] not only the lived experience in which the appearing [*das Erscheinen*] of the object consists . . . , but also the object appearing [*erscheinende*] as such" ([Tübingen: Max Niemeyer, 1901], 2:231 and 349; trans. J. N. Findlay under the title *Logical Investigations: Prolegomena to a Pure Logic* [London: Routledge & Kegan Paul, 1970], 2:439 and 538 [trans. modified]).

14. Husserl, *Logische Untersuchungen* VI, §37, 3:118 / 762 (trans. modified).

15. Ibid., 3:116 / 761. See also 3:118 / 762.

16. Ibid., VI, §39, respectively 3:122, 123 / 765, 766 (trans. modified).

17. Ibid., "Ideale Fülle für eine Intention," §39, 123; Eng. trans., 766; "Ideal der letzten Erfüllung," title of §37, 118; Eng. trans. 761; "Das Ideal der Adäquation," title of chap. V, 115; Eng. trans., 760.

18. "It is obvious that reason, in achieving its purpose, that, namely, of representing the necessary complete determination of things, does not presuppose the existence of an essence [*nicht die Existenz eines solchen Wesen . . . voraussetze*] that corresponds to this ideal, but only the idea of such an essence, and this only for the purpose of deriving from an unconditioned totality of complete determination the conditioned totality, that is, the totality of the limited" (Kant, *Critique of Pure Reason*, A577/B606, trans. modified). This definition of the ideal by Kant—the unconditioned but nonexistent totality that allows reason to determine the conditioned but existent limitation—covers fairly exactly the Husserlian ideal of fulfillment: unconditioned and complete, but not actualized, equality, in relation and comparison to which is measured the aim [*visée*] that is actualized but intuitively poor. The difference concerns the fact that for Kant the ideal of reason coincides strictly with God, whereas Husserl will wait for the final developments of his teleology of spirit in order to identify the ideal of fulfillment with God. See the classic work of Angela Ales Belo, *Husserl: Sul problema di Dio* (Rome: Edizioni Studium, 1985), and the texts that Jocelyn Benoist has gathered and commented upon: "Husserl: Au-delà de l'onto-théo-logie," *Les Études philosophiques* 4 (1991).

19. Husserl, *Logische Untersuchungen* VI, §40 and §63, 3:131, 192 / 775, 825 (trans. modified). Heidegger too speaks of "a surplus of intentions [*ein Überschuss an Intentionen*]" in *Prolegomena zur Geschichte des Zeitbegriffs*, §6, *Gesamtausgabe* (Frankfurt am Main: Vittorio Klostermann, 1976–), 20:77, 119.

20. Descartes clearly indicates that the privilege of the mathematical type of object (and therefore phenomenon) is due to its "pure and simple [*purum et simplex*]" character, which presupposes nothing that experience renders uncertain (*Regulae ad directionem ingenii* II, *Œuvres de Descartes*, ed. Charles Adams and

Paul Tannery, 11 vols. [Paris: Vrin, CNRS, 1964–1979], X:365, 16ff.; trans. John Cottingham, Robert Stoothof, and Dugalf Murdoch as *The Philosophical Writings of Descartes* (Cambridge: Cambridge University Press, 1984–85). Hereafter AT and CSM, respectively; this privilege of certitude is paid for with an equal poverty of intuitive given, of "matter," such that it procures at one and the same time a real content and an irreducible uncertainty. This is also why the *intuitus* ensures certitude only for objects that are without matter (and poor in intuition, if not purely formal), like mathematical idealities, or for objects that are quasi-tautological (and therefore poor in intuition), like "everyone can mentally intuit that he exists, that he is thinking" (See ibid., III:368, 21ff., CSM II:14 and commentary in my *Sur l'ontologie grise de Descartes* [Paris: Vrin, 1975; 2nd ed., 1981], §6, 41–43 and §7, 49–53.) One of the reasons for the progressive abandonment of *intuitus* by Descartes after 1627–28 is undoubtedly found here: an object is known all the more certainly insofar as it requires a *lesser* intuitive fulfillment and content.

21. See Edmund Husserl, *Cartesian Meditations*, §50–§54. I should stress that appresentation—"the surplus [*Überschuss*] in perception of what is not authentically perceived in it"—intervenes not only in order to know another, but already with the knowledge of the worldly object (§55, Hua 1:151). Descartes also admits that adequate knowledge remains impossible not only for the idea of infinity (AT VII:368, 1–3), but also for that "conceptu rerum de ulla alia re quantumvis parva [of any object whatsoever, however limited it may be]" (AT VII:365, 3–5; CSM II:252; trans. modified).

22. Kant, *Critique of Pure Reason*, A58/B82.

23. Ibid., A51/B76.

24. Ibid., A50/B74, A92/B125.

25. Ibid., A239/B298, then A95 and A253.

26. Ibid., A247/B304.

27. [That which can be aimed at, meant, or intended; from *viser*, to aim at.—Trans.]

28. Kant, *Critique of Pure Reason*, A327/B383 (*notwendig*), and A339/B397 (*unvermeidlicher Schein*). Stéphane Mallarmé, respectively, "Variations sur une sujet" and "Prose pour Des Esseintes," in *Oeuvres complètes*, ed. H. Mondor (Paris: Gallimard, 1965), 361 and 56.

29. Kant, *Critique of Pure Reason*, A290–92/B347–49; see A220/B268 and A163/B204. See G. Granel, "Le nihil privatum en son sens kantien," *Philosophie* 14 (1987), reprinted in *Écrits logiques and politiques* (Paris: Galilée, 1990), 71–88.

30. Immanuel Kant, *Kritik der Urteilskraft*, §57, ad n. 1, *Kants Gesammelte Schriften, Akademie Ausgabe* (Berlin: Königlich Preußische Akademie der Wissenschaften, 1902–10), 5:342, hereafter Ak.A.; trans. Werner S. Pluher under the title *Critique of Judgment* (Indianapolis: Hackett, 1987), 215; trans. modified.

31. Ibid., §49, 5:314 / 182; trans. modified. One should not object that the aesthetic idea is here called a "representation of the imagination" and is not related to intuition because a few lines down intuition is purely and simply assimilated to the "representation of the imagination [*Begriff, dem keine Anschauung*

(Vorstellung der Einbildungkraft) adäquat sein kann]" (ibid.). There are other confirmations of this elsewhere: "the power of imagination as the ability of intuition [*die Einbildungskraft, als Vermögen der Anschauung*]" (§39, 292/158); "an intuition (of the power of imagination) [*eine Anschauung (der Einbildungskraft)*]" (§57, note 1, 342/215). Moreover, there is nothing surprising in this, since already in 1787 the second edition of the first *Critique* explicitly specifies this tie: "Imagination is the power of representing in intuition an object that is not itself present. Now, since all our intuition is sensible, the imagination, by virtue of the subjective condition under which alone it can give to the concepts of understanding a corresponding intuition, belongs to *sensibility*" (§24, B151; trans. modified).

32. Kant, *Critique of Judgment*, §57, ad n. 1, twice *inexponible Vorstellung*, 342ff. For the positive use of this rare term, see *exponible Urteile*, in *Logik*, §31. Ak.A. 9:109.

33. [For the translation of *invisable*, see n. 27, above, regarding *visable*.—Trans.]

34. Kant, *Critique of Pure Reason*, A163/B204.

35. Descartes, *Passions de l'âme*, §73, AT XI:383, 7–10; CSM II:254. See §73: "one halts one's attention at the first image of the objects that have presented themselves, without calling for any other knowledge of them" (ibid., 383, 14–17; CSMII:354).

36. Spinoza, *Ethics* III, appendix, definition IV.

37. Paul Claudel, "Tête d'or," *Théatre* (Paris: Gallimard, 1956), 1:210. Glory weighs: the Hebrew says this with one word. Obviously, I am here extremely close to Jean-Louis Chrétien's *L'inoubliable et l'inespéré* (Paris: Gallimard, 1991); trans. Jeffrey Bloechl under the title *The Unforgettable and the Unhoped for* (New York: Fordham University Press, 2002).

38. Plato, *Republic*, 515c and 517a. The term μαρμαρυγη originally designated vibration (for example, that of dancers' feet, in *Odyssey*, 8:265), then the vibration of overheated air, and thus mirage and bedazzlement.

39. Plato, *Republic*, 517bc and 518a.

40. Kant, *Critique of Pure Reason*, B219.

41. Ibid., A177/B220 and A180/B222.

42. Ibid., A177/B220.

43. Ibid., A177/B220 and A179/B222. See also A665/B693.

44. Ibid., A177/B220 and A182/B224.

45. It would be necessary to develop some privileged examples here: the plurality of accounts, of literary genres, of testimonies, and of hermeneutics of the same event (the multiple accounts of the crossing of the Red Sea, the irreducible plurality of the Gospels) clearly indicates that a saturated phenomenon is at issue. But the doctrine of the four senses of Scripture, assigning a plurality of different and compossible senses, proves that even a text can sometimes (in the case of the Jewish and Christian Scriptures, although in essentially divergent senses) appear as a saturated phenomenon. This is true also for texts that are not (directly) religious: thus, it is clear that the irreconcilable plurality of literary treatments of

single themes (dramatic models, the very notion of literary imitation, and so on), even of constantly renewed interpretations and stagings of standard works, points to saturated phenomena.

46. Kant, *Critique of Pure Reason*, A74/B100, A219/B266, and A234/B287.

47. Ibid., A255/B273.

48. Ibid., A225/B273 and A220/B267.

49. See Jean-Luc Marion, "Le sujet en dernier appel," *Revue de Métaphysique et de Morale*, no. 1 (1991): 77–95.

50. "Das Sich-an-ihm-selbst-zeigende," Heidegger, *Being and Time*, §7, 31, 12 / 54, 32. See "permit the in-itself-revealed to be seen from itself [*das an ihm selbst Offenbare von ihm selbst her sehen lassen*]," *Prolegomena zur Geschichte des Zeitbegriffs*, §2, *GA* (Frankfurt am Main: Vittorio Klostermann, 1979), 20:117. "Von ihm selbst her" indeed indicates an appearance "of itself" in the strict sense of "starting from itself."

51. Descartes, *Meditations*, AT VII:371, 25 and 52, 15; CSM II:256 and 36, respectively. Infinity is never potential but always *actu*, 47, 19; CSM II:32.

52. AT VII:46, 8, 12; CSM II:31–32.

53. Respectively, "nihil . . . univoce illi et nobis convenire [none belong to Him and to ourselves in the same sense]," AT VII:137, 22; CSM II:98 (see 433, 5–6 or *Principia Philosophiae* I, §51); *attingere*, AT VII:139, 12; CSM II:99 (see 52, 5 and 46, 21; CSM II: 35 and 32).

54. Descartes, AT VII:114, 6–7; CSM II:82. This is why here, and here alone, *intueri* is equivalent to *adorare*.

55. Kant, *Critique of Judgment*, respectively §25, 5:248; *Formlosigkeit*, §24, 247; *Unordnung*, §23, 246; *über all Vergleichung* and *schlechthin* §25, 248 (and §26, 251).

56. Ibid., respectively §23, 245; *Gefühl der Unangemessenheit*, §26, 252; *ungeheuer*, §26, 253.

57. Ibid., respectively *Unbegränztheit*, §23, 244. See *keine angemessene Darstellung*, 245.

58. Ibid., §23, 245. See *subjektive Unzweckmässigkeit*, §26, 252; *Widerstreit* of the subjective end, §27, 258. Respect [*Achtung*] comes in at §27, 257. Here I follow P. Lacoue-Labarthe, "La vérité sublime," in *Du sublime*, ed. Jean-François Courtine (Paris: Belin, 1988).

59. This is Paul Ricœur's goal, particularly in *Temps et récit*, 3: *Le temps raconté* (Paris: Seuil, 1985); translated by Kathleen Blamey and David Pellauer under the title *Time and Narrative*, vol. 3 (Chicago: University of Chicago Press, 1988). My analyses obviously owe much to his decisive works.

60. See my study on an exemplary case of the saturated phenomenon, the argument of Saint Anselm, wrongly called "ontological": "L'argument relève-t-il de l'ontologie," *Questions cartésiennes* (Paris: Presses Universitaires de France, 1991) or *Archivio di Filosofia* 1–2 (Rome, 1990); trans. Jeffrey L. Kosky under the title *Cartesian Questions: Method and Metaphysics* (Chicago: University of Chicago Press, 1999).

3. Metaphyics and Phenomenology: A Relief for Theology

1. Blaise Pascal, "Mémorial," *Oeuvres complètes de Pascal*, ed. Jacques Chevalier (Paris: Gallimard, 1954), 554.

2. Thomas Aquinas, "Proemium Sancti Thomas," in *Librum Primum Aristotelis de Generatione et Corruptione, Expositio*, in *Aristotelis Libros—De Caelo et Mundo, De Generatione et Corruptione, Meteorologicorum—Expositio*, ed. Raymondo M. Spiazzi (Taurini: Marietti, 1952), 315.

3. Francisco Suarez, "Proemium," *Disputationes Metaphysicae*, 2 vols., vol. 25 of *Opera Omnia*, ed. C. Berton (1866; Hildesheim: G. Olms, 1965), 1:2. See also: "Therefore, this science, which treats these special objects, likewise considers all predications; it (this science) also treats those things that are similarly predicated of other things. This as a whole is metaphysical doctrine [Eadem ergo scientia, quae de his specialibus objectis tractat, simul considerat omnia praedicata, quae illis sunt cum aliis rebus communia, et haec est tota metaphysica doctrina]" (1:25).

4. On the history of this doctrine, see, in addition to the recent work of Jean-François Courtine, *Suarez et le système de la métaphysique* (Paris: Presses Universitaires de France, 1990) (esp. pt. 4), that of Ernst Vollrath, "Die Gliederung der Metaphysik in eine *Metaphysica generalis* und eine *Metaphysica specialis*," *Zeitschrift für philosophische Forschung* 16, no. 2 (1962): 258–83.

5. Such is the scope of the famous declaration, whose radical and complex nature is nevertheless often underestimated: "And the proud name of an ontology that claims to supply, in a systematic doctrine, an a priori knowledge of things in general [*überhaupt* or *in communi*] (e.g., the principle of causality), must give place to the modest name of a simple analytic of pure understanding" (Immanuel Kant, *Kritik der reinen Vernunft*, 2d ed., vol. 3 of *Kants Werke* [1787; Berlin: Walter de Gruyter, 1968], 207 [A247/B304]; trans. Norman Kemp Smith, under the title *Immanuel Kant's Critique of Pure Reason* [London: Macmillan, 1964], 264, trans. modified). See also 546 [A845/B873]; 661. Of course, it would remain to be known whether *ontologia*, in its historical acceptation (from Goclenius to Johann Clauberg), ever claimed to accomplish anything more and anything other than a "simple analytic of pure understanding," since it never claimed being as its object, but only the *cogitabile* (see the documents gathered in Courtine, *Suarez et le système de la métaphysique*, 246–93, 422–35). Has the hypothesis ever been taken seriously that "ontology," understood historically, never dared to confront being as such? Would this fact not have to call into question the immediate possibility of a science of being that would not, first, be a science of being as thinkable and therefore a submission of the *ens in quantum ens* to representation? Would one not have to be amazed that the very term *ontologia* remained unknown to Aristotle and the medievals and was established only by the moderns, in a situation that was explicitly assumed to be Cartesian? See Johann Clauberg, *Metaphysica de ente, Quae rectius Ontosophia* (1664), in *Opera Omnia Philosophica*, ed. Johann Schalbruch, 2 vols. (1691; Hildesheim: G. Olms, 1968), 1:283–340, esp, sec. 8, 283 n.c.

6. Martin Heidegger, *Identität und Differenz* (Pfullingen: G. Neske, 1957), 66–67; trans. Joan Stambaugh under the title *Identity and Difference* (New York: Harper & Row, 1969), 68, trans. mod.

7. Ibid., 68 / 69.

8. Friedrich Nietzsche, "Die 'Vernunft' in der Philosophie," *Götzen-Dämmerung oder Wie man mit dem Hammer philosophiert*, in *Nietzsches Werke: Kritische Gesamtausgabe*, ed. Giorgio Colli and Mazzino Montinari (Berlin: Walter de Gruyter, 1967–91), 6:3:70; trans. Walter Kaufmann under the title "'Reason' in Philosophy," *Twilight of the Idols; or, How One Philosophizes with a Hammer*, in *The Portable Nietzsche*, ed. Kaufmann (New York: Viking Penguin, 1982), 481.

9. Nietzsche, "Ende 1886–Frühjahr 1887" (7[54]), in *Nachgelassene Fragmente*, vol. 8 of *Nietzsches Werke*, 1:320–21 and *Der Wille zur Macht: Versuch einer Umwertung aller Werte* (Stuttgart: A. Kröner, 1980), sec. 617, 418–19; trans. Kaufmann and R. J. Hollindale under the title *The Will to Power* (New York: Vintage, 1967), 330.

10. There are several ways to deny the "end of metaphysics." It can be a matter of postulating that "metaphysics" remains identical with itself, without any real history. But then one runs the risk either of repeating the presuppositions of nihilism without recognizing them (thus Blondel, with the philosophy of will, and Schopenhauer) or of producing ahistorically a philosophy that was never professed (thus Maritain, inserting an "intuition of Being" into the text of Aquinas for the needs of current existentialism; thus Cohen and Natorp for the "return to Kant"). Or, more positively, one runs the risk of having to reconstruct an author against the unanimous tradition that claims him as its own by deforming him (Gilson for St. Thomas). Or, on the contrary, it can be a matter of attempts at "overcoming" metaphysics that reproduce without knowing it (or without wanting to know it) metaphysics' most classic theses and aporias—thus Carnap and the first logical positivism rediscovering the difficulties of empiricism.

11. Jean-Luc Marion, "La fin de la fin de la métaphysique," *Laval théologique et philosophique* 42 (Feb. 1986): 23–43.

12. Aristotle, *De Anima*, ed. W. D. Ross (Oxford: Oxford University Press, 1956), 72 (3.5.430a18); Aquinas, *Existence and Nature of God*, vol. 2 of pt. 1, *Summa Theologiae* [Latin and English], trans. and ed. Thomas McDermott (London: Eure & Spottiswoode, 1989), question 3, art. 2, 24; René Descartes, "Responsio Authoris ad Primas Objectiones," *Meditationes de Prima Philosophia* (Amsterdam, 1642), 108–31; and G. W. F. Leibniz, *Principes de la nature et de la grâce fondés en raison*, ed. André Robinet (Paris: Presses Universitaires de France, 1954), sec. 8, 45.

13. Edmund Husserl, Introduction, *Logische Untersuchungen*, 2 vols. (Halle: M. Niemeyer, 1922), 2:1:19; trans. J. N. Findlay under the title *Logical Investigations*, 2 vols. (London: Routledge & Kegan Paul, 1970), 1:263, trans. mod.

14. Edmund Husserl, *Ideen zu einer reinen Phänomenologie und phänomenologischen Philosophie: Erstes Buch, Allgemeine Einführung in die reine Phänomenologie*, vol. 3 of *Husserliana: Edmund Husserl Gesammelte Werke* (The Hague: Martinus Nijhoff, 1976), pt. 1, 51; trans. F. Kersten under the title *Ideas Pertaining*

to a Pure Phenomenology and to a Phenomenological Philosophy: First Book, General Introduction to a Pure Phenomenology (The Hague: Martinus Nijhoff, 1982), 44, and W. R. Boyce Gibson under the title *Ideas: General Introduction to a Pure Phenomenology* (1931; London: Collier-Macmillan, 1969), 92, trans. mod. [*Source de droit* (source of right or rightful, legitimate source) is the French rendering here of Husserl's German *Rechtsquelle*, which Gibson gives as "source of authority" and which Kersten translates as "legitimizing source"—Trans.]

15. [The French here is *au principe*. Playing on the biblical *in principio*, the passage refers to Husserl's discussion in *Ideas*, sec. 24, of the "genuine sense" of *principium*—Trans.]

16. See Aristotle, *The Metaphysics*, trans. Hugh Tredennick, 2 vols. (Cambridge: Harvard University Press, 1933–36), 1:208–9 (5.1.1012b34).

17. I willingly adopt a formula that Levinas advances only with reservation: "Phenomenology is only a radical mode of experience" (Emmanuel Lévinas, *Le temps et l'autre* [St. Clement: Fata Morgana, 1979], 34; trans. Richard Cohen as *Time and the Other* [Pittsburgh: Duquesne University Press, 1987).

18. One therefore would not have to speak of a (real or supposedly threatening) "general metaphysics" in Husserl, contrary to Dominique Janicaud, *Le tournant théologique de la phénoménologie française* (Paris, Éditions de l'Éclat, 1991, 43; trans. Bernard G. Prusak under the title "The Theological Turn in French Phenomenology," in *Phenomenology and the "Theological Turn,"* ed. Dominique Janicaud et al. [New York: Fordham University Press, 2000], 58), but rather generalize the conclusion of my analysis of the Husserlian "I without Being" [*Je sans l'être*] in *Réduction et donation: Recherches sur Husserl, Heidegger et la phénoménologie* (Paris: Presses Universitaires de France, 1989), 240; trans. Thomas A. Carlson under the title *Reduction and Givenness: Investigations of Husserl, Heidegger, and Phenomenology* (Evanston, Ill.: Northwestern University Press, 1998), and thus radically confirm my *Dieu sans l'être: Hors-texte* (Paris: Arthème Fayard, 1982); trans. Thomas A. Carlson under the title *God Without Being* (Chicago: University of Chicago Press, 1991).

19. See also my *Réduction et donation*, 280–89.

20. Heidegger, *Sein und Zeit* (Tübingen: Max Niemeyer, 1963), sec. 7, 38; trans. John Macquarrie and Edward Robinson under the title *Being and Time* (New York: Harper & Row, 1962), 62; and Aristotle, *The Metaphysics*, 1:456 (9.8.1050.a3–5).

21. ["The given of Being" (*le donné d'être*) defines every being as "a being-given" (*un étant-donné*). With the hyphenation of *étant-donné*, which is translated as *being-given*, Marion creates a single term that resonates on several levels. On the one hand, one can read the simple construction wherein a noun, *l'étant* or *un étant*, is modified by an adjective, *donné*, thus yielding "the given being" or "a given being." On the other hand, one can also read the common French locution *étant donné (que)*, which in its normal usage means "being given (that)" or "seeing that." Phenomenology allows one to think the being-given in every given being, and thus the precedence of donation over beings and their Being.

The term *donation* itself can convey at least three interrelated senses: giving, givenness, and the given—Trans.]

22. Plato, *The Republic*, trans. Paul Shorey, 2 vols. (Cambridge: Harvard University Press, 1956), 2:106 (6.9.509b8–9). I am obviously taking up a direction of research that was opened by Levinas in *Totalité et infini: Essai sur l'extériorité* (The Hague: Martinus Nijhoff, 1961); trans. Alphonso Lingis under the title *Totality and Infinity: An Essay on Exteriority* (The Hague: Martinus Nijhoff, 1979), and especially in *Autrement qu'être ou au-delà de l'essence* (The Hague: Martinus Nijhoff, 1974); trans. Lingis under the title *Otherwise than Being, or Beyond Essence* (The Hague: Martinus Nijhoff, 1981). But it seems to me that this thesis can be generalized to all intuitive donation and therefore, according to Husserl, to all phenomenality without exception.

23. Nietzsche, *Also sprach Zarathustra: Ein Buch für Alle und Keinen*, vol. 6, pt. 1 of *Nietzsche Werke*, 5–6; trans. Thomas Common under the title "The Three Metamorphoses," *Thus Spoke Zarathustra*, vol. 11 of *The Complete Works of Friedrich Nietzsche*, ed. Oscar Levy (New York: Macmillan, 1916), 25–27. For a justification of this allusive judgment, see my study "L'effrondrement des idoles et l'affirmation du divin: Nietzsche," *L'idole et la distance: Cinq études* (Paris: Bernard Grasset, 1977), 49–105; trans. Thomas A. Carlson under the title "The Collapse of the Idols and Confrontation with the Divine," in Marion, *The Idol and Distance* (New York: Fordham University Press, 2001), 27–78.

24. This slogan, moreover, could also translate the *Prinzip der Voraussetzungslosigkeit*. On this debate, see the arguments of Jean-Louis Chrétien, *L'Appel et la réponse* (Paris: Minuit, 1992); trans. Anne A. Davenport under the title *The Call and the Response* (New York: Fordham University Press, 2004), and of Michel Henry, "Parole et religion: La Parole de Dieu," in *Phénoménologie et théologie*, ed. Jean-Louis Chrétien et al. (Paris: Criterion, 1992), 129–60; trans. Jeffrey L. Kosky under the title "Speech and Religion: The Word of God," in *Phenomenology and the "Theological Turn,"* ed. Janicaud et al., 217–41. On the question of phenomenological method, I take as my own this remark by Didier Franck: "Such a method goes beyond the strict framework of descriptive phenomenology, all the while finding support in it. But was this not already the case with the Husserlian analyses of time, of the other, and of the body, and is not phenomenology, from turn to turn, characterized by the fact that it does not cease to distance itself from itself and that these distances end up in a certain way belonging to it?" (Didier Franck, "Le Corps de la différence," *Philosophie*, no. 34 [April 1992]: 86).

25. [For a discussion of the interloqué, see Marion, "L'Interloqué," trans. Eduardo Cadava and Anne Tomiche, in *Who Comes after the Subject?* ed. Cadava, Peter Connor, and Jean-Luc Nancy (New York: Routledge, 1991), rpt. in *The Religious*, ed. John D. Caputo (Oxford: Blackwell, 2002), 131–44—Trans.]

26. [Marion is here using the psychological term *secondarité*, which "is said of persons in whom present circumstances do not immediately provoke any reactions and who constantly refer to their past and to their future" (*Robert*)—Trans.]

27. See Husserl, *Ideen* I:1:122. Husserl evokes "God" here explicitly under the figure and in the function of a "ground" (*Grund*; 155).

28. Heidegger, *Identity and Difference*, 57, 70 / 60, 72.

29. See Jacques Derrida, "Comment ne pas parler: Dénégations," in *Psyché: Invention de l'autre* (Paris: Galilée, 1987), 535–95; trans. Ken Frieden under the title "How to Avoid Speaking: Denials," in *Languages of the Unsayable*, ed. Sanford Budick and Wolfgang Iser (New York: Columbia University Press, 1989), 3–70. Here denial [*dénégation*] has nothing to do with a dogmatic negation, leaves the status of prayer open, and, in a paradoxical fashion, maintains the play of the "divine names."

30. F. Laruelle suggests that I could hardly avoid this conclusion in his otherwise pertinent and constructive remarks in "L'Appel et le phénomène," *Revue de métaphysique et de morale* 96 (Jan.-Mar. 1991): 27–41.

31. [*L'étant-abandonné.* Here as elsewhere, Marion appeals to the resonance of the given (*donné*), in the abandoned (*abandonné*)—Trans.]

32. [In this context, the obsolete English term *to evoid* ("to clear out, empty out, remove"), in conjunction with the common *to void*, nicely translates the French *évider* ("to hollow out") in its relation to *vider* ("to empty, vacate, void")—Trans.]

33. Pascal, "Mémorial," 554.

34. See my essay "Le phénomène saturé," in *Phémenénologie et théologie*, ed. Chrétien et al., rpt. as Chapter 2 of this book.

35. This distinction was very shrewdly noted by Derrida in a text dedicated to Jan Patocka but above all to Christian "logic": "It needs to think the possibility of such an event [revelation], but not the event itself. A major difference that allows one to hold such a discourse without reference to religion as established dogmatics and to propose a thinking genealogy of the possibility and of the essence of the religious that is not an article of faith. . . . The difference here is subtle and unstable, and it would require shrewd and vigilant analyses. On several accounts and in diverse senses, the discourses of Levinas and Marion, and perhaps even Ricoeur, share this situation with that of Patocka; [namely, of offering a] nondogmatic doublet of dogma . . ., in any case *thinking*, which 'repeats' without religion the possibility of religion" (Jacques Derrida, "Donner la mort," in *L'Éthique du don: Jacques Derrida et la pensée du don*, ed. Jean-Michel Rabaté and Michael Wetzel [Paris: Métailié-Transition, 1992], 52). My only disagreement has to do with the identification of this "doublet" indifferently as "philosophical, metaphysical"; when it is matter of thinking the possibility, and especially the radical possibility, of the impossible itself, phenomenology alone is suitable—and not at all metaphysics, which is a thought of actuality par excellence.

4. "Christian Philosophy": Hermeneutic or Heuristic?

1.Émile Bréhier, "Y-a-t-il une philosophie chrétienne?" *Revue de Métaphysique et de Morale* (April 1931): 133–62; and a first discussion in the *Bulletin de la Société Française de Philosophie* (1932). See the brilliant summary of this debate by Henri de Lubac, "Sur la philosophie chrétienne," *Nouvelle Revue Théologique* 63, no. 3 (March 1936): 225–53, published in English as "Retrieving the Tradition: On Christian Philosophy," *Communio* 19, no. 3 (Fall 1992): 478–506.

2. Maurice de Wulf, *Introduction à la philosophie néo-scolastique* (Louvain: Institut Superieur de Philosophie, 1904), cited in an excellent anthology of the present positions by Étienne Gilson, as an appendix to his first contribution to the debate. See Gilson's *L'esprit de la philosophie médiévale* (Paris: Vrin, 1932), 430.

3. See Bréhier's discussion in the *Bulletin de la Société Française de Philosophie* (1932), 59.

4. Maurice Blondel, "Les exigences rationnelles de la pensée contemporaine en matière d'apologétique et la méthode de la philosophie dans l'étude du problème religieux," *Annales de philosophie chrétienne* (May 1896), 34. It is true that Blondel thinking on this topic evolved, as it did on others.

5. Ludwig Feuerbach, *Sämtliche Werke*, vol. 8, *Vorlesungen über das Wesen der Religion*, ed. Wilhelm Bollin, Friedrich Jodl, and Hans-Marin Sass (Stuttgart: F. Fromann, 1903), 58ff.; Martin Heidegger, *Nietzsche: Der europäische Nihilismus—II. Abt. Vorlesungen 1919–1944*, *Gesamtausgabe* (Frankfurt am Main: Klostermann, 1986), 48:162. See my *Dieu sans l'être* (Paris: Arthème Fayard, 1982), 91ff.; trans. Thomas A. Carlson under the title *God Without Being* (Chicago: University of Chicago Press, 1991), 61ff. There is also Husserl's way of putting God "out of circulation" (*Ideen* I, §58). This thesis was prolonged until recently, e.g., in J. Beaufret, "La philosophie chrétienne," in *Dialogue avec Heidegger II* (Paris: Minuit, 1973) or "Heidegger et la théologie," in *Étienne Gilson et nous*, ed. M. Couratier (Paris: Vrin, 1980).

6. Gilson, *L'esprit de la philosophie médiévale*, 33, a formula repeated and defended again in *Christianisme et philosophie* (Paris: J. Vrin, 1949), 138.

7. Maurice Blondel, *Lettre sur les exigences de la pensée contemporaine en matière d'apologétique* (Paris: Presses Universitaires de France, 1956), 40.

8. Maurice Blondel, *Carnets intimes* (Paris: Presses Universitaires de France, 1961), 525ff.

9. Friedrich Nietzsche, *Jenseits von Gut und Böse: Vorspiel einer Philosophie der Zukunft*, in *Kritische Studienausgabe*, ed. Giorgio Colli and Massimo Montinari (Berlin: Walter de Gruyter, 1999), §108, 92; trans. Walter Kaufmann under the title *Beyond Good and Evil: Prelude to a Philosophy of the Future* (New York: Random House, 1966), §108, 85.

10. Irenaeus of Lyon, *Contra Haereses* 4.34.1.

11. Pascal, *Pensées* (Paris: Garnier/Flammarion, 1973), §306.

12. Immanuel Kant, *Kritik der Urteilskraft*, §91, ad n. 4, *Kants Gesammelte Schriften, Akademie Ausgabe* (Berlin: Königlich Preußische Akademie der Wissenschaften, 1902–10), hereafter Ak.A.; trans. Werner S. Pluher under the title *Critique of Judgment* (Indianapolis: Hackett, 1987). I owe this reference to de Lubac, "Sur la philosophie chrétienne," 481, which refers to L. Brunschvicg, *La raison et la religion* (Paris: F. Alcan, 1939), 166.

13. I refer here to my previous work: *God Without Being*, particularly chaps. 3–4; *Réduction et donation: Recherches sur Husserl, Heidegger et la phénoménologie* (Paris: Presses Universitaires de France, 1989); trans. Thomas A. Carlson under the title *Reduction and Givenness: Investigations of Husserl, Heidegger, and Phenomenology* (Evanston, Ill.: Northwestern University Press, 1998); "De la mort de la 'mort de Dieu' aux noms divins," *Laval théologiques et philosophiques* 41, no. 1 (1985): 25–42; and "La fin de la fin de la métaphysique," *Laval théologiques et philosophiques* 42, no. 1 (1986): 23–33.

14. Justin, Dialogue with Trypho II, *Patrologia Graeca* 6.475B.

15. Thus Gilles Deleuze: "On the minor question of a Christian philosophy: yes, there is a Christian philosophy, not as much according to belief, but since judgment is considered an autonomous faculty, requiring therefore God's system and guarantee" (*Critique et clinique* [Paris: Minuit, 1993), 55.

5. Sketch of a Phenomenological Concept of the Gift

1. See Chapters 1 and 2 of this volume.

2. See my *Réduction et donation: Recherches sur Husserl, Heidegger et la phénoménologie* (Paris: Presses Universitaires de France, 1989); trans. Thomas A. Carlson under the title *Reduction and Givenness: Investigations of Husserl, Heidegger, and Phenomenology* (Evanston, Ill.: Northwestern University Press, 1998), and also the commentary by Michel Henry, "Quatre principes de la phénoménologie," *Revue de Métaphysique et de Morale* (Paris: A. Colin, 1991), 1:3–25.

3. Jacques Derrida, *Donner le temps: I. La fausse monnaie* (Paris: Galilée, 1991); trans. Peggy Kamuf under the title *Given Time: I. Counterfeit Money* (Chicago: University of Chicago Press, 1991), 13. Page numbers will refer to the English translation.

4. Ibid., 12.

5. Derrida continues, "this simple recognition of the gift *as* gift, as such, [suffices] to annul the gift as gift even before *recognition becomes gratitude*" (ibid., 13–14). And also: "There is no more gift as soon as the other *receives*—and even if she refuses the gift that she has perceived or recognized as gift" (ibid., 14). This last point can be argued; in fact, it could be that the gift survives its refusal (by ignoring it), as Derrida seems to suggest in the logic of his third and fourth arguments.

6. Ibid., 23. See the "intentional signification" of the gift, which is sufficient to refute it, 157–58.

7. See my study in *Questions cartésiennes*, chap. 5, §5, "La dernière formulation du cogito: La générosité" (Paris: Presses Universitaires de France, 1991); trans. Jeffrey L. Kosky under the title *Cartesian Questions* (Chicago: University of Chicago Press, 1999).

8. Derrida, *Given Time*, 24.

9. Ibid., 14.

10. Ibid., 13.

11. Ibid., 13, 14, and 15, respectively.

12. Ibid., 27.

13. Ibid., 54.

14. Ibid., 12.

15. Spinoza, *Ethics* III, §7: Demonstration.

16. See my "The Final Appeal of the Subject," in *Deconstructive Subjectivities*, ed. Simon Critchley and Peter Dews (Albany: State University of New York Press, 1996).

17. I am not returning here to a regulation of the consciousness of debt, which was certainly eliminated by Heidegger: "*Dasein* as such is guilty or in debt" (*Sein und Zeit*, 10th ed. §58 [Tübingen: Max Niemeyer, 1963; trans. John Macquarrie and Edward Robinson under the title *Being and Time* (New York: Harper & Row, 1962), but we should also not forget the work by C. Bruaire, *L'être et l'esprit* (Paris: Fayard, 1983).

6. What Cannot be Said: Apophasis and the Discourse of Love

1. 1 Corinthians 2:9, quoting Isaiah 64:4: "From ages past no one has heard, no ear has perceived, no eye has seen any God besides you, who works for those who wait for him."

2. Descartes, *Meditations*, Fifth Replies, *Œuvres de Descartes*, ed. Charles Adams and Paul Tannery, 11 vols. (Paris: Vrin, CNRS, 1964–79], VII:368, 2–4.

3. John Chrysostom, *Peri akataleptou*, *Patrologia Graeca* 48, col. 720; trans. Paul W. Harkins under the title *On the Incomprehensible Nature of God* (Washington, D.C.: Catholic University of America Press, 1984).

4. Immanuel Kant, *Kritik der reinen Vernunft*, 2nd ed., vol. 3 of *Kants Werke* (1787; Berlin: Walter de Gruyter, 1968); trans. Norman Kemp Smith under the title *Immanuel Kant's Critique of Pure Reason* (London: Macmillan, 1964), A761/B789.

5. Ludwig Wittgenstein, *Tractatus Logico-philosophicus* (London: Routledge, 1922), 7.

6. Martin Heidegger, "Protocole à un séminaire sur la conférence *Zeit und Sein*," *Questions* IV, ed. Jean Beaufret (Paris: Gallimard, 1976), 83; the German version can be found in *Zur Sache des Denkens* (Tübingen: Max Niemeyer, 1969). 51. Compare with: "It must remain an open question whether the nature of Western languages is in itself marked with the exclusive brand of metaphysics . . . or whether these languages offer other possibilities of utterance—and that means at the same time of a *telling silence*" (Heidegger, *Identität und Differenz* [Pfullingen: G. Neske, 1957], 66, emphasis added; trans. Joan Stambaugh under the title *Identity and Difference* [New York: Harper & Row, 1969], 73).

7. Wittgenstein, *Tractatus Logico-philosophicus* 6.522 (see also 6.432 and 6.44).

8. Jacques Derrida, "Comment ne pas parler: Dénégations," in *Psyché: Invention de l'autre* (Paris: Galilée, 1987), 535–95, trans. Ken Frieden under the title "How to Avoid Speaking," in *Languages of the Unsayable: The Play of Negativity in Literature and Literary Theory*, ed. Sanford Budick and Wolfgang Iser

(New York: Columbia University Press, 1989), 3–70; and then *Donner le termps: I. La fausse monnaie* (Paris: Galilée, 1991), trans. Peggy Kamuf under the title *Given Time: I. Counterfeit Money* (Chicago: University of Chicago Press, 1991); and *Sauf le nom (Post Scriptum)* (Paris: Galilée 1993), trans. John P. Leavey, Jr., under the same title in Derrida, *On the Name*, ed. Thomas Dutoit (Stanford: Stanford University Press, 1998), 35–85, in which he discusses my *L'idole et la distance* (Paris: Bernard Grasset, 1977), trans. Thomas A. Carlson under the title of *The Idol and Distance: Five Studies* (New York: Fordham University Press, 2001); *Dieu sans l'être* (Paris: Arthème Fayard, 1982), trans. Thomas A. Carlson under the title *God Without Being* (Chicago: University of Chicago Press, 1991), and *Réduction et donation: Recherches sur Husserl, Heidegger et la phénoménologie* (Paris: Presses Universitaires de France, 1989); trans. Thomas A. Carlson under the title *Reduction and Givenness: Investigations of Husserl, Heidegger, and Phenomenology* (Evanston, Ill.: Northwestern University Press, 1998).

    9. Derrida, *Sauf le nom*, 70/63.

   10. John Scotus Eriugena, *De Divisione Naturae*, I, 14, *Patrologia Latina* 122, col. 462.

   11. Aristotle, *On Interpretation* 4, 17a4.

   12. See my response to Derrida, "In the Name: How to Avoid Speaking of 'Negative Theology,'" in *God, the Gift, and Postmodernism*, ed. John D. Caputo and Michael Scanlon (Bloomington: Indiana University Press, 1999), 20–42, and then in *De surcroît: Études sur les phénomènes saturés* (Paris: Presses Universitaires de France, 2001), 162–71; trans. Robyn Horner and Vincent Berraud under the title *In Excess: Studies of Saturated Phenomena* (New York: Fordham University Press, 2002), chap. 6, "In the Name: How to Avoid Speaking of It," esp. section 2, 134–42.

   13. Stendhal, *La Chartreuse de Parme*, chap. 28.

   14. Husserl, *Logische Untersuchungen*, 2 vols. (Halle: Max Niemeyer, 1922), 1:26, esp. 2:82ff.; trans. J. N. Findlay under the title *Logical Investigations*, 2 vols. (London: Routledge & Kegan Paul, 1970).

   15. J. L. Austin, *How to Do Things with Words* (Cambridge: Harvard University Press, 1962), 109.

   16. "Thus we distinguish the locutionary act (and within it the phonetic, the phatic, and the rhetic acts) which has a *meaning* [from] the illocutionary act which has a certain *force* in saying something" (ibid., 121).

   17. Montaigne, *Essais*, I, 28, ed. P. Villey (Paris: V. L. Saulnier, 1965), 1:189.

   18. Austin, *How to Do Things with Words*, 15.

   19. Stanley Cavell, "La passion," in the collective work modestly entitled *Quelle philosophie pour the XXIe siècle? L'organon du nouveau siècle* (Paris: Pompidou Center, 2001), 373; the English original can be found as "Performative and Passionate Utterance," in Cavell, *Philosophy the Day after Tomorrow* (Cambridge: Harvard University Press, 2005), 181; further citations will be to the English version. Cavell's discussion of Austin's conditions has been helpful for my own analysis.

20. Austin and Searle should not be confused on this point. Austin classifies "to promise" among the commisives (*How to Do Things with Words*, 157), mentions insincerity (18, 40), and has not a single word to say about "to love." J. R. Searle, *Speech Acts: An Essay in the Philosophy of Language* (Cambridge: Cambridge University Press, 1969), 57–62, gives a thorough analysis of the illocutionary act "to promise" (including the promise without sincerity) but without making the slightest allusion to "I love you."

21. Austin, *How to Do Things with Words*, 109. In this sense, it remains a performative (110).

22. Searle, *Speech Acts*, 25.

23. Cavell, "Performative and Passionate Utterance," 173.

24. Roland Barthes hesitates on this point: sometimes, he is confused: "this word [I-love-you] is always *true* (it has no other referent than its offering of itself: it is a performative)"; sometimes, he sees things correctly, though not without imprecision: "The atopia of love, what is proper to it and allows it to escape from all theses, is that *in the last instance* we can speak of it only according to *a strict allocutionary determination*; in the discourse on love there is always a person to whom one speaks, even if this person takes the form of a ghost or a creature from the future. No one wants to talk about love, if it is not *for* someone" (*Fragments d'un discours amoureux* [Paris: Seuil, 1977], 176 and 88; trans. Richard Howard as *A Lover's Discourse: Fragments* (New York: Hill and Wang, 1978); translation modified for this context. Or rather, no one wants to speak *about* love, if not to someone who is *loved*, for one can very well speak *about* love without love, and without a loved one.

25. Austin, *How to Do Things with Words*, 101 (my emphasis).

26. Cavell, "Performative and Passionate Utterance," 180.

27. Austin, *How to Do Things with Words*, 122 and 119.

28. Cavell, "Performative and Passionate Utterance," 180; cf. Austin: "The 'I' that accomplishes the action does thus come essentially into the picture" (*How to Do Things with Words*, 61).

29. Austin, *How to Do Things with Words*, 119.

30. Cavell, "Performative and Passionate Utterance."

31. Descartes mentions this in *Passions de l'âme*, §82, *Œuvres de Descartes*, ed. Charles Adams and Paul Tannery, 11 vols. (Paris: Vrin, CNRS, 1964–79], XI: 388–89.

32. Barthes' opinion could not be more misplaced: "Once the first avowal has been made, '*I love you*' has no meaning whatsoever; it merely repeats in an enigmatic mode—so blank does it appear—the old message (which may not have been transmitted in these words). I repeat it though it may no longer have any relevance; it leaves language behind, it rambles, where?" (*Fragments*, 175/147; trans. modified). It does not ramble, since it repeats, and it does not repeat in a void, since it thereby maintains the lover's discourse, despite the apophasis that apophasis inevitably provokes. It is only this repetition that gives time to the lover's discourse, its only possible time, possibly precisely despite the impossibility that the present inflicts upon it.

33. Alphonse de Lamartine, "Le poète mourant," *Les Nouvelles Méditations* (Paris: U. Canel, 1823), 125–26.

7. The Banality of Saturation

1. The reproach, sometimes explicit, often implicit, that I remain within "metaphysics" because I take my point of departure from Kant's typology (and Husserl's) seems to me unjust and inadmissible, for several reasons. Methodologically, even if I do start with a "metaphysical" definition of the phenomenon for the purpose of reaching that of the phenomenon as it shows itself from itself and insofar as it gives itself, I am only repeating the Husserlian and Heideggerian movement of starting with a "natural" or "inauthentic" situation so as to pass, by reduction or destruction, to a "reduced" or "authentic" situation. Historically, in defining the phenomenon for the first time as *Erscheinung* and not as mere *Schein*, Kant indicated a way to overcome all metaphysical senses. Heidegger made no mistake about this, as he took the Kantian definition as his point of departure in constructing the "phenomenological" meaning of the phenomenon in *Being and Time*, §7. Finally, conceptually, it would be necessary to define, at least once, what one means precisely, therefore *conceptually*, by the term *metaphysics*, a task all the more delicate (as confirmed by Heidegger's successive positions on its use) because the term has perhaps never received a stable or univocal definition. (See my study "La science toujours recherché et toujours manquante," in *La métaphysique: Son histoire, sa critique ses enjeux*, ed. J.-M. Narbonne and L. Langlois (Paris: Vrin, 1999), 13–36.

2. See my *Étant donné: Essai d'une phénoménologie de la donation* (Paris: Presses Universitaires de France, 1997), §24; trans. Jeffrey L. Kosky under the title *Being Given: Toward a Phenomenology of Givenness* (Stanford: Stanford University Press, 2002), §24. Here, in distinction to my first approach to the saturated phenomenon (see Chapter 2 of this volume), I no longer include revelation in the list of simple paradoxes or saturated phenomena. Supposing that it can enter phenomenality, revelation demands at least a combination of the four figures of saturation, ending up in a radicalized paradox. On this point, see *Being Given*, §25, and *De surcroît: Études sur les phénomènes saturés* (Paris: Presses Universitaires de France, 2001), chap. 6; trans. Robyn Horner and Vincent Berraud under the title *In Excess: Studies of Saturated Phenomena* (New York: Fordham University Press, 2002), "In the Name, How to Avoid Speaking of It," 128–62.

3. Baudelaire, "Three Drafts of a Preface" to *Les Fleures du mal / The Flowers of Evil*, ed. Marthiel and Jackson Mathews (New York: New Directions, 1989), xxvii.

4. Marlène Zarader, "Phenomenology and Transcendence," in *Transcendence in Philosophy and Religion*, ed. James Faulconer (Bloomington: Indiana University Press, 2003), 110. This essay often assumes what it calls a "canonical" phenomenology, which is a puzzling formulation. Would this be a moment in the history of phenomenological doctrines? But then one would need to know who defines the "canon." Husserl? But which period in Husserl's work? And why one

rather than another stage? As things stand, none of these questions receives an answer, since not one of them is even posed. Does this concern an abstract and nontemporal model of phenomenology? But what legitimacy can be granted to this? Often the most dogmatic defenders of the (presumed) orthodoxy of phenomenology also seem to ignore its real history and development (it matters little whether this happens voluntarily or not).

5. Ibid., 113, 110, and 118, respectively.

6. Ibid., 114. This is an allusion to Rudolf Bernet, *La vie du sujet: Recherches sur l'interprétation de Husserl dans la phénoménologie* (Paris: Presses Universitaires de France, 1994), who in concluding evokes the question of "an intentional life without subject or object" (297ff). This concession, one that is inevitable in phenomenological terms (not only in reference to the dispute between Bolzano, Twardowski, Meinong, and Husserl about nonexistent objects, but also in regard to the overcoming of *Vorhandenheit* by *Zuhandenheit* in *Being and Time* §§15–17) already grants a lot, in fact almost everything, to the saturated phenomenon's claim to legitimacy, whose chief ambition is precisely to do justice to phenomena that are irreducible to objectification.

7. Zarader, "Phenomenology and Transcendence," 115. Of course, the devoted [*l'adonné*, see n. 10 below] was never defined in such a way, since it finds itself charged, at the very moment when it receives itself with what gives itself, with the visibility of the very thing that gives itself. Here there is nothing like a simple choice between "activity" and "passivity," with no other option (these are, for that matter, only categories borrowed from Aristotle, radically metaphysical, whose phenomenological usefulness can be disputed). The devoted operates according to the call and response and manages the passage of what gives itself to what shows itself: neither the one nor the other corresponds to these categories. "Passivity" and "activity" intervene only once the characteristics of the devoted are misconstrued. One can make the same observations concerning Charles Larmore's criticisms of the supposed passivity of the devoted in *Les pratiques du moi* (Paris: Presses Universitaires de France, 2004), 221ff.

8. Zarader, "Phenomenology and Transcendence," 114. Obviously the problem consists in deciding not whether the devoted maintains a "character of subjectivity" but *which one*—transcendental, empirical, or something else? The outrageously simplified alternative loses all pertinence. For that matter, why reproach the devoted for *keeping* a subjective function when other criticisms (or even the same ones) give it grief for *losing* this function?

9. Title of the collection *Who Comes after the Subject?* ed. Eduardo Cadava, Peter Connor, and Jean-Luc Nancy (New York: Routledge, 1991).

10. [*L'adonné* designates being "devoted" or "given over" to someone or something and is also used to refer to someone "addicted" to something. Jeffrey Koskey translates the term as "the gifted" in *Being Given* and in his original translation of the present article, but "devoted" seems a more accurate and appropriate translation in light of Marion's treatment. See esp. bk. 5 of *Being Given*.—Trans.]

11. Jocelyn Benoist, "L'écart plutôt que l'excédant," *Philosophie* 78 (June 2003), 89. See "there was nothing to overcome" (ibid., 93). One remark: What

does it mean to say "nothing that can be assigned [*rien d'assignable*]"? Is this the same as seeing absolutely nothing? No, without a doubt, since it is specified that what is at stake is challenging "some *absolute* form of appearing" in the name of some phenomenon (89). "To assign" therefore means *not to absolutize the phenomenon* (77), to accord (to *all* phenomena) only a *relative* phenomenality. But, I ask, relative to what or to whom? Such a presupposition should be argued or at least explained more fully. Once it is admitted, no doubt a saturated phenomenon (not to mention a phenomenon of revelation) cannot be admitted. But does not the entire question rest on the legitimacy of this presupposition?

12. Jocelyn Benoist, *L'idée de phénoménologie* (Paris: Beauchesne, 2001), 102. Let me observe that this question, one far too personal to remain purely philosophical, goes on: "I see nothing or something else, for example, the infinite forest of sensible life or the metamorphoses of the divine in our daily affair of being loved, rather than the monotheistic idol?" (ibid.). Or: "[the phenomenon's] intuitive richness and the unbelievable complexity of the forest of the sensible" (Benoist, "L'écart plutôt que l'excédent," 92). This simple addition calls for some remarks. (a) Can one describe the supposedly "infinite forest of the sensible" and its "frightening complexity" without having recourse to one or several saturated phenomena? (b) How can one describe what is here named quite rightly "our daily affair of being loved" without, once again, a nonobjectifying phenomenology, therefore a phenomenology of saturated phenomena (as I attempted in *Le phénomène érotique* [Paris: Grasset, 2003]; trans. Stephen E. Lewis under the title *The Erotic Phenomenon* [Chicago: University of Chicago Press, 2007])? (c) Finally, with what right and by what procedures can one recognize (once again rightly) "metamorphoses of the divine," indeed, oppose them to a presumed "idol," except by presupposing a rationality of this very divinity, therefore the means to think it, e.g., as paradox of paradoxes (*In Excess*, chap. 6)? But then, if one does not want to remain sunk in platitudes and edifying discourses but reach the level of the concept, what philosophy will allow one to do so? At the very least, one can say it is not a positivism decked out in Husserlian rags, which tries the patience, the diligence, and the effort of the one who describes phenomena as they give themselves in excess and without remaining always in one's measure.

13. I think here of a remark by Husserl: "He [Wundt] refuses to, because he deduces, as the real a priori philosophy, that he can have absolutely nothing like it. Against this a priori, there is no cure. One cannot make oneself understood to someone who both does and does not want to see" ("Entwurf einer 'Vorrede' zu den 'Logischen Untersuchungen' (1913)," *Tijdschrift voor Philosophie* [Louvain, 1939], 335; trans. Philip J. Bossert and Curtis H. Peters under the title *Introduction to the Logical Investigations: A Draft of a Preface to the Logical Investigations (1913)* [The Hague: Martinus Nijhoff, 1975]). I owe this reference to Benoist himself (*L'idée de phénoménologie*, 102), whom I thank.

14. Aristotle, *Metaphysics* 1, 993b 9–11 (or also *Physics* 1, 2, 185a 1–2), commented on by St. Thomas Aquinas, *In Metaphysicorum Libros* 22, n. 282. For the angels, another caution is in order: "Accordingly, just as a man would show himself to be a most insane fool if he declared the assertions of a philosopher to be

false because he was unable to understand them, so, and much more, a man would be exceedingly foolish were he to suspect of falsehood the things revealed by God through the ministry of his angels, because they cannot be the object of reason's investigations" (*Summa contra gentes* 1, 3).

15. Husserl refers here to the "I am" as the sole intentional ground of the entire ideal world, even that of the other. I would gladly substitute the saturated phenomenon as the official model of phenomenality, even (as we will see) for poor or common phenomenality.

16. Edmund Husserl, *Formale und Transzendentale Logik, Versuch einer Kritik der logischen Vernunft*, Hua VII, §95; trans. Dorian Cairns under the title *Formal and Transcendental Logic* §95, (The Hague: Martinus Nijhoff, 1969), 237.

17. Efforts that, for the most part, remain in vain, since the criticisms of the saturated phenomenon, while calling for precise and concrete analyses, most of the time do not consider the descriptions offered in *In Excess* (and thereafter) but stick to the still abstract schema in *Being Given*, if not just to the 1992 essay (Chapter 2 of the present work).

18. Benoist: "I believe instead that it is necessary, continuing some Husserlian analyses, and like numerous philosophies today, to recognize the fundamental and relatively uniform *richness of intuition*. What need is there to go looking for exceptional intuitions?" ("L'écart plutôt que l'excédent," 87). This is to say too much and to say it too quickly. (a) What are these "Husserlian analyses" and these "numerous philosophies"? (Are not these precisely ones that the author rejects elsewhere?) (b) Why, after all, could this "fundamental richness" of intuition not exercise an influence in defining the phenomenon itself, perhaps even modifying this definition? (c) Does the "relatively *uniform* richness of intuition" designate some specific characteristic for this uniformity or not? If it is the case, does it not suggest a model common to all phenomena endowed with this "rich" intuition, and would it not therefore join my attempt to establish a new paradigm of phenomenality?

19. Dominique Janicaud, *La phenomenology éclatée* (Combas: L'Éclat, 1998), 69 (though the same author had previously denounced a "watered-down experience," in *Le tournant théologique de la phénoménologie française*, ed. Dominique Janicaud, Jean-François Courtine, et al. (Combas: L'Éclat, 1991); trans. under the title *Phenomenology and the "Theological Turn": The French Debate* (New York: Fordham University Press, 2000), 50.

20. On this apparently unexpected point, see *Being Given* §23 (and in fact also §§3–4), which already sketch this banality without, admittedly, formulating it as such.

21. St. Augustine, *Confessions* 11.22, 28, in regard to time; trans. Rex Warner (New York: Signet, 2001), 270–71, trans. modified.

22. The confusion of these two questions (whether willed or not) weighs heavily on Janicaud's criticism in *La phénoménologie éclatée*, in particular chap. 3, 63ff., to the point of leaving it too confused to be really useful and worth discussing.

23. Reproduced in Diane Waldman, *Mark Rothko, 1903–1970: A Retrospective* (New York: Abrams, 1978), plate 173. See the analysis of other paintings by Rothko (and Klee), as well as other phenomena saturated in terms of quality (idol), in *In Excess*, chap. 3, §2–§4.

24. [Marion uses different examples in the French text.—Trans.]

25. The detailed and argued application of the concept of the saturated phenomenon to music itself (and not just to listening) has been more than sketched by Sander van Maas, "On Preferring Mozart," *Bijdragen: International Journal in Philosophy and Theology* 65, no. 1 (2004): 97–110.

26. Derived uses are attached to the objective sense of touch: touching in the sense of taking possession (money, military equipment) or else of hitting a distant target (i.e., in fact not touching directly, from flesh to thing). To its sense in terms of the saturated phenomenon, other uses are attached: to touch someone in conversation (wound or move him or her, beyond what is said or without saying anything specific to the other), to touch on something or other while with someone (without saying anything, without the intention of saying anything specific, but doing so nevertheless), to stay out of touch (in fact, to lose all contact with society or a group).

27. Descartes, *Principia Philosophiae* [*Principles of Philosophy*], I, §45, in *Œuvres de Descartes*, ed. Charles Adams and Paul Tannery, 11 vols. (Paris: Vrin, CNRS, 1964–79), VIII-A:22; trans. John Cottingham, Robert Stoothof, and Dugalf Murdoch as *The Philosophical Writings of Descartes* (Cambridge: Cambridge University Press, 1985), I:207–8; trans. modified. Hereafter AT and CSM, respectively. Even taste can admit coding in terms of order and measure, insofar as one can assign it causes that, in extension (intelligible and producing intelligibility), determine it as their effect.

28. Signification, in the sense of what can be communicated clearly and distinctly in language, is lacking here, but this shortcoming opens space for public discussion about the least communicable intuition—as if the chasm between common and private language had became blurred.

29. "Hence a perception can be clear without being distinct, but not distinct without being clear" (Descartes, *Principles of Philosophy*, I, §46 / CSM, 209). One could introduce a distinction: certain clear items of knowledge become distinct, though without a unique concept, such that it is indeed clear but not necessarily clear for just anyone. There is an excellent description of the saturation of taste in P. Delerm, *La première gorge de bière* (Paris: Gallimard, 1997). (But why stick with just poor old beer?)

30. Baudelaire, "Correspondances," *Les Fleurs du mal*, 12; trans. modified.

31. Baudelaire, "La chevelure," ibid., 32; my emphasis.

32. Baudelaire, "Le poison," ibid., 62; trans. modified.

33. In the correct formulation of Janicaud (*La phenomenology éclatée*, 112). I am contesting nothing save that such a banality impugns the hypothesis of saturated phenomena. To the contrary, it implies them.

34. One thinks of M. Aymé's character: "Vouturier knew to recognize the evidence and, in the same moment, to refuse its consequences. . . . He gave up

the blessed springs of paradise in favor of remaining faithful to his lieutenant and to his ideal of secularity" (*La Vouivre*, chap. 8 (Paris: Gallimard, 1974), 3:581.

35. An objection often raised, though with very different intentions, among others by: Janicaud, in *La phénoménologie éclatée*, 67; Béatrice Han, in "Transcendence and the Hermeneutic Circle," in *Transcendence and Philosophy of Religion*, ed. James Faulconer, 136ff.; and Ruud Welten, in "Saturation and Disappointment: Marion According to Husserl," *Bijdragen: International Journal in Philosophy and Theology* 65, no. 1 (2004): 79–96.

36. Immanuel Kant, *Kritik der reinen Vernunft*, 2d ed., vol. 3 of *Kants Werke* (1787; Berlin: Walter de Gruyter, 1968); trans. Norman Kemp Smith under the title *Immanuel Kant's Critique of Pure Reason* (London: Macmillan, 1964), A5/B7.

37. Ibid., A111 (my emphasis). See also A158/B197.

38. Leibniz had already seen this: "Does the soul have windows? Is it similar to writing tablets, or like wax? Clearly those who take this view of the soul are treating it as fundamentally corporeal. Someone will confront me with this accepted philosophical maxim, that there is nothing in the soul that does not come from the senses. But an exception must be made of the soul itself. *Nihil est in intellectu quod non fuerit in sensu excipe nisi ipse intellectus*" (*Die Philosophischen Schriften*, ed. Karl Gerhardt [Berlin: Akademie-Verlag, 1962], II.1, §2; trans. Peter Remnant and Jonathan Bennett under the title *New Essays Concerning Human Understanding* [Cambridge: Cambridge University Press, 1981], 110). Even *rasa*, the *tabula* remains a tablet erased and therefore available for the *self*, for the *ego cogitans* before the experience cogitated—in short, it already posits an a priori, in a certain fashion. If empiricism itself already implies a transcendental posture (consciously or not, it doesn't really matter), one can be free from it only by one path: thinking the *ego* as the devoted, for the devoted does not precede the given that it receives (as a *tabula rasa* already there awaiting it still does), since it *receives itself* from what it receives (see *Being Given* §26).

39. Let me refer to the analyses of the infinite (Descartes), of the sublime (Kant), and of the originary impression of time (Husserl) as nonobjective phenomena sketched in *Being Given*, §22.

40. There is no greater misreading than to imagine that I attribute an *intuitus originarius* to the devoted so as to permit it to experience directly, clearly, and distinctly the divine absolute (Han, "Transcendence and the Hermeneutic Circle," 137). There is no better illustration of the devoted's situation of saturation than what Kant identifies with reason as our *intuitus derivativus* because here this finitude is not limited to sensible intuition but determines the entire experience of phenomenality.

41. In the (arbitrarily) privileged case of God, for example, Jocelyn Benoist objects: "But *is it enough not to be a concept to be God?*" (*L'idée de phénoménologie*, 86). Or: "repeating my criticism of your thought, *it is not enough not to be a concept to be God*" (ibid., 96). Let me pass over the fact that respect for the basic rules of mystical (so-called "negative") theology would have resulted in avoiding

this syntactical error. To speak more precisely, several remarks are called for. (a) Of course, God is not a concept, but it happens too often that we want to identify him by a concept (albeit only the very concept "God"). (b) Yes, God should not be identified with *a* concept, since his incomprehensibility requires all concepts (*via affirmativa*). (c) Agreed, it is not enough that God exceed each concept (and demand them all), but that nevertheless remains a necessary, though not sufficient, condition; as soon as we invoke a concept, it is no longer a question of God. (d) God *is* not a concept, for a more radical reason: he does not have *to be*, by contrast to everything that this polemic supposes in continually returning to the opposition between "atheist" and "believer" ("I am an atheist, you are not," ibid., 84), without at any time accepting the need to dispute the grounds or even the meaning of this opposition. It could be that "believer" is opposed no more to "atheist" than to "theist," "deist," or what have you, but rather to "nonbeliever," designating someone who refuses to believe what he or she already knows well enough, be it only so as to have the power to refuse it.

42. See esp. *Being Given*, §22 and §30, and *In Excess*, *passim*.

43. Stéphane Mallarmé, "Prose pour des Esseintes," in *Stéphane Mallarmé: Selected Poems*, trans. C. F. MacIntyre (Berkeley: University of California Press, 1957), 63. One can also speak of "the eye exceeded by light" (Emmanuel Levinas, *De Dieu qui vient à l'idée* [Paris: Vrin, 1982], 57; trans. Bettina Bergo as *Of God Who Comes to Mind* [Stanford: Stanford University Press, 1998], 30).

44. On bedazzlement, see *Being Given*, §21. Benoist notes, as an objection, that "the only bedazzlement I know of is that of our organs' sensibility, sometimes submitted to a stimulation too strong for them" ("L'écart plutôt que l'excédent," 91). But who ever asked for a different definition of bedazzlement? I can only suggest the following. (a) The "organs" submitted to this stimulation "too strong for them" cease to give us an object exactly in the sense that I indicated. (I suggest elsewhere that "this bedazzlement counts for intelligible intuition as well as for sensible intuition"; *Being Given*, §21.) (b) In such a situation, "our organs" extend more broadly than to sensation understood in the most sensualist sense, as I have just suggested in §4. (c) Theology itself (to return to the case always privileged by my reader) always considered the "spiritual senses" to be the senses of "our organs," suggesting only that the sensibility of the latter is not limited to sensualism. It is in this sense that one must understand the sensibility of categorical intuition in Husserl (See my *Réduction et donation: Recherches sur Husserl, Heidegger et la phénoménologie* [Paris: Presses Universitaires de France, 1989]; trans. Thomas A. Carlson under the title *Reduction and Givenness: Investigations of Husserl, Heidegger, and Phenomenology* [Evanston, Ill.: Northwestern University Press, 1998]).

45. I owe it to Ruud Welten ("Saturation and Disappointment: Marion according to Husserl") to have drawn my attention to this essential point.

46. Let me note that this hypothesis is quite contrived, indeed inconceivable. Who, how, and by what right could convince me that I do not experience the excess of light that makes me blink, indeed, close my eyes? Descartes' argument

(and its exegesis by Michel Henry) are fully valid here: "For example, I am now seeing light, hearing a noise, feeling heat. But I am asleep, so all this is false. Yet I certainly *seem* to see, to hear, and to be warmed. This cannot be false; what is called 'having a sensory perception' is strictly just this" (Second Meditation, AT VII:29, 12–16; CSM II:19).

47. On this resistance, see *In Excess*, chap. 2, §5, and chap. 4, §5. If one neglects it, the decisive phenomenological gap between "giving itself" and "manifesting itself" disappears. Then one remains stuck in misreadings that give rise to objections concerning the supposed passivity of the devoted or the supposed infinity of manifestation, etc. [The explanatory part of the note is not in the French version.—Trans.]

48. Descartes, *Meditations on First Philosophy*, AT VII:22, 6 (See also 28, 27; 79, 14).

49. St. Augustine, *Confessions* 10.23, 226–27 (trans. modified).

50. In the sense of *gaudium de Deo* or *de veritate* (as in *Confessions* 10.29–22, 33, or *De vita beata* 4.35) or of Pascal's "Truth is so obscured nowadays and lies so well established that unless we love the truth we shall never recognize it" *Pensées* §739 (New York: Penguin Books, 1966).

51. St. John of the Cross, *Llama de amor viva*, 4.11. Hans Urs von Balthasar has commented: "The illuminating light is in the first instance predominantly purificatory," such that we can speak of an "experience of the absolute in the non-experience of all content or finite activity" (*Herrlichkeit*, vol. 2, *Fächer der Style* [Einsiedeln: Johannes, 1962], 527; trans. under the title *The Glory of the Lord* [San Francisco: Ignatius Press, 1986], 138). Kevin Hart offers an excellent commentary on this formula in "The Experience of Non-experience," in *Mystics, Presence, and Aporia*, ed. Michael Kessler and Christian Sheppard (Chicago: University of Chicago Press, 2003), 196ff.

52. One should therefore take quite seriously—as is rarely the case, in my experience—the fact that Descartes himself avoids these terms. No doubt because for him, at least, the *ego* (as well as the *mens* or the *anima*, etc.) never exerts itself toward an object, according to the rules of the method, but sometimes admits an affection.

53. See *Being Given*, §1. If only for this reason, there is no occasion for theologians to be worried about the surreptitious reestablishment of a transcendental condition of possibility assigned to Revelation. See, e.g.: V. Holtzer, "La foi, ses savoirs et sa rationalité: Esquisse des débats fondamentaux en théologie catholique contemporaine," a presentation at the conference L'intelligence de la foi parmi les rationalités contemporaines, Institut catholique de Paris, 5 March 2004; or Kathryn Tanner, discussion at the conference *In Excess*: Jean-Luc Marion and the Horizon of Modern Theology, at the University of Notre Dame, 9–11 May 2004. For that matter, *Being Given* already explicitly evokes this possible objection and answers it (235–36 and 243), thereby taking up the analyses of 1988; see Chapter 1 of this volume.

54. See *Being Given*, §22.

8. Faith and Reason

1. St. Augustine, *City of God*, 8.1.

2. St. Thomas Aquinas, *De Potentia*, Q.7, A.5, ad. 14.

3. Friedrich Nietzsche, "Von den Verächtern des Leibes," *Also Sprach Zarathustra: Ein Buch für Alle und Keinen*, I, 4, in *Nietzsches Werke: Kritische Gesamtausgabe*, ed. Giorgio Colli and Mazzino Montinari (Berlin: Walter de Gruyter, 1967–91); trans. Thomas Common under the title *Thus Spoke Zarathustra*, vol. 11 of *The Complete Works of Friedrich Nietzsche*, ed. Oscar Levy (New York: Macmillan, 1919).

4. Descartes, *Discourse on Method* VI, in *Œuvres de Descartes*, ed. Charles Adams and Paul Tannery, 11 vols. (Paris: Vrin, CNRS, 1964–79), trans. John Cottingham, Robert Stoothof, and Dugalf Murdoch as *The Philosophical Writings of Descartes* (Cambridge: Cambridge University Press, 1984–85).

5. *From the faith in things which one does not see*, chaps. 2 and 4.

Perspectives in Continental Philosophy Series

John D. Caputo, series editor

1. John D. Caputo, ed., *Deconstruction in a Nutshell: A Conversation with Jacques Derrida.*

2. Michael Strawser, *Both/And: Reading Kierkegaard—From Irony to Edification.*

3. Michael D. Barber, *Ethical Hermeneutics: Rationality in Enrique Dussel's Philosophy of Liberation.*

4. James H. Olthuis, ed., *Knowing* Other-*wise: Philosophy at the Threshold of Spirituality.*

5. James Swindal, *Reflection Revisited: Jürgen Habermas's Discursive Theory of Truth.*

6. Richard Kearney, *Poetics of Imagining: Modern and Postmodern.* Second edition.

7. Thomas W. Busch, *Circulating Being: From Embodiment to Incorporation—Essays on Late Existentialism.*

8. Edith Wyschogrod, *Emmanuel Levinas: The Problem of Ethical Metaphysics.* Second edition.

9. Francis J. Ambrosio, ed., *The Question of Christian Philosophy Today.*

10. Jeffrey Bloechl, ed., *The Face of the Other and the Trace of God: Essays on the Philosophy of Emmanuel Levinas.*

11. Ilse N. Bulhof and Laurens ten Kate, eds., *Flight of the Gods: Philosophical Perspectives on Negative Theology.*

12. Trish Glazebrook, *Heidegger's Philosophy of Science.*

13. Kevin Hart, *The Trespass of the Sign: Deconstruction, Theology, and Philosophy.*

14. Mark C. Taylor, *Journeys to Selfhood: Hegel and Kierkegaard*. Second edition.

15. Dominique Janicaud, Jean-François Courtine, Jean-Louis Chrétien, Michel Henry, Jean-Luc Marion, and Paul Ricœur, *Phenomenology and the "Theological Turn": The French Debate*.

16. Karl Jaspers, *The Question of German Guilt*. Introduction by Joseph W. Koterski, S.J.

17. Jean-Luc Marion, *The Idol and Distance: Five Studies*. Translated with an introduction by Thomas A. Carlson.

18. Jeffrey Dudiak, *The Intrigue of Ethics: A Reading of the Idea of Discourse in the Thought of Emmanuel Levinas*.

19. Robyn Horner, *Rethinking God as Gift: Marion, Derrida, and the Limits of Phenomenology*.

20. Mark Dooley, *The Politics of Exodus: Søren Keirkegaard's Ethics of Responsibility*.

21. Merold Westphal, *Toward a Postmodern Christian Faith: Overcoming Onto-Theology*.

22. Edith Wyschogrod, Jean-Joseph Goux and Eric Boynton, eds., *The Enigma of Gift and Sacrifice*.

23. Stanislas Breton, *The Word and the Cross*. Translated with an introduction by Jacquelyn Porter.

24. Jean-Luc Marion, *Prolegomena to Charity*. Translated by Stephen E. Lewis.

25. Peter H. Spader, *Scheler's Ethical Personalism: Its Logic, Development, and Promise*.

26. Jean-Louis Chrétien, *The Unforgettable and the Unhoped For*. Translated by Jeffrey Bloechl.

27. Don Cupitt, *Is Nothing Sacred? The Non-Realist Philosophy of Religion: Selected Essays*.

28. Jean-Luc Marion, *In Excess: Studies of Saturated Phenomena*. Translated by Robyn Horner and Vincent Berraud.

29. Phillip Goodchild, *Rethinking Philosophy of Religion: Approaches from Continental Philosophy*.

30. William J. Richardson, S.J., *Heidegger: Through Phenomenology to Thought*.

31. Jeffrey Andrew Barash, *Martin Heidegger and the Problem of Historical Meaning*.

32. Jean-Louis Chrétien, *Hand to Hand: Listening to the Work of Art*. Translated by Stephen E. Lewis.

33. Jean-Louis Chrétien, *The Call and the Response*. Translated with an introduction by Anne Davenport.

34. D. C. Schindler, *Han Urs von Balthasar and the Dramatic Structure of Truth: A Philosophical Investigation*.

35. Julian Wolfreys, ed., *Thinking Difference: Critics in Conversation*.

36. Allen Scult, *Being Jewish/Reading Heidegger: An Ontological Encounter*.

37. Richard Kearney, *Debates in Continental Philosophy: Conversations with Contemporary Thinkers.*

38. Jennifer Anna Gosetti-Ferencei, *Heidegger, Hölderlin, and the Subject of Poetic Language: Towards a New Poetics of Dasein.*

39. Jolita Pons, *Stealing a Gift: Kirkegaard's Pseudonyms and the Bible.*

40. Jean-Yves Lacoste, *Experience and the Absolute: Disputed Questions on the Humanity of Man.* Translated by Mark Raftery-Skehan.

41. Charles P. Bigger, *Between* Chora *and the Good: Metaphor's Metaphysical Neighborhood.*

42. Dominique Janicaud, *Phenomenology "Wide Open": After the French Debate.* Translated by Charles N. Cabral.

43. Ian Leask and Eoin Cassidy, eds. *Givenness and God: Questions of Jean-Luc Marion.*

44. Jacques Derrida, *Sovereignties in Question: The Poetics of Paul Celan.* Edited by Thomas Dutoit and Outi Pasanen.

45. William Desmond, *Is There a Sabbath for Thought? Between Religion and Philosophy.*

46. Bruce Ellis Benson and Norman Wirzba, eds. *The Phenomoenology of Prayer.*

47. S. Clark Buckner and Matthew Statler, eds. *Styles of Piety: Practicing Philosophy after the Death of God.*

48. Kevin Hart and Barbara Wall, eds. *The Experience of God: A Postmodern Response.*

49. John Panteleimon Manoussakis, *After God: Richard Kearney and the Religious Turn in Continental Philosophy.*

50. John Martis, *Philippe Lacoue-Labarthe: Representation and the Loss of the Subject.*

51. Jean-Luc Nancy, *The Ground of the Image.*

52. Edith Wyschogrod, *Crossover Queries: Dwelling with Negatives, Embodying Philosophy's Others.*

53. Gerald Bruns, *On the Anarchy of Poetry and Philosophy: A Guide for the Unruly.*

54. Brian Treanor, *Aspects of Alterity: Levinas, Marcel, and the Contemporary Debate.*

55. Simon Morgan Wortham, *Counter-Institutions: Jacques Derrida and the Question of the University.*

56. Leonard Lawlor, *The Implications of Immanence: Toward a New Concept of Life.*

57. Clayton Crockett, *Interstices of the Sublime: Theology and Psychoanalytic Theory.*

58. Bettina Bergo, Joseph Cohen, and Raphael Zagury-Orly, eds., *Judeities: Questions for Jacques Derrida.* Translated by Bettina Bergo, and Michael B. Smith.

59. Jean-Luc Marion, *On the Ego and on God: Further Cartesian Questions.* Translated by Christina M. Gschwandtner.

60. Jean-Luc Nancy, *Philosophical Chronicles*. Translated by Franson Manjali.

61. Jean-Luc Nancy, *Dis-Enclosure: The Deconstruction of Christianity*. Translated by Bettina Bergo, Gabriel Malenfant, and Michael B. Smith.

62. Andrea Hurst, *Derrida Vis-à-vis Lacan: Interweaving Deconstruction and Psychoanalysis*.

63. Jean-Luc Nancy, *Noli me tangere: On the Raising of the Body*. Translated by Sarah Clift, Pascale-Anne Brault, and Michael Naas.

64. Jacques Derrida, *The Animal That Therefore I Am*. Edited by Marie-Louise Mallet, Translated by David Wills.